The Royal Nonesuch

Also by the author

Tuscaloosa

The Royal Nonesuch

GLASGOW PHILLIPS

In which the Author, a failure at literature, fails likewise at pornography; founds a corporate branding consultancy and a New Media Empire; impersonates the Antichrist; plays nursemaid to a homeless street performer in a bear suit; battles oblivion and The Big She; and attempts to answer the one great question that troubles his generation:

What will I do when I grow up?

Black Cat
New York

a paperback original imprint of Grove/Atlantic, Inc.

Printed in the United States of America
Published simultaneously in Canada

FIRST EDITION

Library of Congress Cataloging-in-Publication Data

Phillips, W. Glasgow, 1969–
The royal nonesuch : in which the author, a failure at literature, fails likewise at pornography, founds a corporate branding consultancy . . . / by Glasgow Phillips.
p. cm.
ISBN-13: 978-0-8021-7028-6
ISBN-10: 0-8021-7028-5
1. Phillips, W. Glasgow, 1969–   2. Authors, American—20th century—Biography.   3. Hollywood (Los Angeles, Calif.)—Biography.   4. Screenwriters—United States—Biography.   5. Motion picture industry—United States.   6. Motion picture producers and directors—United States—Biography.   I. Title.
PS3566.H528Z46 2006
813'.54—dc22
[B}   2006043361

Black Cat
a paperback original imprint of Grove/Atlantic, Inc.
841 Broadway
New York, NY 10003

Distributed by Publishers Group West

www.groveatlantic.com

07 08 09 10 11 12   10 9 8 7 6 5 4 3 2 1

For Heather

Author's Note

Most of the characters in this book are my friends. They have been incredibly generous in allowing me to use their names and tell stories about our adventures together. Even so, I'd like to emphasize at the front that this account is one person's subjective version of what happened, acknowledge that not everyone agrees with all of it, and request that the reader give equal credence to any other version of the same events. With regard to the facts, I do think I got most of them right, but I wouldn't advise using this book for anything other than amusement.

A handful of people requested that their names be changed or omitted. I've done my best to make them as anonymous as possible within the bounds of telling a true story, by referring to them in general terms and/or giving them pseudonyms. The last gets a bit confusing, because some of the people in this story use pseudonyms in their daily lives. Rather than including a list of which names are pseudonyms, an action that seems like it would only make readers more curious about who those characters "really" are, I humbly make a second request, that you try to avoid the temptation to figure it out, or, if you just can't resist the investigative urge, that you keep your suspicions to yourself.

Still other people I was unable to locate. I have left some anonymous, used pseudonyms for others, and used real names when it seemed that I wasn't writing anything that would cause offense, regret, or sadness. I have also used the real names of public figures, since changing their names would be weird and cause this story to make even less sense than it does.

Well, all day him and the king was hard at it, rigging up a stage and a curtain and a row of candles for footlights; and that night the house was jam full of men in no time. When the place couldn't hold no more, the duke he quit tending the door and went around the back way and come onto the stage and stood up before the curtain and made a little speech, and praised up this tragedy, and said it was the most thrillingest one that ever was; and so he went on a-bragging about the tragedy, and about Edmund Kean the Elder, which was to play the main principal part in it; and at last when he'd got everybody's expectations up high enough, he rolled up the curtain, and the next minute the king come a-prancing out on all fours, naked; and he was painted all over, ring-streaked-and-striped, all sorts of colors, as splendid as a rainbow.

—Mark Twain, *The Adventures of Huckleberry Finn*

Prologue

This may be of interest to no one but myself. It's just an account of some things that happened, as well as I can remember them. If it is about anything, I suppose it is about growing up, which is something my generation seems to do late, and in that respect I am just one more unremarkable exemplar. It is also about money, money and fame, our gods. I have achieved very little of either, certainly not enough to write an instruction manual on how best to get them. I tried pretty hard for both of them, though, and so in that respect I suppose my story may serve as a cautionary tale. Then again, you'd have to be an asshole to make the decisions I made.

What happens? I can honestly say, some good stuff. Some silly shit that went down on two separate levels of the American cultural economy, the top and the bottom, though sometimes it was hard to tell which was which, that I had the opportunity to witness and at times be a part of perpetrating. From 1998 to 2001 I was a principal member of two different companies, a fringe entertainment company and a corporate brand strategy consultancy, both started with old friends. Neither of these undertakings was a big success in financial or any other terms, but both were real attempts to interrogate a question that troubled me in my late twenties and continues to trouble me even as I slide into my late thirties: What will I do when I grow up?

This is a deeply self-indulgent question to be entertaining so late in life. As such, personal memoir, the most self-indulgent form imaginable, with the possible exceptions of spoken word and interpretive dance, feels appropriate to an account of its interrogation. In advance defense of these pages, a great many members of my generation—I was born in 1969—seem still to be struggling with the question, even now, when we're supposed to be all grown up.

Because I was unable to arrive at a satisfactory answer, these pages will be descriptive rather than prescriptive. There will be celebrities, though not much dish. There will be violence, albeit some of it simulated. There will be sex, some between consenting puppets, and some between real people. There will be crime, but as usual, only the little guys get in trouble. We will have cancer, but I feel obliged to reveal up front that she makes it. We will descend into madness with a charismatic clown, and I am deeply sorry to inform you that he doesn't. It is customary to begin these things with a moment of action and high excitement. I will start by crashing my motorcycle.

One

1

I slid facedown with a leg pinned under it through an intersection in downtown Austin, Texas. My protective gear was first-rate: full-face helmet, lace-up boots, Kevlar-reinforced gauntlets, and set of black leathers made for high-speed tumbling on the Autobahn. Unfortunately, most of this equipment was safe in my closet when the Camry rolled into the intersection, and I hit the pavement in just the helmet, the boots, and a Hawaiian-print bathing suit. At the far side of the street, I untangled myself from the bike and stood to take an accounting. There was no apparent structural damage to my person, but quite a bit of meat was missing from my hands, forearms, stomach, and legs. As the white, scooped-out places where the flesh had been welled up red and spilled over, I sat down on the curb to await further developments.

This was in the summer of 1997, and I had been awaiting further developments for some time. I was twenty-eight years old, living there in Austin and working on a doomed second novel. Four years earlier I had published a first one. I had worked hard on it, typing secretly in the afternoons of my last semester at Brown University. I desperately wanted to believe it was truly original, the first slim entry in a giant

3

literary career, but I knew in my heart it was little more than accomplished Southern voice fan fiction. It even included a passage that I dreaded someone would notice and accuse me of plagiarism, an exchange about yard work remembered from *Red Sky at Morning,* one of my favorite books when I was a kid, run through my Walker Percy distortion box. No one ever noticed the passage, but the results of publication were castastrophic nonetheless: encouraging reviews, translations, a paperback sale, a film option, and a Stegner Fellowship at the Stanford University Creative Writing Program, where my father had been a Fellow and then a lecturer twenty years before.

The atmosphere at Stanford during my fellowship could not possibly have been more conducive to good work. There were nine of us; all we had to do was show up twice a week, chat amiably about one another's pages in the presence of whichever accomplished faculty member was running our seminar that trimester, and cash the checks. We sat on couches in a book-lined room I remembered from childhood, kept cool by thick stone walls and the shades of departed giants. Wallace Stegner's ghost extended benevolently from the corner office, and Raymond Carver's lumbered melancholy through the halls.

My fellow fellows were phenomenally talented, but none of them had yet published a book. Determined to lengthen my lead, I spent a year at Stanford grinding out the first few chapters of a second book, reading what I had written, and throwing it away to begin again at the beginning. I did this three times within the academic calendar, and by the end of the year had produced not a single page I could look at without feeling an upwelling dread combined with a terrible sleepiness. A horrible, secret thought had taken hold in me: Perhaps, just possibly, whatever talent I had was of the kind that would never be more than promise.

I retained the humble objectivity to judge that I was as technically skilled as the other eight Stegner Fellows, who like me had been skimmed from a swarming pool of literary polliwogs. They were my friends, but I knew better than to share my concerns. Already I had had better luck than anyone else, so I could hardly look to my fellow fellows for sympathy. After the first year, I bought the motorcycle, a brutish old KZ 750 with an aftermarket pipe, and drove it to Austin, where I stayed instead of returning for my second year.

Austin's main appeal was that I knew hardly anyone there. If I continued to fail, at least I would do so in privacy. I rented a cottage under oaks behind the home of a University of Texas librarian, which came with a screened-in porch and a reading chair upholstered in comic plaid. The cottage was right around the corner from a seedy strip bar called the Crazy Lady, where I liked to drink sodas and smoke cigarettes after a long, hard day of sitting around in my underwear. I started dating a funny girl and working on another book, and in no time I had another hundred pages to throw away. I spent two years like that, poring over Nabokov, Updike, and Roth, gradually coming unglued. How do they do it—sound like themselves and no one else? I went from my laptop to a manual typewriter so that I couldn't delete my work and, when that failed to gain me anything but shredded cuticles and an overflowing wastebasket, to filling giant spiral notebooks like a serial killer.

When the money from options and translations started to run out, I wangled a couple of assignments from *Rolling Stone*. The first one was on spec, but they paid my expenses; I traveled to Las Vegas to cover the AVN Awards, the porn industry's equivalent of the Oscars. For the second I documented a Survival Research Laboratories robot fiasco at a speedway near Austin. Neither piece ran. I could hardly blame the editor who commissioned them for killing them, as neither one was printable. The first ended with me jacking off in a hotel room while a hooker squatted over me, and when the editor had the poor judgment to give me another assignment, I sent him, in the hopes he would mistake me for David Foster Wallace, eleven thousand words instead of the thousand requested. I wrote little snatches of cultural criticism for *Might*, a hopeful magazine in San Francisco, and I did some other freelance work, but I knew it was over. I was done, washed up before I was thirty. I made maudlin examinations of the weapons at Guns, the bluntly named shop down the street from my second apartment, and drove the KZ way too fast on Austin's looping overpasses.

Except for summer months that I spent with my father in Tennessee, I grew up in the Bay Area—in San Francisco until I was eight, and then north across the Golden Gate, in Marin County. The Marin of my late childhood was a suburban playground of postdisco decadence, of liberal privilege and Tahoe vacations, of hot tubs and pot-smoking parents, of gurus and gourmet groceries. It was the high seat of the "bohemian bourgeois" culture David Brooks would identify in his book *Bobos in Paradise,* the same culture that would give rise to our most famous native son of the twenty-first century, American Taliban John Walker Lindh—poor bastard.

The town where I lived was called Ross. It was contiguous to San Anselmo, the hometown of Lindh's childhood. The location of our home within the boundaries of Ross proper allowed me to attend Ross School, generally regarded as the best public grammar school in an area of excellent public schools, and gave us a 94957 zip code, which came, in one of those bizarre inversions of convenience understandable only to the very rich, with the privilege of collecting mail from the dumpy post office rather than having it delivered.

When we ran out to grade school recess on the Ross School soccer field—the "Ross Common," as it was called in imitation of East Coast nomenclature, as though anybody had ever grazed a sheep there—attractive mothers in tennis skirts could be seen across the street, chatting on the post office steps or beneath the kiosk erected beside them where lost-dog and maid-service postings were tacked. The eagle-eyed moms could see us, too. More than once my playground misdeeds were reported from the post office aerie to my own mother, who worked in San Francisco.

We were watched. But that makes it sound unpleasant, and it was anything but unpleasant—it was idyllic, more outrageously safe and free from care than I would understand until I was older and saw more of how other people lived. During the school year we went to school and played soccer, basketball, and baseball in seasonal sequence, and in the summer we rode our BMX bikes wherever we wanted to go. We played tennis until we had blisters, swam until we were burned and pickled, and then found good sheltering shrubs from which to throw small hard plums, which grew abundantly everywhere, at each other and at passing cars.

This makes it sound like my family was rich. And of course we were rich, outrageously, obscenely rich by any standard other than that of the community around us. The difference between our family and most of the other families in town was that my mother worked. She had been working like an animal since my parents divorced in 1973, at the same temporary-personnel agency where she had been the first employee. I hardly noticed this and certainly didn't think of it as unusual, as for me it wasn't—it simply was how things were. Only in retrospect did I realize that few if any of my grade school friends' moms had that kind of job, the kind where you commuted into the city at dawn every day and came home after dark.

My mother, Margaret, worked in order to provide me with a stability she had not enjoyed as a child. She had grown up in Alabama, in Tuscaloosa—not in rural poverty or anything like that, but it was a pretty chaotic situation. Her paternal grandfather was the director of Bryce Hospital, the state mental hospital, which was a respectable post in town, but her father was a lawyer who didn't practice that much law. By inclination and talent he was a tennis player, and by obscure entitlement some kind of sketchy state official, a post that sometimes allowed him a car and driver he could use to run weird errands out in the country. He also liked to fly a small plane, which he would get into with his dog and a bottle of whiskey and return when he returned. But mainly he was a charming schemer, perpetually importuning friends and relatives to invest in sure-thing Argentinean mining investments, radio-wave health products, and the like. At one point he even had my dad, Bert, peddling a special "aluminized soil." The soil was supposed to have preservative properties: Stick a bag of it in the back of your fridge, and all your perishables would last a few days longer than they would otherwise. After that venture's demise the leftover samples were wryly referred to as Bert's Dirt.

My mother's second marriage and our move to Marin surely had some footing in a desire to provide me even more safety and security. Not that she and my stepfather didn't like or even love each other; my stepfather was charismatic, handsome, and funny, and I was fond of him, too. But my mother and he weren't perfectly compatible, and had the marriage not offered a simulacrum of nuclear stability for her offspring, she might not have entered into it.

We had moved to Marin when they married, and we stayed there after they separated, the summer before I started high school. After the divorce, my mother found herself even more alienated from the social center of our town. Her close friends were wonderful and continued including her in everything they did, but she was shy, and the rotating dinner parties thrown by a wider circle, the barbecues and weekend getaways with a combined herd of kids, were de facto couples events. I know my mother was lonely for companionship I was unable to provide.

But that was an adult problem, which held little interest for me at the time. On the contrary, I was living the high life in every way I could get my hands on it. That fall I was matriculated into the rolls of the Branson School, the fancy private high school in Ross; and there I soon fell among peers who shared my principal interest—to wit, getting super-duper fucked up.

Jason McHugh was my best friend. I was not alone in having this privilege—everybody in our group of friends would say the same thing. On Friday evenings our recreation was organized through the communications center in his bedroom, a yellow telephone with a weird curved handset that was always slipping off onto his belly or under his arm. If we weren't already lying stoned on the beanbags or big green dinosaur pillow in his bedroom, looking up at the ceiling plastered over with psychedelic posters, we called him when it was getting dark and found out where we were supposed to go, who would be there, whether we would be sleeping over, and what was on the psychotropic menu.

With his utilitarian attitude toward fun, endlessly plotting how the most could be had by the largest number of people, Jason existed at the center of an exclusive clique ruled by a resolute open-door policy: All you had to do to be a part of it was commit to having as much fun as possible, all the time. On weekday nights, when our parents could prevail on us not to drive in swerving lines from party to party in Marin and San Francisco until we swarmed to a reeling, laughing stop in the kitchen or basement rec room of someone's big house full of art and antiques that needed to be spilled on, bumped, and broken, the yellow phone murmured long past midnight with the secrets of pretty girls.

Jason himself was pretty back then, with green eyes and what seemed an unfair share of luck. His astonishing physical laziness—he was capable of spending all of a weekend day propped up under a blanket in the corner of the L-shaped leather couch in the den at his mom and stepdad's house, watching football, taking calls, and nibbling like a princeling at the snacks with which his mom kept the kitchen stocked—was belied by surprising strength and a canny competitive instinct. He was sly and well coordinated, and when at the spun-out ends of weekend binges we all fell in piles and fought like seals at mating season, he ended up sitting on me as often as I ended up sitting on him.

Our unique friendship coalesced in our sophomore year, at our first Grateful Dead show. We had secured five grams of psilocybin mushrooms and ill-advisedly turned to Ward, a kid one year our senior, for advice on dosage. He recommended that we split the bag into four equal parts, each take one of the parts before the concert, and at halftime take the rest. These mushrooms turned out to be the strongest I would ever get my hands on, and by the time the noise stopped and the lights came up, Jason looked decidedly strange in the seat next to me at the Berkeley Community Theater. We were both confused to the extent that we clung to the only structure left to us, the plan about taking the rest of the mushrooms; after a fragmentary conversation, we gobbled the contents of the two remaining packets and sat back to see what would happen next.

What happened next is unclear. I do know that the kid from school whose dad was the Grateful Dead's dentist, and who had supplied both the tickets and the ride to Berkeley, dropped by our seats and saw that something was amiss. But all he could think of to stave off disaster was a couple of Carnation malts, the kind that come in little paper cups like at a ballgame. I didn't feel like eating my malt, so I didn't, but Jason dutifully spooned his up. After that he quit talking. The next thing I recall is rolling around in sticky brown gurp, which turned out to be his vomit, and an episode of convulsive soul searching that culminated in a flight through the dreadlocked goblin horde out the front door of the theater, where I collapsed and fell down the steps before crawling across an immense courtyard to take shelter in a puddle under a park bench. At some point later I rounded the corner of a large stone building, déjà vu swarming, to enter the courtyard I had crawled across, only now it was filled with people I knew. Jason still couldn't talk. He had been struck dumb by the mushrooms, and he was being held up by the collar by a big kid from school, who took my collar in his other hand. Jason didn't say a word on the entire ride home in the backseat of the dentist's sedan, but the wide-eyed looks of stunned significance he directed to me during that long ride said it all: Whatever it was, we had been through it.

At teen rehab two years later, where my dear exhausted mom—to whom I had been an odious little shit for the first three years of high school, raging relentlessly about the horrific injustices of my existence in her house, where I had a huge bedroom suite with French doors onto one porch and the pool, and another private porch under oaks off the palatial bathroom, where I got high and made myself inaccessible even when she was at home—finally managed to park me between my junior and senior years of high school, the counselors told me my friendships had not been real. Those people were not true friends, they were *using* friends—they *used me,* and I *used them,* so that we could *all use.*

That dismal pun may have accurately described the peer relations of most of the kids I shared the ward with, but I knew it wasn't right for mine. On my seventeenth birthday—

a real shit sandwich of a day, on which the counselors sat me in the center of a loser horseshoe and had all the other kids tell me how often and badly I had hurt their feelings with my big long words and snotty superior attitude, until, finally, I sobbed with the unbearable pain of being such an asshole—group therapy was interrupted when Jason and the rest of them ringed the building, a prefab unit out in a parking lot of Marin General, and started slapping HAPPY BIRTHDAY signs up on the windows. It drove the staff crazy— our *using* friends were supposed to have forgotten we existed the instant we entered the hospital. For the remainder of my stay the therapeutic agenda was set. My commitment to sobriety would be measured by my willingness to shut out my old friends. And afterward I did to a large extent, forsaking a social life in my senior year for Aftercare and AA meetings and allowing my closeness with Jason and the rest to attenuate.

Not for that long, though. Almost all of them would cycle through rehab or a twelve-step program in the next five years, and by the time some decided they still preferred getting high to not getting high, we had collectively determined that the prevailing wisdom about using friends was wrong. For better or worse, and on whatever side of the divide any of us stood at a given time, we were the regular kind.

After high school Jason went to the University of Colorado at Boulder, came back home after one semester for rehab at Marin General, worked with retarded adults for a while to be reminded of how fortunate he was, and returned to Boulder to major in film. Film was a marginal department, with a smaller annual budget and crappier equipment than the

football team's media room. But there were a few good professors, among them the avant-garde director Stan Brakhage.
Jason directed a couple of short films as an undergraduate,
my favorite of which was *Search for Shamu,* a *Wild King-
dom* spoof in which a diminutive classmate named Dian
Bachar played a yuppie who is shot with a tranquilizer gun,
examined, and released back into his natural environment,
an upscale café, with a huge tag stapled to his ear.

But really Jason was a producer. In film he found a perfect application for his natural ability to build consensus
among disparate parties around an unlikely central proposition and then launch the assemblage off a cliff. The role
of the movie producer is notoriously ill defined, but
the ability to generate goodwill is its first requirement. In
Jason's last year of college, while I was typing away earnestly in my apartment in Providence, he formed a production company called the Avenging Conscience with three
other CU Boulder film students, two of whom were Matt
Stone and Trey Parker.

In school Trey had written and directed, and Jason, Matt,
Dian, and several other classmates had sung and danced in,
a gag trailer for a nonexistent musical about legendary Colorado cannibal Alferd Packer, a prospector who had led a
mining party into the Colorado wilderness in the 1800s, got
them lost, and ate them. When the trailer was screened, everyone at film school wanted to know when the movie was
coming out, so Trey wrote an *Oklahoma*-style musical, complete with seven catchy original show tunes. Even then it was
clear that he was freakishly gifted, but when Jason told me
that he, Jason, was raising money for a feature-length, filmed
musical telling the story of a historic Colorado cannibal who,

in the film, was in love with his whorish horse, I thought he was out of his head.

Nevertheless, he got it done, pooling a hundred or so thousand dollars from the financing sources recommended to first-time producers in the books about independent filmmaking: family, friends, and fools. The Avenging Conscience shot the movie in Colorado as winter was ending, freezing their asses off in real mountains covered in real snow. During production Jason demonstrated a flair for promotion, finagling quite a few enthusiastic write-ups and convincing MTV to cover their adventures in renegade filmmaking. When *Cannibal! The Musical* was completed, the Avenging Conscience held a screening in Boulder. They rented a limousine that circled to ferry every member of the cast and crew from the back side of the block to the red carpet at the theater's entrance.

The Sundance Film Festival was effectively the only domestic market for an independent film at that time. When the Avenging Conscience submitted their film for consideration, Sundance didn't even respond with a rejection letter. Festival crashing was not yet a common practice. The Sundance Film Festival still had some marginal claim to being "independent"—though that term, like its music business analogue, "alternative," was losing meaning in proportion to the frequency and volume of its use as a marketing tool—but there were no alternatives to the independence of Sundance. The Slamdance Film Festival, the Sundance publicity parasite that would grow into a legitimate screening and sales venue in its own right, hadn't been founded yet. Its founders would meet at Sundance that year, the same year Jason et al. drove uninvited to Park City, rented a conference room at the Yarrow Hotel, and screened *Cannibal!* for anyone they could get in the door. They didn't secure distribution for the film, but they did meet a number of people who offered representation or a floor to sleep on in Los Angeles.

The Avenging Conscience went to Hollywood. There had been a falling-out with one of the original four, and now it was just Jason, Matt, and Trey. There followed a couple of difficult years, but eventually, championed by a young development executive at Fox Kids named Pam Brady, the Avenging Conscience made two separate pilots, spaced a year apart, for a kids' show called *Time Warped*. By the end of shooting the second pilot they were all exhausted and cranky. Soon after they delivered it, the network disbanded Fox Kids and shelved all the division's projects. Things were looking bleak.

But just before the offices were emptied, Pam's boss, Brian Graden, gave Trey and Matt a personal check for a few thousand dollars to make a cut-paper animated video short called *The Spirit of Christmas*, a more polished sequel to an earlier short called *Jesus vs. Frosty*. Graden planned to distribute the videos as holiday gifts. In the meantime, Jason's dad was moving out of the warehouse where he lived in Boulder, which had doubled as a storage and production space for the second *Time Warped* pilot and still contained important items like the front end of a fake woolly mammoth and props and costumes for *Beowulf on Ice* (never completed, but a trailer had been shot in the warehouse on roller skates). While Trey and Matt worked on the video holiday card, Jason drove to Boulder to clear out the warehouse.

During the slack time between pilots, Trey had written another feature script, *Orgazmo*, about a Mormon who becomes a sex superhero. Jason and Matt cobbled together money for *Orgazmo* from several different sources. A good bit of its million-dollar budget came from a Japanese porn company called Kuki that wanted to feature its girls and products in American mainstream media. Meanwhile, the Christmas video had been mailed by Graden to everyone who was anyone in Hollywood, and the dubs were being dubbed. In short order a nerd would digitize it and post it to the Internet.

But when I met Jason in Las Vegas for the porn convention—the one I was supposed to be covering for *Rolling Stone* in January 1997, for which he was my tour guide—nobody knew that yet. The producer who had come in with the Kuki money was pushing him out of the picture as much as possible. Jason had done his part in banging the drum for the unlikely project when it was just a script and some comic book drawings, and now he was charged with maintaining relationships in the world of actual pornography for the production. His specific errands in Las Vegas were to cast one of the last remaining roles in the film, Very Old Porn Star, and possibly to secure product sponsorship from a lube company.

In Las Vegas Jason introduced me to Farrell Timlake, impresario of a porn company called Xplor Media based in San Diego. Farrell was consulting on *Orgazmo,* and like Jason he was a dreamer with the gift of gab. His company's bread and butter was the category of pornography, then still a fringe category, known as amateur. Their main label, which they had bought out of bankruptcy to start Xplor, was called Homegrown Video. Tapes on the Homegrown label were compilations of homemade porn sent to the office by couples all over the country. The company paid twenty dollars a minute for footage that it used, then packaged the material and sold it to people who liked amateur porn, many of whom happened to be the same people who made it in their homes. My opinion was that if anything should be left to professionals, it was pornography, but Homegrown titles like *Overweight, Oversexed, and Over 40* were absolutely destroying in the marketplace. The Homegrown business model was a perfect expanding loop of production and consumption.

When I got back to Austin, the girl I was dating, who had no connection to anyone I knew in California, popped a cassette into a VCR. The image that came up on the television, barely discernible beneath the static of ten generations of tape, was a line of little round-headed cartoon kids talking like Matt and Trey. Soon afterward a mild bidding war erupted between MTV and Comedy Central, and the *South Park* pilot was scheduled for production in the summer.

Jason worked on the pilot, but *South Park* was not his show. He had been moving stuff out of the Boulder warehouse when *The Spirit of Christmas* was made, and it would have been way out of character for him to fight for top billing on a show he had not been instrumental in putting together. And in light of having produced two features, he didn't much feel like working a midlevel animation production job under his partners when the completed pilot got a six-episode order. When the first episode of *South Park* broke all cable ratings records a few months later, it was way too late for any change of heart—had Jason been given to changes of heart, which he was not.

October Films bought *Orgazmo* right after its first screening at the Toronto Film Festival. The movie sold for a million dollars. That was its production budget on the nose, which meant the financiers got their money back, but that was it. No matter how gracious Matt and Trey were in talking about Jason and their earlier projects in interviews—and for the most part, they were gracious—no one was listening. Now, retroactively, *Orgazmo* and even *Cannibal! The Musical* had been made by just Matt and Trey. The two of them were about to be featured on the covers of *Time, Newsweek, Spin,* and *Rolling Stone.* The ten thousand dollars that had been Jason's producing fee on *Orgazmo* was long gone. He was now broke and unemployed, like me.

2

It took about three weeks for the skin on my hands to heal up after the crash, and afterward my left hand still wasn't working right. X-rays revealed a small broken bone in my wrist, which meant my arm would be put in a cast, and I would be out of action for a few more weeks. It also meant my medical costs would go up considerably, but by then that did not come as bad news. After the crash, which really wasn't my fault except insofar as I was an idiot for: a) owning a motorcycle in the first place; and b) riding it without adequate protective equipment, I had asked of the Camry driver's insurance company only that they pay for my ambulance ride and emergency room visit, and for repairing the motorcycle. They had refused to pay for repairing the motorcycle, which they claimed didn't have sufficient value to merit repair. That may have been true, but fixing it would have cost only a few hundred bucks, and that was all I had in the bank.

One of my friends in Austin was a personal injury attorney. He had offered to represent me for free right after the crash, but since all I had wanted was my costs covered, I had declined. Now I called him again, and he took up my case. The increase in medical expense due to the fracture was nice in that my "pain and suffering" increased commensurately. "Loss of income" would have been a hard sell, since I didn't have any. We toyed briefly with adding "loss of consortium with self" to the litany of my agonies, since I had been unable to use either hand for three weeks, but my friend could find no record of a prior case in which that claim had been made as a basis for damages, and we decided that trying to set a precedent might put the whole enterprise in jeopardy. With my forearm wrapped in a fiberglass cast that I used to wedge half-gallon tubs of peach ice cream against my stomach, I sat on the porch of my apartment with my feet against the rail and spooned myself into creamy, sugared bliss, contemplating the world of opportunities that lay before me.

My life had hardly changed materially, but in just a few short weeks I had come to feel completely different about it. Right before the accident I had started taking Paxil, a second-generation selective serotonin reuptake inhibitor manufactured and marketed by SmithKline Beecham. The psychiatrist who prescribed it had told me I wouldn't feel anything for several days at the earliest, but that was not my experience. Less than an hour after eating the first half-tablet I felt a mild, euphoric dizziness like the first pulse of ecstasy, which I hadn't taken since 1986, back before it even came in pills and you had to lick the bitter powder off the bindle. Sitting alone at my desk I laughed out loud at the profound interest I suddenly felt in the mundane goings-on in a picture postcard taped to the wall in front of me.

I hadn't been interested in anything for months; the post-card was an unlikely first subject. It depicted a standard Venetian canal scene: a gondola tied off to a stone building, with some tiny people in it who broke down into a swarm of benday dots if you looked at them very closely, which I was doing now. My nose was about three inches from the wall. Marvelous, that we ingenious creatures had found a way to capture an image on film, separate the image into its component colors, and compose those colors in dot patterns that could be laid over one another in transparent inks to reconstitute the original picture. I flipped up the postcard. It was from my mom, to whom only days before I had been sobbing on the phone about the sorry state of my life. I called her now and told her how great it was.

The fascination with every person, object, and sensate experience that came my way did wear off in a few days, but the relief did not. I felt better. I felt *good*—so good that a few days later I called a customer-service 800 number at SmithKline Beecham to say so, freaking out some nice lady on the phone bank. Despite being out of money, I immediately put myself on vacation. I closed the scribbled-over notebooks and basked in the simple pleasure of being me. I had been on the way to one of Austin's gorgeous spring-fed municipal pools, to glory in sunshine and my own magnificent muscled body when I crashed. I hadn't been killed, and now I was eating ice cream by the bucket and waiting for an insurance payout. Things could not have been better.

Jason and I had been in close touch all summer. With their series pickup, Matt and Trey were moving out of the beach apartment where the three of them had been living. The rent was eminently reasonable, just fifteen hundred to split three

ways, and Jason had no trouble convincing me to move out
to Los Angeles and into one of the vacated bedrooms. Maybe
in Los Angeles I would write some screenplays or something,
make up dumb stories with Jason and type them up in a few
short weeks, and then Jason would produce them. Maybe that.
But no more of what I thought of as "real" writing—no more
of this literary fiction assfuckery with which I had been making myself miserable for the entirety of my middle twenties.
The insurance settlement, twenty-five thousand dollars, came
through in the fall. I loaded my few possessions into a U-Haul
and headed west, arriving at the beach in November.

Our apartment was in a scruffy little town called Playa del
Rey, roughly in the center of the curve that makes up Santa
Monica Bay. Playa was situated on the south side of Ballona
Creek, the drainage that ran past the last undeveloped wetland in the coastal basin. Just north across the drainage was
Marina del Rey, a paradise of cheezy glitz, fake tits, and high-
rise condominiums, but somehow Playa had dodged improvement for decades. It was reasonably accessible to Los Angeles proper, but wedged as it was between Ballona Creek to
the north and the flight easement of LAX just to the south,
it felt like a world apart. There was no Starbucks or
7-Eleven or McDonald's, just a local coffee shop called
Tanner's, a little market called Gordon's, and a handful of
bars and burger joints. Property owners in Playa rarely listed
vacancies in the paper, preferring to tack up signs on phone
poles. Many tenants in the neighborhood had been there for
decades, moving from apartment to ratty apartment. Egrets
and pelicans mucked around for fish in the nearby wetland,

and crew teams from UCLA and Loyola Marymount sculled in the dirty but placid creek.

Our section of Playa was a cul-de-sac called the Jungle, either for the vegetation that grew wildly in the alleys between the densely packed, ramshackle houses and condominiums or for the beery luau parties that spilled out onto the sand on weekends. The apartment was in a stucco triplex right on the sand, painted the color of doll's flesh. It was soggy and filthy, but in the evenings the sunset coming through a big bay window turned our living room a mellow shade of orange. In the mornings, pro volleyball players in bikinis practiced on the nets beyond our patio. You weren't supposed to have fires on the beach, but the lifeguards didn't care as long as you had them at night, which was the only time you wanted to have them anyway.

Jason and I had no clear plan, but we each held the unspoken hope that somehow together, after small successes and subsequent spirals into failure, we would be unstoppable. I felt the last few years of my life had been wasted, not only because I had failed to produce anything of merit, but because I had not enjoyed them. I realize that sounds like claptrap, and of course it is, but the point that life is short cannot be disputed. And despite the positive attitude Jason maintained and his continued friendship with Matt and Trey, who now lived together just up the street, I knew that he couldn't be entirely happy with how things were turning out for him, either.

He had stayed sober for five or six years after rehab, and then a couple of years back he had started getting high again. Whether his getting high was a symptom or a cause of difficulties within the Avenging Conscience—or whether it was either—was not my business. But Jason had been sober when they had started working together, and now he wasn't, and whether he got high too much had been the subject of several arguments between Jason and the two of them. Matt was an inveterate recreational arguer, and he knew full well that the getting-high thing was a solipsistic torpedo. Once introduced as a problem, it was one by virtue of having been introduced; on the other hand, that didn't mean getting high wasn't a problem. Jason's only course of defusing the torpedo would have been to stop getting high, but even that wouldn't really have defused it, because it would have been an admission that there had been a problem—and it would have meant that he couldn't get high. So it was a complicated business, the getting-high thing, though as I say, not mine.

The heat from *South Park* brought Matt and Trey the opportunity to work with the Zucker brothers, the film-makers who had made, among other fine films, *Airplane*. *BASEketball*, a sports-movie spoof conceived by the Zuckers in which a game similar to horse becomes a national pastime, was obviously an absurd idea, but the production was the real deal, a studio feature at Universal. After years of scrounging for burrito change in the sofa cracks, between *South Park* and now *BASEketball* the two of them were both incredibly busy and flush with cash. If Jason had been thinking that the three of them would keep making features while those two worked on *South Park*—because one way of looking at *South Park* was that it would lend new feature projects momentum—that wasn't how things were going.

The third roommate in our apartment was Dian Bachar, Jason's old classmate, the actor who had been tagged and

released in *Search for Shamu*. Dian had also play
of a sex-crazed virgin miner in *Cannibal*. Dian
credibly talented actor, an absolute natural at
whatever character he chose, but after college he had returned
to Littleton, the Denver suburb where he and Matt had grown
up, to become a bricklayer. He was perfectly proportional
but small, not much over five feet and slight as an elf, and in
light of that and his stupendous laziness, beside which Jason
looked like an engine of industry, bricklaying seemed an odd
choice of profession. But Dian was an odd creature.

It had been a herculean task to for Jason to convince him
to leave his bright future in masonry and come out to Los
Angeles to play Choda Boy, the dildo-helmeted sidekick in
Orgazmo, even though—or rather, precisely because—the part
had been written expressly for him. Dian suspected the entire
project had been conceived with the sole aim of getting him
in front of a camera with a dick on his head. He tended to
suspects plots were being hatched against him—and, in fairness, they sometimes were. His paranoia made hatching plots
against him, or pretending to be hatching plots against him,
which if you think about it pretty much the same thing, nearly
irresistible.

Like Jason, Dian was a chronic pot smoker, but unlike
Jason, Dian always thought he was about to quit smoking
pot, so it was quite rare that he bought pot of his own. He
"borrowed" pot from Jason, or when Jason was out of the
house, he simply stole it. No matter how far up in a closet
or deep down in a sneaker Jason had hidden his bag of good
green weed, upon arriving home he would find it shrunken.
In order to protect his good green weed, Jason started

leaving a daily ration of mediocre brown weed out in the open for Dian to steal. Since Dian would steal and smoke the first pot he came across, the Dian bowl actually kept Jason's good pot pretty safe. Dian was sneaky but not particular. He also came with a reputation for violence. The previous summer at the *South Park* office, where he had been employed as the worst production assistant in the history of production assistants, he had stabbed Matt in the ass with an X-acto knife.

I realize that I have not painted the portrait of an ideal roommate, and I will not pretend that Dian was one. He never washed a dish, he flew into a rage if you disposed of the weird food he left to rot in the refrigerator, and he played the same songs over and over on his stereo at top volume. I now know definitively that "It's a Long Way to the Top (If You Wanna Rock 'n' Roll)." But he was hilarious, and beneath the interpersonal quirks he was a sweet, even sentimental guy. The key to enjoying him as a roommate was to think of him not as a conventional domestic partner, who might pitch in when it was time to scrub the bathroom, but as an unruly exotic animal—a hundred-pound ferret, a monkey with a drinking problem—that you were lucky to have for a friend.

Jason had literally hundreds of friends in Los Angeles, and we were never at a loss for something to do at night. If we weren't having a bonfire on our own beach, there were parties in the hills and shows at clubs in Hollywood. I felt a little weird that I didn't have to go make friends of my own, but I was with Jason, and he knew where the good times were to be had. Everyone was hilarious, all the girls were gorgeous, it was summer all the time, and we were welcome everywhere we went. I gave myself over to his tour of the glittering idiot city. We had a ball, and I felt immune to consequence.

*   *   *

It was with that feeling of immunity to consequence that I took a role in Farrell Timlake's magnum opus. As he described it, this great work was to be a porno comedy with dozens of different characters, combining virtually every genre of filmmaking into one big hilarious sex festival. My character was named El Niño, a masked *luchador* Jason and I cooked up for the occasion. El Niño wore motorcycle boots and a Speedo and, because I could not get my hands on a Mexican wrestling mask fast enough, a black Spandex hood I found at the Pleasure Chest, a bondage emporium in West Hollywood.

The hood was creepy rather than silly. It didn't have eyeholes, and it blotted out my features entirely, but since I wasn't sure I wanted a future in porno, that seemed like a good idea. I could make out basic shapes through the fabric, but that was all, so when I put the hood on I had to walk with my hands outstretched, and I tended to trip and bump into things, so the net effect returned to being ridiculous. Farrell said he would decide later how to slot in El Niño, plotwise—maybe El Niño would be a bungling assassin, or maybe he would be a bodyguard to Shiny Jim, the hairless alien pimp character Dian had developed and was in talks to portray.

Farrell had an ingenious technique for securing upscale locations for free, which was telling the people who lived in them that if they let him shoot at their homes, they could watch. While this proposition obviously wasn't for everyone, it was for more people than you might imagine. Farrell never had a problem finding locations. El Niño was scheduled to make his debut in a tacky Hollywood mansion rented by four or five entertainment types in their twenties, former frat guys from UCLA who had made it into independent producing or the middle ranks at established entertainment companies.

What Farrell had neglected to tell me—probably because he hadn't thought it worth mentioning—was that an informal rider to the free location agreement stipulated that the hosts could invite a few friends over to watch, too. When we arrived at the house, there was already a small party going on, and by the time everything was set up, there were forty or fifty people, mainly but by no means exclusively male, milling around the house and yard. I knew a handful of them, but most were strangers. I wasn't sure which was more regrettable, doing this in front of people who knew me or doing this in front of people who didn't.

Another guy would also be performing that evening: Manny, one of Farrell's regulars, a very nice guy with a great set of junk, who took his profession seriously. I asked him if he planned to take off his sunglasses for the shoot—we were inside, and it was getting dark outside. He shook his head and told me they were his trademark.

Farrell had booked two girls for the shoot. In the interest of taking the nervous edge off things, I approached them to make a little small talk. One was an astonishing beauty, a brunette with blinding blue eyes, flawless milky skin, and a figure without defect or even idiosyncrasy except in how closely it resembled the *Maxim* readership ideal of physical perfection. She was from Romania, or some other benighted Balkan porn recruitment ground, and spoke absolutely no English. The other was a girl from Costa Mesa, with an ass the size of a washing machine. This one spoke perfectly good

English but seemed already to have taken a strong dislike to me.

The Romanian beauty was a real pro and performed only with people who had current AIDS tests, which Manny naturally had. I would be performing with a condom, but I didn't have the right paperwork, so the girl from Costa Mesa and I were stuck with each other. Neither one of us was happy about it. I will spare the reader a description of the next hour or so, except to say that I spent much of it watching waves of ass rippling through a gauze of black spandex, the scene was taped in the living room in front of the entire party, and my antidepressant made it nearly impossible for me to climax by conventional means. Most of the tape was spent on me all by myself in boots and a spandex hood, jacking off on the couch under the disgusted gaze of the girl from Costa Mesa and a dwindling crowd of onlookers. The night would have been a total bust except that I first met my attorney later in the evening, when even more people showed up and the shoot turned into a party. I believe I am the only writer in Hollywood who can claim to have first met his attorney while wearing just a Speedo, motorcycle boots, and a spandex bondage hood, right on the heels of masturbating publicly—but then again, who knows?

That was the beginning and end of my career in Adult, unless I count the scene we shot later, which had no sex in it, which was part of Farrell's "plot." I have no idea what part, as I never saw the finished product, but in the scene Dian as Shiny Jim chases El Niño around the streets and alleys of Playa del Rey on a Friday night—no mean feat, to sprint blind and naked except for heavy boots through a neighborhood where lots of parties are going on. A professional makeup artist had come over to do Dian beforehand, and he looked freaky beyond belief, with his eyebrows waxed over and his hair covered by a rubber dome. As Shiny Jim, he pitched his voice up about three octaves, so for me, it was like being menaced by a tiny villainous eunuch afflicted with alopecia.

Shiny Jim was supposed to catch El Niño under the streetlight illuminating the public restroom out on the beach, where he and El Niño would engage in martial arts combat. Dian was going to kill me by reaching up my ass and yanking out my heart. Jason was propmaster for the shoot. He was supposed to get a beef heart at the butcher's, and the heart and Dian's arm were supposed to be covered in Hershey's syrup, which he was also supposed to get, and which could pass for blood in low light. If I were positioned on my hands and knees and Dian were situated behind me, it would be a simple enough piece of movie magic to angle the camera from low in front of my face and make it look like Shiny Jim was pulling the heart out of my ass. All Jason came back with from the store, though, was a Styrofoam platter of liver—not a great heart substitute—and he forgot the Hershey's altogether, so we had to use Mrs. Butterworth's from our cabinet for the blood.

It was a foggy night, and I couldn't see shit out of the mask, but eventually we made it to the pool of illumination cast by the streetlight, where we were suppposed to have the fight. Dian and I did some wrestling and kung fu moves—Jason was running camera—and then when Farrell thought he had enough of that, we got into position for the kill. I was on all fours screaming into the camera with my faceless face, and Dian was behind me, shrieking his victory over El Niño and holding up a handful of maple-slathered liver that he had pulled out from under my stomach, when the police car pinned us in its lights. I don't know who was more bummed, us or the cops. Jason had the Mrs. Butterworth bottle in one hand and the camera in the other as he gave them some stuttering bunk about a student film, which they clearly didn't buy—but how else to account for a naked guy in a bondage hood play-fighting with a syrupy, hairless alien midget with his hands full of raw liver? They shook their heads and let us go.

I had been in Los Angeles for more than a month; it was time to get to work. Jason had two feature films going to festivals in Park City that winter. Though *Orgazmo* had already secured distribution, Sundance invited it to screen that winter—an irony not lost on Jason, whose first film had not even been formally rejected but was simply ignored. *Cannibal! The Musical* had video distribution by now, but Jason called the directors of Slamdance, the barnacle festival that had not yet brokered its uneasy peace with Sundance, and got *Cannibal* a screening slot in their venue, just to be a dick. Going to Park City sounded like fun to me, but I didn't want to be the only person in town without a film to promote.

Jason showed me set stills from something called *Le Petit Package,* a short Matt and Trey had shot the previous summer but never edited. The pictures were of a bunch of fools with fishing line tied around their dongs so they could be worked like marionettes. If penis shorts were the ticket to Hollywood superstardom, I thought I could deliver. I had been a genital origami practitioner for years, and already had half a dozen tricks in my repertoire. My first inclination was to present them in a magic-show environment, but my old girlfriend from Austin suggested that a kung fu angle might be better.

With Jason's help I made a short film, *The Sound of One Hand Clapping,* in which a Shaolin monk destroys his adversaries with devastating manipulations of his cock and balls. We laid the plans over the Thanksgiving holiday in Marin, roping Jason's younger sister, Brody, into coming down to Los Angeles and helping with the physical production after Christmas. In every obvious way, Brody was Jason's opposite: orderly, practical, presentable, etc. By virtue of knowing Jason, I had known her since she was a freckled kid in grade school. She was no longer a freckled kid. Whereas Jason and I were taking the shortest available routes from clear-eyed youth to dirty bumhood, Brody had become a pert, attractive young woman with excellent professional prospects. She lived in New York, where she worked in commercial production, and doing a project with us would be a pointless sidestep from her normal job. But we convinced her it would be fun.

We filmed *The Sound of One Hand Clapping* in a couple of days on Super 8, using the beach for one location and an empty quadrangle at UCLA for the other. A solemn monk in an ochre robe walks from the beach to his temple. In the temple courtyard he is assailed by ninjas, whom he destroys as described. I was the monk. Jason and Dian were ninjas, as were Andy Kemler (one of Jason and Dian's film school friends who now lived in Playa del Rey), Dian's friend Marcus, and Tony Mindel, a good friend of Jason's and mine from high school.

A professional transfer to digital video would have been expensive, so we set up a Mini DV camera next to a film projector on my desk and taped the raw footage as it played against my closet door. This ghetto transfer gave the image a rich, flickery look with lots of scratches and pops, exactly what I had hoped for, and now the media was in a format that could be edited on a nonlinear system, where we could also add sound. Farrell was kind enough to lend a Media 100 and the services of one of the Xplor editors down in San Diego, who was delighted to get a break from cutting an amateur anal compilation. We cut for a couple of days, added music and titles, and were done. The whole thing cost less than three hundred dollars. I had never had so much fun in my life.

So Jason now had three films going to Park City, and he worked the phones with characteristic brio. Lampooning Sundance's insider politics and self-congratulatory air, he told a reporter from the *New York Times Magazine* that he was starting a new festival called Undance that was so independent it would feature only one film, *The Sound of One Hand Clapping*. The Slamdance organizers, when he informed them of his plans, put their hackles up a little at the idea of another outsider festival; that was supposed to be their territory. But Jason convinced them it was just a joke, and they said we could set up a viewing monitor in their venue. *The New York Times* prefestival magazine issue came out the week before we went to Utah, and we giggled to see that Undance and *The Sound of One Hand Clapping* led a short piece on underground festivals.

In Utah we stayed with most of the cast and crew of *Orgazmo* in a ski condo that was supposed to sleep twelve. In actuality it slept thirty comfortably, as long as you didn't mind sleeping on the carpet, and there was a hot tub outside the sliding-glass doors downstairs. Except for one guy's wife, there were no women at the condo. The place smelled gamy immediately. We were all in our twenties or thirties, with the exception of a single real grown-up, Lloyd Kaufman.

Lloyd was the president of Troma Films, the company that was distributing *Cannibal* on video. Troma was the world's premiere purveyor of haute schlock, with such titles as *The Toxic Avenger, Surf Nazis Must Die,* and *The Class of Nuke 'Em High* in its catalog, and Lloyd tirelessly carried the company message of high-camp gore, bunking down on junkets in the same dumps as the off-kilter film geeks who wore the costumes of his Troma characters at events. The main characters aside from the company mascot, Toxie, the melted-faced, mop-wielding mutant of *Toxic Avenger* fame, were Sergeant Kabukiman (half NYPD cop, half Japanese thespian) and a six-foot Killer Condom with fangs. There were usually also a few juicy promotional girls, but none of those was staying with us at the condo.

Lloyd's enthusiasm for traveling the world with a squad of kids half his age would have been creepy were he himself not so emphatically uncreepy. He was the most urbane of all the film industry people I would ever meet: an impish little man appearing always in his trademark blue blazer and bowtie, who had been a Chinese language scholar at Yale and was married to a lovely woman who was the New York City film commissioner. He was a brilliant conversationalist with an encyclopedic knowledge of film history, and though he knew absolutely everyone who was anyone, he was perfectly happy to sit up all night talking vintage sci-fi with aggressive dweebs. Troma was a private joke he had been perpetrating for more than twenty years. You had to love him, and I instantly did.

Troma's business was predicated on video sales. Occasionally, Troma financed its own productions, which Lloyd directed, but for the most part the company acquired comprehensive rights to produced films that no one else would dream of buying, just when their directors and producers had reached the point of utter despair. The advantage of buying at the bottom of the market was that Troma rarely had to pay a penny up front. So it had gone with *Cannibal*. But Jason, in a typically byzantine but possibly prescient financial maneuver, had raised a small second round of financing to form New Cannibal Society, an LLC that bought back all the ancillary rights (because video was the important set of rights, the ancillaries were theatrical, sound-track, stage, and merchandise) from Troma.

This arrangement had the potential to be a genuine win for both Jason and Troma. Troma knew what its business was—video—and had built its war chest by never once incurring a significant marketing expenditure. Any momentum Jason could generate with a midnight theatrical run, stage play, or merchandise line would increase the value of Troma's asset. Troma's inclusion of *Cannibal* in its cult catalog combined with the interest of core *South Park* fans created the possibility of a small but real market for the assorted *Cannibal* crap Jason envisioned peddling.

Tony Mindel, our friend who had been one of my ninjas, was the principal investor in New Cannibal Society. The bond between Jason and Tony was special, not subject to the natural tides that slowly shift relationships. Their friendship went back to third grade. Tony was one of the sweetest people I will ever know, and certainly savvy enough to realize that there were better investments than those in independent film —or in media undertakings even less sensible, as will be seen—but he was always willing to go one more to keep people together or to keep a dream alive.

Tony had invested in all of Jason's projects up to and including New Cannibal Society. He did not work in a conventional way but lived happily in the cozy maze of the basement apartment under his mom's house in the Marina district of San Francisco, where he managed his investments, smoked pot, did yoga, and quietly fostered the careers of his friends. In addition to the investments in Jason's projects, Tony managed a band called Vinyl, an instrumental octet composed of our high school friend Jon Korty and seven others. Insofar as both *Cannibal* and *Orgazmo* were properties in which he had invested, the festival week was a big one for Tony, too. Projects he had believed in and seeded were coming up in the middle of a media frenzy.

For that was what Sundance was, to a point past parody: rented SUVs bumper to bumper in the streets or stuck to the wheel wells in snow, camera crews taping each other on every corner, cell phones frozen to every head. Mixed in with those who had real business, there were hundreds, maybe thousands, like myself—nobodies from nowhere, aspiring directors, writers, actors, and producers. In fact, it seemed as though there might be more of us than there were of them.

The Gap sponsored Sundance that year and outfitted the official staff in bulky orange jackets. Sundance volunteers wearing the Gap jackets bustled importantly through town, muttered into walkies, and strode head-down on urgent errands. These were supposedly the people in charge. But among the motley hoi polloi there was a palpable air of rebellion. The people in the Gap jackets weren't in charge at all, I realized in the parking lot outside the grocery store, when I saw a grumpy volunteer in a sponsored orange parka get smacked in the face with a snowball. They were targets. A media underclass had come to Utah in a mob.

A carpool of us returned from that grocery expedition to find, wet and shivering at the kitchen table behind steaming mugs of cocoa, the last thing it would have been reasonable to hope for, in light of how much the condo already smelled like a shoe: two absolutely beautiful girls. One of them was without question the most gorgeous girl I had ever seen. She looked a little like Audrey Hepburn, with anime eyes and impossible lips—but it was hard to get more than a glimpse. Andy Kemler skulked between them and the rest of us like a hyena caught by the pack over a stinky carcass he wanted to eat all by himself.

The story that emerged from between impossible lips was this: Heather and Shana—Heather was the one I was already preparing to fall in love with, if she would condescend to speak to me—were actresses who had moved to Los Angeles together from New York the summer before. They were programmers for the Slamdance short film program, but Slamdance was still a shoestring operation, and volunteers were expected to be resourceful. The girls had come to Utah in Shana's ragtop Jeep, trading the ride against lodging with a Slamdance filmmaker whose aunt had a condo in Park City. The Jeep's canvas top had provided no insulation from the bitter cold that started seeping in the moment they left the salt flats two thousand feet below, and by the time they arrived in Salt Lake City, they were frozen. But apparently the filmmaker had not called ahead, because when he reached his aunt from a pay phone, she said they couldn't use the condo. Unfazed, he had directed the girls to his cousin's place in the wilderness toward Park City.

The cousin had opened the door in nothing but a silk kimono, and his eyebrows were shaved off—fine, if slightly *Silence of the Lambs*. Then the cousin led them back to the room where they were supposed to sleep. The entire house was decorated with progressively more elaborate and uncomfortably sexualized shrines to Ariel, the mermaid in *The Little Mermaid*—unsettling, but still in the realm of the acceptable. But the back room to which he had them follow him was completely unfurnished and unadorned, except that one wall was covered in the ragged pelts of cute little furry animals the drag queen country cousin had slain and skinned himself.

Combined, these circumstances constituted a genuine emergency. The girls had been on the road for eighteen hours, there was not an available motel room within fifty miles, and if they fell asleep in the Jeep, they would freeze to death. Heather remembered that a friend of hers in New York had a brother, Andy, who was supposed to be there in Park City. Heather had miraculously reached her friend in New York, gotten Andy's cell phone number, and reached him at our condominium. She had apologized for getting in touch in an emergency but explained the circumstances and asked if there was any chance at all that she and her friend Shana could stay at the condo where Andy was staying. Of course, they would be happy to chip in for its cost.

Andy had declined the request categorically. No way. But let's meet somewhere for drinks. Well, asked Heather, could we come over for long enough to warm up and figure out where we're going to stay?

ANDY: No.

HEATHER: What do you mean, no?

ANDY: There's just not room.

HEATHER: To use the phone?!

ANDY: No. Sorry.

HEATHER: Do I have to call your sister again?

ANDY: Okay, okay, you can come over.

Kemler sulked as the story came out. Now we all had seen the two of them, and there was no way we were going to let them stay anywhere else, even if they wanted to. Jason and I outlasted the rest of the lurkers one night and kept Heather and Shana up talking by the fire until dawn. It would take another month, but eventually I would bamboozle Heather into dating me.

Slamdance had promised a monitor in their main room for *The Sound of One Hand Clapping,* but they realized at the last minute that a monitor placed there would impede traffic through the venue. As an alternative they offered a storage closet in a back hall, accessible from either the restroom area or from behind the main screen. The closet could hold a standing audience of five or six. I was disappointed, but it was their venue. Maybe over the course of the party they had scheduled that night, a few people would find their way back to the closet.

The venue, a club called the Underground, was tunnelly and confusing, with the result that we had steady traffic of lost twos and threes as soon as the party started. Farrell had the idea of offering a shot of Jaegermeister and a viewing for a dollar. When people got drunker, they seemed to like the movie more, and they demanded repeat viewings. Those outside became unruly, pressing in from both directions. It was our good luck that a camera crew from E! arrived just as things got completely out of hand. The cameraman managed to get his Betacam high enough to see over people's heads, and he captured a snatch of my ass off the TV screen. He put the lights on Jason and me, and we yelled an interview on the subject of independent media until the firemen came and herded everyone out into the slush.

3

Back at the condo we decided to form a company. Precisely what the company would do was somewhat beside the point. We were friends who wanted to do something together. In other times or other circumstances we might have started a magazine, a social club, a religion, or a gang. It was the late 1990s, so we started an Internet company.

The first idea for making money was to do something Jason was already trying to do, sell merchandise derived from his intellectual properties. New Cannibal Society had regained from Troma the exclusive license to make *Cannibal* merchandise. Jason hoped to make a similar arrangement with October Films to make *Orgazmo* merchandise and to make still another with Comedy Central to develop *South Park* merchandise. Farrell told us that retail and wholesale sales could easily be conducted online.

But what we really wanted to do was make new movie and television properties of our own. And we wanted to tap into, and provide a platform for, the media underclass that had thronged uninvited to Park City. We knew we weren't alone in feeling alienated from most of what could be seen on TV or in theaters. Everyone we knew, from my most high-brow academic friends to Jason's most reprobate stoner associates, felt alienated from it. What was available on television and in theaters simply did not say what we felt. This was true of network programming and studio movies—but of course it was true of those. What was more distressing was that it was also true of purportedly alternative and independent media, where we might hope to find our values echoed and amplified.

On television there simply was no "alternative" media, not even in the distant reaches of cable. With *Beavis and Butthead* gone, MTV was just a shit factory, and *South Park* was the first hint that Comedy Central might be anything but the junior varsity for toothless network comedy. The same was even more true of the movies. Sundance was first and foremost a marketing outpost for slumming studio talent. Whatever independence it might once have represented had been completely co-opted by mainstream entertainment companies that were using "independence" as a marketing angle. You could find politically correct mewling in the Sundance program—same-sex domestic dramas, vague documentaries about down-trodden brown people—but not much that was really funny or angry, or that pointed specific, non-sponsor-friendly blame.

It didn't have to be that way. The cost of production was becoming absurdly low, as witnessed by our own short film having cost almost nothing. All over the country, people were out there making their own media. They were making it at school. They were making it in basements and bedrooms, using consumer cameras, hardware, and software. We didn't know much about the market for this stuff, but there were useful case studies right at hand. Homegrown Video, with its circle of production and consumption, demonstrated how media could be an instruction manual for the production of more media. Look: Anyone can do it. Troma provided an object lesson in how the marketing of such media could work over the long haul, as long as you never overreached and started incurring big expenses. And *South Park* was the perfect example of how something small and weird, provided it had a genuinely unique voice, could break big overnight.

Operating under the umbrella of New Cannibal Society was discussed as a possibility, but I wanted to start with a clean slate. The ownership structure of New Cannibal Society was already confusing, and I had had nothing to do with the production of Jason's feature films. I was happy to help him organize the production and marketing of merchandise for his finished projects—he wasn't the most organized dude, and it seemed a manageable task. But what really interested me was starting new projects, for which this company would be a launching pad.

Back in Los Angeles we kicked around ideas for the name of the new enterprise, eventually settling on Certified Renegade American Product, or CRAP. Jason liked the idea of an acronym, and crap was what we proposed to sell at first. I liked the idea that anything could be "certified" as "renegade," because it got to the heart of what was so sinister about the American culture machine as a whole, its ability to effortlessly absorb any objection to it and then regurgitate the objection as a commercial product.

Our first company slogan we stole: "Commodify Your Dissent" (*Commodify Your Dissent: Salvos from* The Baffler, edited by Thomas Frank and Matt Weiland). Jason thought the big words were fancy-college bullshit, but really he was of the same mind. Scoop Misker, the newsman on KFOG, the FM station in the Bay Area when we were kids, used to sign off by saying, "That's the news, and if you don't like it, go make some of your own." Misker's diction was more Jason's style, but it all got back to the same thing. The book's point was that "commodify your dissent" is the prime imperative issued by American marketers: Drink this, drive this, buy this product to express your individuality. Our point was slightly different: The most effective mode of criticism isn't criticism but embedding a point of view in your own cultural production, so what you should do is make your dissent into a commodity. There was a very real, if stymied and ironic, idealism in the name we chose for the company, whose first move would be to try to sell T-shirts and other licensed garbage.

Tony Mindel was in for twenty-five thousand dollars of seed financing. Farrell proposed to build the company's Internet presence and run our online sales through Xplor's warehouse in San Diego. Jason was to be the company's president, creative genius, and impresario. Based on what imaginary credentials I have no idea, I proposed to be our strategic and business visionary. These were all broad duties that would leave little time for minutia, so we tricked Brody into moving out to Los Angeles. Somebody would have to run the books and deal with reality if we were going to get anything done.

None of us would be getting paid at first, not until the company had some cash flow. Until then we would all get by on what we were already doing. Tony had his own money, and he was developing a driving range up in northern California. Xplor and Homegrown in San Diego were Farrell's main businesses. Jason had his morass of *Cannibal* and New Cannibal Society stuff, and he and Tony and Farrell were already involved together in another business that was winding down, a record label and party-promoting company called Global Underworld. At the same time as this was happening, I was starting a consulting business with another friend, Alex Frankel, called Quiddity, which will receive its own treatment in these pages. Brody actually had the most dependable skill set in the group; she could freelance as a production coordinator in Los Angeles.

This was 1998, and screwing in a lightbulb without a Web site to celebrate it would have been unthinkable. If our company's first foray into commerce would be online sales, then we needed a Web site immediately. The World Wide Web was still something of a mystery to me. I used e-mail, and I used a browser to look at things, but I had no idea how any of it really worked. At that time Jason had an even less developed understanding of the Internet than I did. He seemed to be under the impression that the World Wide Web was a magical wonderland in which you had only to imagine something, and so it would be.

Xplor Media had been selling videos on the Web for years, and they were supposed to be CRAP's interactive partner, but that partnership began to unravel almost as soon as it began. At the first design meeting between Farrell, Jason, and myself in San Diego, Jason and Farrell pulled massive preparatory bong hits and began to conceptualize. A visitor would come to the site's home page and then have choices about looking at stuff or going to a store to buy something. So far, so good. But Jason and Farrell both strenuously resisted the idea of a hierarchical structure of any kind, arguing instead for an exploratory, psychedelic user experience, in which a visitor might fall though trapdoors, enter tunnels, ride spaceships, be absorbed into rainbows, and so on.

About an hour into this design meeting—I was slow on the uptake—it became clear to me that Farrell didn't have the slightest idea what he was talking about, either, which in light of Xplor's responsibilities as the interactive provider in our undertaking was troubling. Farrell explained that he did the high-level conceptual work for Xplor's Web sites, and the actual *technical* work of Xplor's site development was carried out by still another company, which was Xplor's interactive partner. As far as I was concerned, this stunk. Jason and Farrell both thought I was being a pill, but I left the meeting determined that Xplor Media would not be the interactive partner for whatever it was we turned out to be doing. As soon as we returned to Los Angeles, I began to conspire with Brody, who hated all the porn stuff from the start, about how we could separate from the San Diego contingent.

As it turned out, the conspiracy was unnecessary. Shortly after our design meeting, Farrell had some kind of disagreement with the two shady guys who hosted the Xplor sites, and they shut down the Xplor Media servers, an action that had the unintended effect of curtailing Xplor's ability to host a Web site for CRAP. Needless to say, I was delighted, despite the inconvenient timing.

After Utah, in a postfestival interview with a *Variety* reporter, Jason had announced that we were planning another of what he termed "barnacle festivals" in Cannes, which would be timed to coincide with the Cannes Film Festival and International Film Market that spring. While it was true that in

Park City we had joked about the possibility of staging an event in Cannes and naming it Cannes You Dig It?, it was patently untrue that we had a plan to put on such an event. None of us had ever even been to Cannes.

The joke turned out to be on us. *Variety* ran its alternative-festival follow-up piece, and several inches down in the text was the announcement of the upcoming Cannes You Dig It? Film Festival. It seemed a harmless if pointless prank Jason had perpetrated, until a few days later when the videotapes started arriving. Our address wasn't listed in the article, but within a week more than twenty tapes had come to our door, and by the end of two weeks it was more like a hundred.

After watching three or four of the tapes at random, I knew for certain that I wanted no part of programming a film festival—ever. Even Jason's patience was tested. But Dian had nothing better to do, and Heather, who by this time had succumbed to my advances, actually liked to watch hours and hours of tedious, self-indulgent dreck intermittently spiced with poignancy, excitement, or comedy—and she had the Slamdance programming experience to prove it.

So Dian and Heather became the Cannes You Dig It? Film Festival programming committee. They sat in the living room for days on end, watching submissions. Jason and I came out of our rooms when they laughed loudly or groaned in pain. Dian at one point became so incensed at the shittiness of a submission that he ejected the tape from the VCR, found the number on its label, and called the filmmaker at home. He identified himself as the Cannes You Dig It? Film Festival programming committee and told the poor filmmaker to go fuck himself for making something so stupendously shitty.

The filmmaker at first was taken aback, but then he became equally pissed off and started yelling back at Dian, who screamed that if the filmmaker wanted his ass kicked, he should come right over and Dian would kick it for him. This truly was how film criticism should be conducted, in person, and it was at that moment that I began to believe in the Cannes You Dig It? undertaking.

But now we had a company without a Web site, and it was having its first event, which naturally also needed a Web site. The smart thing to do would have been to go down to the bookstore and purchase a beginner's book on HTML, but I wouldn't have that brainchild for two more years, until I had run one Internet company into the ground and offered my expert advice to countless others.

We had the good fortune right then to be introduced to Jolon Bankey and Martha Clayton. Jolon and Martha had just arrived in Los Angeles from Boston in a van containing themselves and all their earthly possessions—two cats, a lot of books, a fiberglass tub full of koi, and some computers— and they had moved into an apartment about a mile away from our place. Jolon was a few years younger than we were, maybe twenty-five or twenty-six. He wore tattered skateboarding clothes and had scabs all over his hands and knees from falling down. But he seemed confident that he and Martha could make a Web site for the Cannes You Dig It? Film Festival, and in short order they did.

From that beginning Jolon and Martha became CRAP's interactive partners, and they became our friends. Having lazily accepted so many of the conventional advantages myself, I had tremendous respect for autodidacts, and to a great extent Jolon was one. At fifteen, enrolled in public school in Dallas, he had called a meeting of his parents and principal and calmly informed them all that he was no longer challenged by the school curriculum. He took his GED, moved out, and lived in a squat for a couple of years, skating and doing crimes. When he got bored, he moved up to Providence, Rhode Island.

We figured out that he had lived there during my last couple of years of college, and that he had known several of my professors. While living in Providence and supporting himself as a house painter, he had simply walked in and audited close to a full course load at Brown. After his then girlfriend, who was a student there, graduated, and they broke up, he moved to Boston. In Boston he took all the computer classes available in the local community college system and went to work at a Web shop called Strategic Interactive Group. While at SIG, he had been a lead designer on L. L. Bean and SmithKline Beecham Web sites. As the company moved toward its initial public offering, he learned about options packages and found out he didn't have one, so he quit.

Martha had worked at a boutique ad agency in Boston, and she had also been a bike messenger and bartender. They met at the bar where she worked, where Jolon was the last drunk standing night after night. They were now a business partnership as well as a couple. In Los Angeles they were perfectly happy to hole up for days in their apartment taking downers and speed, playing with the cats, feeding the fish, and coding massive, secure, bug-free Web sites. They fought all the time, but you had the distinct impression that if you fucked with one of them, the other would smash something on the back of your head. Martha's temper put mine in the shade, and though from time to time we all had spectacular blowouts, we were lucky to count them as partners.

The Cannes You Dig It? site was simple, just a page with the logo—a big cartoon question mark—contact information, and a listing of the films selected by our crack panel. Among these films were some gems. This was the stuff: movies too weird to be seen anywhere else, too weird even to be accepted by normal film festivals, that nevertheless were great.

Junky was made by Tony Nittoli, a filmmaker who made wrenching, gritty, no-budget Super 8 puppet dramas all by himself. *Junky* told the story of a cracker-addicted parrot forced to perform humiliating acts by its keeper. Tony used a combination of stop-motion and live-action, and since he couldn't afford actors, he used his girlfriend as a secondary character. Unfortunately, she thought his movies and puppet obsession were stupid, so the only way he could get her into scenes was to affix the parrot to the end of a broomstick and chase her around the house with the camera rolling. *Junky* featured a poignant flight sequence in this vein, with the bird croaking entreaties and rounding corners just as the girlfriend disappeared around farther corners. The sequence ended with a heartbreaking squawk as a door slammed shut on the parrot.

Dog People was a documentary made by Brad Jarvis, a kid who had recently graduated from USC. Brad was depressed because he had just found out that USC had a cruel policy preventing student filmmakers from actually making any money on films they had made as students if any of the university's equipment had been used in the making, but Brad still hoped to reach an audience with *Dog People*. The film profiled three obsessive pet owners: a plushy/furry couple who got married in mascot costumes and used their dogs as groomsmen and bridesmaids; a wealthy single woman with a clearly unwholesome attachment to her big-balled Rhodesian ridgeback; and a sweet old lady whose beloved poodle, memorialized in a gilded shrine of photos, had been gulped down whole by the escaped python of an unapologetic metalhead up the street.

Scout's Honor was an incredibly graphic hard-core porno movie whose cast consisted entirely of inflatable sex dolls. Because the dolls were smaller than real people, about three-quarter scale, the filmmakers, Steve Hall and Cathee Wilkins, had been forced to build elaborate miniature sets, and they had hand-sewn fantastic costumes for the different vignettes. The voices were great, and the puppetry and camera work were fantastic. Watching *Scout's Honor* you went from laughing, to getting a little turned on, to remembering you were just watching plastic dolls have nasty sex, and back to laughing again.

None of these films or filmmakers was going to get the Cannes You Dig It? Film Festival to France. We had enough money for one plane ticket, and that was about it. Having solicited all these fine entrants, semiaccidentally or not, we now were in danger of not being able to provide a screening venue. Succor arrived at the last minute in the form of *Lucinda's Spell,* a feature-length celebration of sexual wizardry written, produced, directed by, and starring an Englishman named Jon Jacobs; more accurately, succor arrived in the form of Jon Jacobs himself.

Lucinda's Spell was Jon Jacobs's third or fourth feature. The star of a Jon Jacobs movie was always Jon Jacobs, and the salient characteristic of the Jon Jacobs character, whether he was a cowboy, rock star, druid, or postapocalyptic high-wayman, was a sexiness so overpowering that it obliterated any evil that dared to challenge it. In *Lucinda's Spell,* Jon Jacobs had cast himself as a warlock in contemporary New Orleans. His character was Merlin's direct descendant, who had to find among all the witch-prostitutes in the French Quarter the one possessed of sufficient sexy magic to accept his sex-magical seed and bear the sex-magical reincarnation of Merlin himself.

To say that Jon Jacobs was a living, breathing Austin Powers would be unfair to the singularity that was Jon Jacobs. You even were sad that Mike Myers had invented Austin Powers, for Jon Jacobs had been Jon Jacobs for al-most four decades, and to have one's self so overshadowed by billboards, to have one's heartfelt utterances echoed and drowned out by catch phrases, must have been the height of personal tragedy. Or maybe not. Jon Jacobs was so overflow-ing with positive vibes that he may have been entirely un-aware of any resemblance he might have borne to Austin Powers.

But Jon Jacobs was indeed an International Man of Mys-tery. He loved spangled costumes. He got out of impossible situations in the nick of time. And he had a big infectious smile full of crazy English teeth, though there the physical resem-blance ended. Jon Jacobs was a good-looking guy, lithe and tan. He wore shiny shirts, fancy sweatpants, suede train-ers, and silver rings: a Euro-club-DJ personal style.

But the real reason it would be unfair to compare the two is that the ladies surrounding Jon Jacobs at all times put Austin Powers's pussy posse to shame. Jon Jacobs was such a sex superstar that wherever he went, there were always at least three incredibly, incredibly, *incredibly* hot ladies with him—and we were pretty sure he got to sleep with them *all*. They didn't even fight over him. They just took turns, or had threesomes, foursomes, fivesomes—whatever caught everyone's fancy—was our impression. And he was such a nice guy that you couldn't even be jealous about it. Jon Jacobs deserved to be Jon Jacobs.

He had finished *Lucinda's Spell* for far less money than he had raised to make it, and as a result he had the kind of promotional budget indie filmmakers were supposed to only dream about. While we were trying to figure out how Jason could afford to rent the right format TV/VCR combo over in France to screen the movies, Jon Jacobs casually offered to drop ten grand on a Cannes You Dig It? Film Festival party. If he went to France, he would of course be bringing the Jon Jacobs ladies, and he would be happy to put them to work on the Croisette, the beachfront walk in Cannes, promoting the Cannes You Dig It? Film Festival along with *Lucinda's Spell*.

At dawn the day before The Cannes Film Festival started, I gave Jason a ride to the international terminal at LAX. He looked like a lonely camel on the curb, bleary and loaded down with duffel bags. The bags contained his clothes, a sleeping bag, a wadded banner we had made, and the twenty or thirty videotapes that were the Cannes You Dig It? Film Festival. A huge surge of pity for him—for both of us, for the sad jokes we were making of our lives—spiked out from my heart.

There had been a time when we both showed tremendous promise simply as bright young people who would *do* something. The school where we had met had pulled the brightest children from an area without match in liberal intellectual values or the capital to make a *Free to Be You and Me* ideal come true. Jason and I had been at the center of our spoiled and drug-crazed fun-times mob; but between us, even during all that, we had captained sports teams and gotten ourselves elected to silly high school offices. After getting caught smoking pot, Jason, Tony, and I had been called before the judicial council, on which Jason was supposed to be holding a seat. I had been made one of our student body presidents right before being put in rehab. Even with all the disciplinary disasters on our records, we had each won faculty-judged awards at graduation. Was it too much to hope that we wouldn't grow up to be total losers?

But then a few of the Cannes You Dig It? filmmakers who had dropped by the beach apartment in the past few days separated from the check-in line to greet Jason—and then a few more. They surrounded him, helping with the bags. I hadn't realized until then that they were all going to France, too. But of course they were. Wouldn't you scrape together the airfare, if your film was going to be screened in Cannes? The motley Cannes You Dig It? Film Festival, led by my scattered and balding but still inspired and indomitable best friend, was on.

He kept us posted by telephone over the next few days. Lloyd Kaufman of Troma was a regular at Cannes and let Jason sleep at the suite that was Troma's headquarters, on the floor between Toxie and Troma's ultraluscious promo girl, Tiffany Shepis (well worth a Googling). Jason and Jon Jacobs struck a deal with one of the restaurant owners on the Croisette; now Cannes You Dig It? had an actual venue.

The Troma squadron and the Jon Jacobs ladies costumed up (the Troma team as their usual selves, the ladies as the *Lucinda's Spell* sex witches several of them had played) and held daily parades on the Croisette to promote the Cannes You Dig It? Film Festival and party, which now was also a Troma event. The parades sounded to me like the worst kind of humiliation, but Jason was having an awesome time. He said everybody loved the parades.

To prove him right, the cameras ate it up. The E! *Wild On* crew—ever dependable, we were learning, when there might be nudity in the offing—was all over our festival. Kelly, the most absolutely flawless of the Jon Jacobs ladies, was pulled from the parade by a photographer from Italian *Vogue* for a surfside mermaid photo shoot. The night of the Cannes You Dig It? Film Festival party, it was the hottest ticket in town. Attendees packed the venue on the sand, and the hordes who did not get in were kept off the chain-link fence by hired guards with Dobermans.

Jason returned in exhausted triumph. And so, another success, in the vague way we were coming to define success at Certified Renegade American Product: More people wanted to be there than could fit, it was written up in a few places, and afterward in Los Angeles we met people who had heard about what we were doing.

4

By holding a weird little film festival, we had stumbled into a great way to meet more of the kind of people with whom we might want to work. But nothing had actually been sold at the Cannes You Dig It? Film Festival. We had plenty of ideas for movies and television shows that we wanted to make. But we had no source of financing for them. In business terms we were in worse shape than when we started.

Most of Tony's initial investment had gone into the design and manufacture of *Cannibal* merchandise and the wholesale purchase of *South Park* merchandise. It was too late to make a licensing deal with Comedy Central, and we didn't have the capital or infrastructure to negotiate one anyway. No licensing deal was coming together for *Orgazmo,* either. October Films had marketed it as a big movie, and its performance in relation to its marketing budget had not been good. October was being sold to Universal, and the last thing anyone at October cared about was what to do with merchandise rights to an underperforming comedy they had paid too much to market. They were worried about losing their jobs.

The electronic store Jolon and Martha were building was also costing money. We were paying them a nominal fee, shopping-cart software had to be licensed, and a merchant account had to be set up at a bank—hard costs we hadn't considered. At the end of winter we had made the bad decision to send a few boxes of merchandise off with the Snowcore rock tour that Primus was headlining. (Primus: alt-prog-funk-rock trio led by bassist Les Claypool, who is generally regarded by fellow musicians and perennially named in popular polls as "The Best Bass Player in the World." Because Les is such a Monster of Rock, there comes a certain discomfort in introducing him too familiarly, but he is a buddy who will pop up from time to time in this saga, so he has to be introduced. It had been Jason's job to contact Les and ask him to do a theme song for *South Park.*

Later on, Matt showed Les my dick movie, and then Les got in touch with me to talk about something he wanted to do—a kids' show called *Johnny Cod* that sadly never came to fruition—and by the time mentioned above everybody was palsy-walsies.) But none of us had accompanied the merchandise on its journey, and most of it simply got lost. For that venture I had loaned the company five thousand dollars. Now that was gone, and it was my own company that owed it to me. Maybe I could pay myself back someday, but by summer, CRAP was pretty much out of cash.

Technically, I was still represented by ICM, the agency that had negotiated my book deal. The book division in New York and entertainment divisions in Los Angeles were separated by more than just geography, but in the course of film option sales my New York literary agent had introduced me to the film rights agent in LA. I proposed that now I would develop the relationship, and maybe we could bridge it into some kind of representation for CRAP. I called the film rights agent and told her that I now lived in town. I was "moving into film and television," and in fact I "already had a few projects going" that I hoped to discuss with someone at the agency. She kindly set up a meeting for me with one of the agency's young TV reps.

I still didn't have a car, and after the accident I wore my leathers whenever I was on the motorcycle. In hot weather they made me sweat profusely. By the time I arrived at the agency's Wilshire Boulevard office, I was coated in horsy slime. Sweat continued to pour off my face as I entered the white marble foyer. I was certain the reception staff could hear the sucking sounds coming out of my boots. Stinky steam rose from the puddle in my helmet, cradled under my arm, and I had a messenger bag strapped across my back. One of the receptionists tried to direct me to the delivery entrance. With affected breeziness I said that no, I was a client, and I had a meeting with so-and-so. The receptionist cocked a shaped eyebrow, spoke quietly into his headset, and directed me to the seating area.

In due course the assistant of the agent with whom I had an appointment came down to the foyer to collect me. I followed her upstairs, the false confidence with which I had clarified my status at the reception evaporating faster than my sweat. The leathers, in addition to smelling bad, made lots of noise when I moved, a creaking accompaniment to the clonk and squish of my boots. The worst part was that wearing this getup to the meeting had been a deliberate decision. I could easily have brought some khakis and a button-down in my bag and found a place to change before the meeting, but instead I had hoped to make a singular impression of "edginess."

My understanding was that being "edgy" represented the peak of desirability in the entertainment industry, and it had been my thought that the Mad Max outfit would signify that I was a wild, unpredictable, slightly dangerous creative type. But in the air-conditioned halls of the agency I just felt like a fraudulent, sweaty clown.

"I understand you have a short film to show us!" the agent said brightly, once we sat down in her office.

She regarded me expectantly, sitting on the edge of her chair in a prim blouse, an engagement ring sparkling on her hand. Her assistant sat with pen poised, a pad balanced on her knee in case I said something worth writing down. I did have a short film to show them. Oh yes I did. But the last thing I wanted to do now was show it to them. I wanted to flee, clomping, creaking, and squishing, back out those hallways and into the street, where I could bang my forehead against the asphalt. With an almost out-of-body sense of disbelief at what I was doing, I pulled the videotape from my messenger bag and handed it over.

"Oh! I didn't know you were an actor," cried the agent with obligatory enthusiasm, when I came up on the screen in my ochre robe. I mumbled that really I wasn't and cringed back into the cushions of her sofa. The first two minutes were interminable for all of us—for them because the first two minutes were just of me walking around to the accompaniment of birdsong and lame flute sounds, and for me because I knew what was coming. When my ass filled the screen with a brassy gong sound, the agent tried a smile, but the sight of my stretched and twisted genitalia a few seconds later wiped it right off her face. After that the movie went on *forever*. Neither one of them made a peep. I thought the assistant might start crying. When the screen finally went black, the agent popped the tape from the VCR and turned around to face me, holding it out by a corner like a plastic-bagged turd.

"That's nice," she said. "But I'm not sure what we can do with it."

With the bridge of major agency representation in cinders behind us, CRAP forged onward. Up in Utah the past winter, Jason had met a producer named John Frank Rosenblum, who had a new production company called On Track Entertainment that was financed to produce a couple of low-budget television pilots. Developing one of these for On Track was the subject of our initial meetings with John Frank and his assistant, Larry laBeouf.

John Frank was about our age, but his bearing and dress made him seem a decade older. Nerds by now having long had their revenge, I don't think he would be hurt to see himself characterized as something of a nerd—not the fake kind with a fancy haircut and four-hundred-dollar goggles, but the real kind with true passion for unusual pursuits and not much of an eye for fashion.

In his childhood he had been a serious fan of the British sci-fi serial *Dr. Who*. At the age of twelve, without his counterparts in England having any idea he was only twelve years old, John Frank had negotiated to become the exclusive American merchandise licensee for the show. John Frank became even more involved with the show in his early teens. He talked his parents into getting him an apartment out of town, then set up the phone so that calls would be relayed to another phone he had set up in England. Soon he was flying regularly to and from England and actually writing on *Dr. Who*—he even appeared in a few episodes—all before he was old enough to drive, without his parents having any idea he was leaving the country.

He retained an abiding affection for sci-fi and its relics, and he had been using the Internet since it was called ARPANET. When we met with John Frank he still had a spectacular mullet, and he had been continuously enrolled as an undergraduate at USC for nearly ten years. The latter was not because he was stupid (he was not) or even lazy (he was, but only in very specific ways), but because the conditions of his educational trust stipulated that he would receive a generous stipend until, but only until, he completed an undergraduate degree, and only so long as he didn't flunk or drop out of school at any point. For almost a decade John Frank had carefully rigged his schedule, shifting majors when necessary and failing or dropping a class when to pass it would have advanced him too quickly toward a cap and gown. In the meantime he continued his professional career. He had made a few easy dollars through the sale of domains registered in the early days of the commercial Internet (scifi.com being one of them), worked for several years with *Taxi Driver* producer Michael Phillips, and on his own sold a show called *Trailer Park,* a clip show featuring campy trailers from old horror and sci-fi movies.

John Frank lived with his collections—videotapes, comic books, posters, memorabilia—in an apartment complex not far from us and ventured out or answered the phone only when absolutely necessary. If you really wanted to talk to him, you had to drive over and bang on the gate, which he could see on a closed-circuit feed. The apartment was fed by redundant media inputs in addition to the closed-circuit feed: cable modems on two different networks, so he would never lose Internet access and his servers would never go offline, plus both cable and satellite television. John Frank recorded practically without remit. The comics and memorabilia had a whole room. The back wall of the living room was completely eclipsed by cardboard file cartons containing every production document generated during the making of *Taxi Driver,* which John Frank had rescued from destruction. The only places in the apartment not filled by John Frank's collections were the area around a bench press machine in the middle of the living room and a cozy nook facing the media center.

John Frank had met his assistant, Larry laBeouf, during one of his rare visits to the USC campus. Larry was barely behind schedule at the USC film school, just a year or so, and he had gone to work for On Track just as he was graduating. He was ready to take the entertainment industry by storm. When he first arrived in our living room with John Frank, he gave every appearance of having his shit together, at least in the way senior salespeople at Best Buy have their shit together. Firm handshake, polo shirt with the collar erectly brushing his earlobes, blond hair gelled straight up from a chubby, earnest face. Like all film school students, Larry planned to be a big director, and he was getting his start at On Track. It was a dizzying opportunity for such a recent film school grad, for in addition to being John Frank's assistant, Larry was slated to direct whatever project we developed for the company.

"Lock and load!" was his favorite expression, but after that first meeting, I don't think he ever appeared on time or with whatever he was supposed to have with him in the entire time I knew him. His highest ambition was to play Anakin Skywalker in *Episode Two,* which had not been cast yet. In the meantime he was learning the entertainment business at the feet of his Jedi Master, John Frank. Larry would have put it that way himself. "Jedi Master" was the highest compliment in Larry laBeouf's lexicon, and he bestowed it freely and with touching disregard for actual rank in the Rebel Alliance—Jason, Dian, and I were all Jedi Masters, too.

Larry loved nothing more than to trap you in a corner and put you to sleep with paeans to your mastery of the Force.

Larry happened to live in the same Hollywood apartment building as Dave Stotts, the freelance still photographer who worked on Farrell's porn shoots. Larry laBeouf, Dave Stotts, and a third tenant named Bridget formed a microcommunity within the apartment building, centered around smoking stupendous amounts of killer bud. Bridget was a mantislike pre-op transsexual close to seven feet tall in heels, with a one-person performance art band called God's Girlfriend. She had a beautiful lipstick-butchy girlfriend, but she also let straight guys suck her dick for money—the whole thing was pretty confusing. It warmed the heart, though, to see how marijuana could bridge the social gaps between an earnest *Star Wars* geek, a straight porn photographer, and a gargantuan cross-gendered succubus.

The pilot CRAP made with On Track was a parody of entertainment magazine shows like *Entertainment Tonight* and *Access Hollywood,* called *The Business.* Jason and I hosted the show, doing wraparounds and reviews from a set designed to look like the living room of cohabiting entertainment moguls. We shot a title sequence on 16mm of me and Jason driving around Beverly Hills in a Z3 roadster, swapping cell phones and waving gaily at pedestrians. At the end of the sequence we arrived at our mansion (the home of the parents of John Frank's financing partner), where Dian, as our truculent houseboy, greeted us with fruity drinks. For the body of the show, we already had a Cannes segment hosted by "foreign correspondent" Lloyd Kaufman and Kelly the hot mermaid, which Jason had taped when he was there. Jason and I discussed a new TV show *(Love Boat: The Next Generation)* and reviewed movies *(Titanic* and *Lost in Space),* for which Dian performed reenactments of key moments, and we did a location interview with the hip-hop artist Kool Keith, also known as Doctor Octagon, the Funky Gynecologist.

On the way over to our studio shoot, Dian decided he wanted to be called Steve rather than Dian, which was typically weird but fine. John Frank tried to gang the studio shoots for two On Track pilots into one day, but the girl hosting the other pilot, *Digital Access,* a news show about the video game industry, couldn't read off the teleprompter. When our turn came, there were only forty-five minutes left to tape. We did a run-through, but we sucked, so we had to roll over into the following day.

We sucked marginally less the second day, and eventually we got it all done. The three of us—Jason, "Steve," and I—had a pretty good time. But for Larry laBeouf, the day was a disaster. Directing a multicamera shoot, even a crappy little multicamera shoot like *The Business,* was not the easiest thing in the world, and at USC Larry had never done anything of the sort. In the course of two hours he was demoted by John Frank from director to assistant director, then to production assistant, then to Larry will you please just shut up and hold still. Larry felt this fall from grace no less keenly than Luke Skywalker felt his plunge down the middle of Cloud City toward the surface of the gas planet Bespin. But Larry did get another job out of the shoot, so the opportunity wasn't completely wasted.

At the end of the second studio day, the whole show was in the can except for the location interview with Kool Keith. Getting that interview proved more challenging than we had anticipated, but we had already shot the wraparounds and teased the interview at the front of the show, so cutting it was not an option. Keith was from New York, but he lived in Hollywood, in two separate apartments just a few blocks from each other. He didn't drive, traveling instead between the apartments by BMX bicycle, so he should have been relatively easy to pin down, but in addition to not driving, Keith didn't use the telephone.

Appointments with Keith were booked exclusively through Money D, an extremely likable man who enjoyed a nebulous sidekick-caretaker-dependent relationship with Keith. Money D did use the telephone, but he didn't drive, either—nor, hilariously, did he ever have any money—so at the end of hanging out with Money D, you would usually have to drive him to one of Keith's apartments, or to Hawthorne or El Segundo, where he had to meet a lady or transact some imaginary piece of business. To complicate matters further, while Money did use the telephone, Keith still didn't, so unless Money happened to be with Keith when you spoke with Money on the telephone, Money was in no better position to reach Keith than you were. And when Money and Keith were together, they were more likely to be riding around Hollywood on BMX bikes in trademark capes and thongs than to be sitting in an apartment by a phone.

Despite these logistical hurdles, the interview with Kool Keith did come to pass. It was staged poolside at one of the buildings where Keith had an apartment. Feeling bad for Larry laBeouf after the directing debacle, we decided to let him do the interview with Keith instead of doing it ourselves. But our largesse came at a price: Larry would have to do the interview as a die-hard Kool Keith fan, which meant that he would have to wear a Kool Keith costume while he did the interview. Larry had some body-image issues, so talking him into an American-flag thong took all our powers of persuasion, but eventually he suited up like a champ.

Though Keith was already known as both Kool Keith and Doctor Octagon, at this time he was developing two more identities, Black Elvis and Benny Wilcox. I never got a handle on who Benny Wilcox was, but Keith's transformation into Black Elvis required only the addition of a rubber Elvis wig and some Elvis glasses to the cape-and-thong ensemble. Keith elected to do his interview as Black Elvis, so a second rubber Elvis wig and pair of Elvis glasses were secured for Larry laBeouf. I have seen few sights more ridiculous than Larry laBeouf in his cape, thong, Elvis glasses, and rubber wig interviewing Keith in his. But Keith proved highly articulate on the subject of Black Elvis. Artistically, Black Elvis represented an escape from the "rapper" label, which Keith deemed constrictive—he considered himself an artist in the line of Elvis Presley, Johnny Cash, and Miles Davis, working beyond category—and politically, Black Elvis represented a simultaneous transcendence from and affirmation of blackness. Larry nodded along like he was thinking about anything but whether his ass had dimples.

Later, Money D explained to Jason and me that Keith's multiple personalities had a business function, as well. Keith might be under contract to one label as Kool Keith, but if the label didn't want to get behind his concept for a second album, even if he had a deal with them for it, he could record another album on another label as someone else—because, you see, then he was someone else. In the same conversation, Money D told us that he himself had already developed a second personality of his own (or third—presumably "Money D" was not his given name) as insurance against a sequence of events in which he first got a recording contract himself and then found its bonds constrictive. He said extra identities were also good for when you got rich and your exes came after your money. They might be entitled to money made by the old you but not to money made by the new you. Masks were good, too, because then you could say, "No, baby, that's not me—that's just a dude who kind of *looks* like me," and they'd never know for sure. Money D's extra identity was Sour Cream 'n' Onion. We laughed our asses off. But that fall Keith did have two records out, as different people on different labels.

In the course of attempting to organize the poolside shoot, Larry laBeouf had made friends with Money D. The apartments where Keith and Money lived were only a few blocks from the apartment building where Larry, Dave, and Bridget lived. Money shared their interests, Larry and Money both had plenty of time on their hands, and it was only natural they should start hanging out. I mentioned that working on *The Business* led to new employment prospects for Larry laBeouf. These came through his association with Money D.

Keith and Money were underground rappers, not mainstream rappers. Though from an outside perspective, hip-hop may seem to be just a thumping morass of indistinguishable beats and rhymes, it is a divided culture. Mainstream rap is about one thing—money and its manifestations. My cars, my houses, my diamonds, my bitches—look at me, I have them, and you don't. But when Keith wore a football jersey and draped himself in huge gold chains, it was a joke, a lampoon of mainstream rap, not a celebration of its values. Keith made money, but he didn't even own a *car*, the elemental signifier of hip-hop success. He rode a *bicycle*. Similarly, Money D would have liked to have some money, and in fact was often trying to figure out how to get some money, but he had not named himself Money D for any reason other than that he was the clown prince of ghetto fabulosity.

Even ghetto fabulosity had its requirements, though, which brings us back to Larry laBeouf and how Larry ended up at a party at Ice T's house with Money D and another underground hip-hop comedian associate, H Bomb, and how Larry afterward came into the employ of a truly terrifying old-school pimp named Sky.

Larry, H Bomb, and Money D had cooked up a business concept that combined escort booking and talent management. The idea was that if you were a girl in their employ, they would book you on both tricks and auditions, helping you pay the rent with sexual services until you got your SAG card, whereupon you would stop turning tricks and become a full-time actress. The operation was going to be very talent friendly, with equitable revenue sharing and comprehensive health and dental for the girls. Larry's work for Sky was supposed to be a sort of internship in the escort side of the business.

Oh, Larry, how far you fell and how fast! From graduating in cherubic flush with dreams of Padme Amidala to driving meth-crazed hookers named after cars on small-hours assignations in the Valley. Larry got the shit scared out of him on the first run. He let Porsche and Mercedes out in front of a house in Encino and was sitting nervously in the parked car when the girls ran back out screaming for him to start the car and get moving. He was on the highway with his rabbit heart hammering before he asked if the guy had attacked them or what. They looked at him like he was an idiot. "We robbed him, fool!" yelled Porsche. She held up a wallet. Larry almost barfed at the thought that he was now an accessory to robbery, as well as being a driver for a terrifying pimp, but he kept his foot on the gas.

Jason and I met Sky the pimp several weeks into Larry's internship, when Larry brought Sky over to our apartment for a "pitch meeting." What Larry had told Sky they had to gain by pitching to us, we had no idea—and when they arrived, we were a little worried about it, because Sky really was terrifying. He had a barrel chest, scarred and corded arms, and a pit-bull mug no less menacing than that of his longtime associate and fellow pimp, Ice T. Sky was *seriously* old-school—he had been hustling before there even *was* hip-hop. We didn't want to be on Sky the terrifying pimp's shit list, especially now that he knew where we lived.

Larry and Sky were working on a screenplay. The story started in the 1970s, with an innocent girl getting off the bus in Hollywood and meeting a streetwise young pimp named Sky. Okay, true crime story of a Los Angeles pimp, Tarantinoesque blaxploitation period piece, hookers and drugs and guns, love it, continue. The story meandered on in that vein, moving through the decades, presumably heading for its climax in the present time. But then about fifteen minutes into the "pitch" Sky introduced a scene by saying, "And then in this scene that happened last night—" and went on to describe an event that had happened the night before: Larry laBeouf getting chased around a motel parking lot by an angry john. We looked at Larry quizzically. He just nodded like Yep, that's what happened. We realized that not only had the screenplay not been put to paper yet, its events hadn't even all occurred.

The meeting ended okay, but the story did not have a satisfying ending for Larry laBeouf. At the end of the summer, a disillusioned young man, Larry left a bunch of his *Star Wars* relics at our place and drove home to Arizona to move back in with his mom.

Larry wasn't the only one having a hard time in Hollywood. Since the releases of *Orgazmo* and *BASEketball*, people had been recognizing Dian in the street, screeching to stops in traffic and rolling down their windows to yell, "Choda Boy!" These surprise fan attacks frightened Dian, as they would have frightened anyone. Being recognized did have its advantages—strangers wanted to buy him drinks, and now that he was a movie star, more girls were interested in him—but he was unable to enjoy his good fortune wholeheartedly.

In addition to being discomfited by the fan assaults, Dian felt he had been the object of mistreatment in his work. There was the *Orgazmo* dick-on-head thing, and in *BASEketball* his character, Squeak, was called Little Bitch and shot in a pineapple suit from a cannon. Dian completely stole both shows, and everyone from friends to reviewers said so, but he felt he was being laughed at, not laughed with, and then his feelings were hurt by the way a *Playboy* reporter quoted Matt and Trey about him. They didn't say anything they wouldn't have said to Dian himself, but in print their comments were divorced of affectionate tone.

At the same time, Dian was running short of cash. *BASEketball* had been a studio and therefore SAG production, so the money had been good, and his role had come with the usual perks. All the previous summer he had been picked up for work every day in a black Town Car, and at the end of the shoot, the studio had given him a huge television—a truly thoughtful gift, for Dian loved his TV. But by late summer, Dian was considering a return to the job he had held before *BASEketball* started, as a waiter at a nearby restaurant called Acapulco. It was your basic sucky job, and now that strangers were recognizing him, the idea of a service industry job was even less appealing. Wearing a turquoise Aztec-patterned shirt and staggering around under platters of brown gurp was bad enough in the first place, but doing it with drunk frat guys calling him Choda Boy would be much worse.

On the beach by the embers of a dying fire, Dian opened his heart to me and Jason on the subject of his future as an actor. He didn't have a good agent, and his new auditions weren't going that well. He did love acting. He even knew he was good at it. But presuming he ever landed another role, he despaired that he would never be allowed to read for anything but weird character parts. He was typecast. After the dick and the pineapple, how would anyone ever consider him for a dramatic lead?

Dian sad was very sad, and on this night he was particularly sad—and also nauseated, having smoked lots of dope with Jason, eaten a ton of vanilla ice cream, and then drunk too much red wine, some nasty jugged swill called Paisano that Jason kept around. As Dian paused occasionally to burp pink foam, he was the very image of the tragic hobo by the campfire, the wizened drunk at the bar, the bitter beat reporter whose time as a newsman has passed. Dian inhabited his entire *life* as a character. Not only was he physically suited to playing interesting roles, but he was magnetic, absolutely riveting, veering recklessly between comedy and tragedy in a way that was impossible not to watch. Jason and I shook our heads. We were the ones whose lives were in shambles.

Dian should have been on top of the world. We told him as much. He said we just didn't understand and staggered back into the apartment.

Out by the fire, Jason and I discussed Dian's predicament. Maybe he was right. Maybe we didn't understand. Maybe it really was a bummer to know, as an actor, that no matter how good you were, you would never play the beefcake.

That night on the sand Jason and I laid out the basic beats of *The Jockey:* the story of Wick Milligan, a disgraced jockey trying to get back in the game. Wick has a hot girl, a stripper, sure, who believes he still has what it takes. And the villain—right, a corrupt owner who made Wick take a fall at the peak of his career. The jockey's agent, a sleazy but lovable Bill Murray type, is the jock's best friend. They're each other's only hope for a comeback. The girl used to date the owner—jealousy, romantic tension. The owner has a new horse, the ultimate stallion: Blackjack! The owner makes Wick the offer Wick can't refuse. Is it payback for the fall— or is he using Wick again? Gambling, drinking, payoffs, drugs, sex, horses, violence, redemption! The Sport of Kings! We giggled and went inside to tell Dian about it. He had vomited in the living room, leaving a trail of pink foam all the way back to his bedroom.

Jason had met Amanda Demme, formerly a hip-hop producer and now the wife of movie director Ted Demme, when he snuck into the *Vanity Fair* Oscar party back in the winter. Amanda had said she wanted to start producing movies. They had traded numbers. Now Jason called her up and set a meeting. We went over to the Demmes' house in Hollywood and talked out by the pool, and Amanda seemed to like the idea. With some outside interest, we started to think maybe it wasn't such a silly idea after all. She said she wanted to talk to her husband about it, and she would get back to us.

They always say they will get back to you, but Amanda actually did get back to us. Ted Demme was then directing *Life,* a comedy with Eddie Murphy and Martin Lawrence, so it was a couple of weeks before a meeting time could be worked out, but in due course we were invited to ride out to the Disney Ranch where *Life* was shooting, so we could meet Teddy (the familiar address), eat lunch, and talk about *The Jockey.*

The Disney Ranch featured the dun hills and oaks that you realize, upon seeing them, you have seen a hundred times. They are the Wild West, they are Vietnam, they are the Planet of the Apes; and now a valley between two hills was a Mississippi prison camp. Teddy met us in a golf cart on one of the access roads. He was a big, friendly guy, fat but also hugely strong, built like John Belushi in his prime. He put us instantly at ease and led us around the set. I had never been on a big one before. That's the crane. That huge bank of stadium lights is for fake moonlight, that building is the barracks, those guys in stripes by the craft service table are prisoners. That's Martin Lawrence. Eddie Murphy never comes out of his trailer.

Teddy put on a self-deprecating act that he hardly knew what was going on himself. He was just some guy, and look! They put him in charge of all this stuff, can you believe it? We ate in the lunch tent—salmon, steak, and grilled vegetables, which were a pleasant change from the toaster-oven cooking in Playa. After lunch in Teddy's trailer, Amanda led us through pitching *The Jockey.* He had already heard it from her, so really it was just getting to know us a little bit, feeling around to see if doing something with us would be fun. Apparently so. He said he liked the idea and was glad we had somebody in mind for the lead, especially someone relatively unknown. He was glad it wasn't Tom Cruise or something, because dealing with the politics of doing a huge movie was a job in itself. *Life*, at seventy million dollars or so, was much larger than anything he'd done before. While he would be on this movie for at least a couple more months, Jason and I should start shaping up the story. We should start having all our people call each other's people, haha, steal some snacks on the way out, ya bums, and come visit again when we do this big interior fantasy thing on a stage at Universal. With a major motion picture in development, we smiled all the way back to town.

Two

1

By the fall of 1998 I had been in Los Angeles for a year. The situation with *The Jockey* paid only in hope, and the practical reader will have realized that by now I should have been running out of money. Not long after arriving in Los Angeles, I had come into a significant amount: eighty thousand dollars from the sale of land and a lake house in Tennessee. My paternal grandfather had originally developed the property, and after my grandmother's death it had belonged to my father and me jointly. The eighty thousand was my share of the proceeds when it sold.

My father, Bert, and I had spent at least a month of every summer together there from the time I was two until my early twenties. I had mixed feelings about the windfall, though not only for sentimental reasons. My high school and college educations had been paid for with money my paternal grandfather had set aside for that purpose. They had been expensive, and I had lived comfortably throughout them, and by the time I graduated from college, the principal in my educational trust was down to a few thousand dollars, which I promptly withdrew and pissed away. My share in the sale of the property was the end of my dead grandfather's beneficence.

I knew that the smart thing to do with the money would be to stick it in a mutual fund or use it as a down payment on a house. But my mixed feelings about the money forbade such a sensible course. On the one hand, I didn't feel like I deserved it, since I hadn't earned it. This wasn't selflessness but a mixture of pride and superstition. Despite having enjoyed all the conventional advantages myself, I didn't think much of people whose alternative lifestyles were comfortably underwritten from home. Allowing myself the security of a nice starter portfolio or equity in a cozy two-bedroom was out of the question. That was the pride part, but the superstition was just as powerful: If I gave myself that security, then in some weird, magical way, it would keep me from achieving success on my own terms; or if I did achieve it, it would be somehow illegitimate. The nice thing would have been to give the money to charity, but I didn't want to do that, either. I wanted to place a big, hairy bet on myself. If I multiplied the money, then it would be mine. And if I lost it—well, it had never been mine in the first place.

I immediately put half the money into the consulting business to which I have referred. On what subject did I believe myself qualified to consult? The only job I had held since college was a part-time gig at Kaplan right after graduation, teaching tricks to rich kids for a few hours a week so they could do better on the SAT, which already favored them. You could hardly call the magazine writing I had done a job, since it rarely paid, and when it did pay, it was for a piece of puff around which ads could be sold: four hundred words on the poetry of telemark skiing—which I had never done—so *Esquire* could sell a few inches to resorts and retailers of rugged outdoor gear. Curiously, the small talents required for these two types of work prepared me well for consulting. Teaching SAT test-taking techniques required the rote explication of a few simple principles and the desire to be seen as a Promethean genius by an audience of captive rubes. Writing the puff pieces required basic ability with language and a propensity for fraud.

The consulting business, as mentioned, was called Quiddity. We were a brand strategy firm specializing in naming, and it was every bit as ridiculous as it sounds. Alex Frankel, another friend from high school, was my partner in the business. Our perspectives on the experience differ considerably. Since we closed it down, Alex has written a book called *Wordcraft* about corporate naming practices, which I recommend to anyone interested in the subject. Any opinions contained herein with regard to what we did and the people to whom we did it are mine and mine alone—that should go without saying, but on that point I wish to be especially clear. Alex and I made some money with the business, and for the most part we had a good time, but we also argued a lot. Some of our arguments were the normal arguments that are part of the day-to-day running of a partnership, but the big ones sprang from differences of worldview rather than differences of opinion.

He was two years my junior, along with Brody among the youngest members of our high school mob, and after graduation, he, too, went to Brown. I dropped out for a year halfway through, and when I came back, Alex was only one academic year behind me. We spent my final year and his penultimate living together in the decaying bottom floor of a mansion the city had declared historic, a designation that apparently relieved the landlords, a set of brothers known locally as the Three Little Pigs, of any obligations with regard to heat, water pressure, security, or fenestration. But the place was huge, with chandeliers and flocked wallpaper that must have been glued up in the twenties, and it was only five hundred bucks a month.

We both concentrated, as majoring was called at Brown, in English and American literature, but we also took a class together in the Anthropology Department, called Hunter-Gatherer Adaptations. It was a real class, not one of the goofy electives with which I occasionally padded my schedule, and it was taught by a Professor Gould, a jolly scholar in a fisherman's sweater who had spent his doctoral years in the Australian Outback, wandering around and digging for grubs with Aborigines. Frankel and I loved Professor Gould, and we lived for Hunter-Gatherer Adaptations that semester. The central premise of the class was that you could understand people better by observing them than by asking them what they were up to, since people would rarely give you a straight answer, or if they tried to give you one, it would be so rooted in their own cultural assumptions that you would probably misunderstand it, anyway.

As an exercise, Gould had us chart our own food acquisition and consumption patterns. Since Frankel and I lived together, we proposed to make the chart together as a hunter-gatherer affiliation group. Gould jovially assented, and the resulting charts showed clearly that Alex was a much better hunter-gatherer than I was. Whereas Alex was willing to postpone shopping indefinitely so long as we had beans and rice in the apartment—and we weren't going to run out of those, since we had twenty-pound bags that Alex had brought from his summer job as a cook for a biological research facility—I wanted to go shopping the instant we ran out of cookies. If he wouldn't go with me, I would go alone to the mini-mart, buy bags of cookies, and eat them all before returning to eating rice and beans.

This was the equivalent of an Aborigine leaving his affiliation group in the middle of harvesting a safe, nutritious root field and running off into the desert by himself in the hope of finding a tasty grub infestation—Gould had slides of himself grinning around mouthfuls of thumb-sized larvae, which he said tasted sort of like vanilla and were the Aborigines' favorite food. Left to my own devices as an Aborigine, I would probably die of hunger and thirst in a dry wash, and Alex would fare just fine on the long walkabout that is life. The charts graphically demonstrated the differences in character that would make us a suitable consulting team, for a while, with his conservative instincts balancing my grub greed and vice versa.

While I was sweating it out in Austin in 1996, Frankel was back in the Bay Area writing for magazines that actually paid and earning even more money doing the kinds of vague freelance creative work through which thousands of other information-age hunter-gatherers were making comfortable livings at that time. Entire businesses were growing up just to serve their networking needs. Craigslist teemed with opportunities for educated people without traditionally defined job skills, and private companies were getting into the game. Hotjobs.com burned, Monster.com roared. I was only dimly aware of what was happening out in San Francisco, but Frankel was right in the middle of it, writing pieces for magazines like *Fast Company*, *The Red Herring*, and *CIO*. He was primarily interested in being a journalist, but he could hardly believe what he was reporting.

The naming thing started with a piece he wrote for *Wired*. In the piece, Alex reported on naming firms in the Bay Area, interviewing their founders and freelancing as a participant in creative sessions. That there even were such companies was weird. But if you thought about it, it made a kind of sense; it was just the furthest extension of the outsourcing concept. Every new product had to have a name, and there were always new products being introduced. Businesses outsourced the design of their new brands to design companies. In the case of really big new brands or venerable brands that needed overhauling, businesses farmed the work out to corporate identity companies. We had known someone in college whose father ran one of those, overseeing a redesign of American Express and the development of Nissan's Infiniti sub-brand. It made sense that a few companies might specialize in doing branding work one step closer to the product than designing its logo.

Alex reported that the leader of Bay Area naming firms was Lexicon, headquartered in Sausalito. Lexicon had been rolling along since the eighties, when it was founded in response to a perceived need for this type of niche service by a senior "creative" at an ad agency. At the time Alex wrote the piece for *Wired,* Lexicon had already named Apple's PowerBook line, among other premiere brands. Idiom, Metaphor, Master-McNeil, and NameLab were four other companies in the niche market of naming. Each professed to have a unique, proprietary "methodology," the best way of divining the core of a new brand and expressing it in a single word, and each had its own language for describing its methodology. Lexicon's line was about building a "vessel," a container for the brand that would float it over the seas of commerce. A couple of the companies had linguists and semioticians on retainer, which lent academic weight to their methodology spiels. But even the word *methodology* was transparently pseudoscientific—hilariously so, when the result was something like Funions.

My favorite of the companies was NameLab, which admittedly did have a unique methodology. The owner had developed software that mixed phonemes, or word parts, into combinations that were supposed to evince a specified set of emotionally loaded characteristics (like, say, *speedy, trustworthy, efficient*). One problem with this approach was that there was a limited set of characteristics that virtually all companies aspired to express through their brands. Very few companies wanted their brands to say *slow, evasive, wasteful*. But the NameLab guy was my favorite because Alex told me off the record that he was maniacally hung up on Monorail as a name. Apparently, his phoneme software said Monorail was perfect for almost any product, and the guy kept trying to push it off on somebody. But to his great frustration, no client wanted to call its product Monorail.

Could there truly be a living to be made in telling other people what to call their products? It seemed so goofy a scam that I could hardly believe it was working. But clearly it was. Frankel continued to freelance as a namer, working for the companies he had profiled; one of them had paid him more for the work he did for them during his research than *Wired* paid him for the article resulting from it. There was an easy couple of hundred dollars to be made by participating in a single brainstorming session. Jobbing on for an entire project, which usually consisted of an initial session, some list-making at home, and participating in another session or two, could pay even more. Between that and his writing, Frankel had more work than he could handle. He started e-mailing me descriptions of the products he was supposed to name, along with lists of the characteristics the clients hoped to project through the new names. I made him lists of candidate names, which he added to the lists he had made, and he sent me checks.

It was his idea that we should start a naming company of our own. The barriers to entry appeared to be few and unimposing. You didn't need any skills or equipment we didn't already have. Perhaps you didn't even need to live in the same place. Alex thought it would be best for me to move to San Francisco if we were going to be serious about it. And he was probably right, but I wanted to go to Los Angeles and dick around with Jason—Alex and I were in the early stages of this while I was still in Austin—and we seemed to be doing okay as a "virtual" freelance team.

All we had to do to get started as a naming company was say we were a naming company. We had to say it with a straight face, though, which was more difficult for me than for Alex. Despite the checks he sent me, I found it astonishing that people were willing to outsource this. It wasn't just new products for which we were being asked to generate lists of potential names, but also start-ups, whole new companies. Wasn't deciding what to call your company the most fun part of starting one? Because after that, you'd have to work there. Already I was missing the point, though. People weren't starting companies to have fun. People were starting them to make money.

The moneymaking possibilities of a naming company were compelling, at least from our lowly hunter-gatherer perspective. We estimated that the companies we worked for were probably charging between ten and thirty thousand dollars for each naming engagement. Lexicon was probably charging a good deal more, but we couldn't even think at that scale. The prospect of moving up a rung on the ladder and making a few thousand dollars, instead of a few hundred, for thinking of names for something sounded fantastic. The most either of us could hope to make writing for magazines was a dollar a word. The generous stipend Stanford provided a Stegner Fellow (and I do mean generous, because it was tremendously generous, a gift) was something like fourteen thousand dollars a year. By the simple math here, that would be two or three words. The advance on my novel had been seven thousand dollars, and I had worked hard on that for months. Selling a single word for the same amount was a delicious prospect.

Naming ourselves was our first task. We struggled over it for some time, laughing at the absurdity of that struggle. If we couldn't get this one right, we were fucked. I am not sure we did get it right, but we decided on Quiddity, which means "the essential nature of a thing." It was a weird word, hardly used anymore, and it could also mean "a quibble" or "a hairsplitting difference." But we liked the sound of it, and its primary meaning did express the character of what we proposed to provide clients. Ours wasn't supposed to be a consumer brand that would appeal to everyone. It was supposed to appeal to people who were looking for somebody smart to help them with a language problem. If our clients had to look up the name of our company in a dictionary, then maybe they would think we were smart.

The URL quiddity.com was registered to a guy in Minnesota who used the address as the home of his Multiple User Dungeon, an electronic play-space for online role-playing game aficionados. None of the members was particularly attached to the name, so the Dungeonmaster—he was a very nice guy—sold us the URL for nine hundred dollars. It was a lot of money for us to spend, but we reasoned that if this was to be our business, we had better get the domain.

We also needed a logo—or more properly, a "brand mark," as we learned logos were supposed to be called. "Logo" was down-market. Surfwear companies had logos. Enterprise corporations had brand marks. A friend of ours who worked at Landor & Associates, the first and most highly respected corporate identity firm, suggested that a baby might be a good symbol for Quiddity. You had to name babies, people thought of their new products and companies as their babies —yes, it was a good idea.

Jane was a designer Alex knew in San Francisco; she had left a swank design outfit when it was rolled up and began operating as Sapient, a big interactive firm. She and Alex rode in the same weekend cyclocross league, racing gnarly circuit courses in empty lots that always sent somebody to the hospital for tetanus shots. Her portfolio was awesome. Before the roll-up of her old employer, she had designed the brand mark for Organic, one of the other big interactive firms; her work was up on the side of their headquarters in SOMA. Jane was starting her own boutique design firm, and she took us on as her first client.

She wanted two thousand dollars for her services. We thought that was an insane amount of money for making us a baby head and putting it on some business cards, and also figuring out our typography and colors and laying out some stationery and an attractive saddle-stitched brochure describing our services, plus selecting stock and managing the printing of everything at the nicest print house in San Francisco. Jane snorted. She knew the same thing would have cost us a minimum of fifty thousand dollars if we were getting it through her previous employer. She was the one who told us about "brand marks," and she also told us we had better start calling the printed stuff "collateral." Alex convinced me the two thousand dollars was a bargain, and it was. Jane designed collateral that made us appear completely legit, at least until we opened our mouths: thick, creamy stocks printed with a full bleed in black and school-bus yellow inks, our own methodology baloney composed in elegant complementary fonts, and a Sanrio-style baby head that struck just the right mix of cute and serious. It made us look like a real company.

We still didn't have clients, though, or any idea how to get them. We paid a visit to my cousin Ted, a junior partner in a venture capital firm in San Francisco, hoping he might have a start-up for us to name. Instead, he was kind enough at the end of a long day to subject us to a three-hour grilling on what in the hell it was we thought we were doing. After the first hour we were ready to thank him and go home, but he cracked open Diet Cokes, put us back in our chairs, and kept us there until nearly midnight. We emerged with something much more valuable than a gig. Ted gave us the beginning of a business vocabulary, the language we would need in the fantasyland we were preparing to enter.

That night was my first real exposure to the world of grown-up business, a crash course in "best practices" and "competitive differentiation," in "market size" and "growth strategies." Ted explained to us that there were two kinds of businesses: real businesses, which were the kind he invested in, and what he called "lifestyle" businesses. What we were proposing sounded to him like a lifestyle business. He explained that this wasn't a pejorative term, not exactly. You could make lots of money with a lifestyle business. It just wasn't going to go on without you, because you were the business—when you went on vacation, the business went on vacation. But you could go on vacation whenever you wanted, hence his term *lifestyle*. He didn't see how a naming company could be scaled into a business worth hundreds of millions of dollars, and so it probably wouldn't be a candidate for venture financing.

That was all okay with us. We were starting a lifestyle business. Lots of money and vacations sounded just fine. By now CRAP was starting to be something, whatever it was, and Frankel was still writing for the New Economy rags. All we wanted to know was what we were supposed to do next. We needed clients. Ted suggested that before we turn our energies to finding those, we should take a closer look at the companies with which we hoped to compete. What did they do? How did they make money? How did they exploit labor, build a pyramid of freelance creative drones? Most of all, how did they convince people of the value of their services?

The freelance "creatives" the other naming companies used had no special qualifications. They were journalists, artists, teachers, bike messengers, Scrabble players, temp workers, poets—people who liked words and needed a little extra cash. The assembled freelancers were used as engines for the development of huge lists, sometimes thousands of words long, of potential names for clients. Sometimes the freelance sessions were simple brainstorming sessions, and sometimes little games were employed. For instance, at first the freelancers might be told the product was a fine cigar, when it was a luxury sedan. Sometimes the actual nature of the product was revealed to the freelancers at some point, and sometimes it wasn't. The lists generated could be used as grist for a recombinant mill that generated even more candidates in the form of "compound" names: PowerBook, PeopleSoft, and the like. Whatever the case, at the end of a session with freelancers, the naming company had a thousand candidate names for the present engagement. And the naming company could keep those names in its files for use in future engagements.

None of this was criminal—neither the fact that the actual work was contracted out to slackers, nor the fact that a solution developed for one client might just as easily work for another. It just could never be acknowledged, because to acknowledge it would tear a gaping hole in whatever balloon of hot air you were inflating to justify charging thousands, or tens of thousands, of dollars for one word. If it were acknowledged that in almost no case was there a single perfect solution that was not also a perfectly good solution to many other cases, the sensible purchaser of naming services would simply ask for a master list of good names. If you admitted to having a tremendous file of those—or if you even let the idea of a tremendous file come up—then you were in trouble, since you couldn't *own* all those good names. They were just a bunch of words.

There was some real work that had to be done on an engagement. You had to come up with new names—even if you had some good ones in the files, you had to come up with new ones. And we actually liked doing it, so for the most part we did it ourselves. There were also URL and trademark hurdles. Finding a domain that was still available was already nearly impossible, and invariably that was one of the things a client wanted. But if a client was big enough to pay top dollar for naming services, that client generally could afford to purchase whatever domain it wanted, so long as that domain was not owned by a major competitor, in which case it was not a good name for the client, anyway. Simple trademark research could be conducted on the USPTO Web site, but definitive trademark research had to be done by an attorney or a search company like Thompson & Thompson. It was easiest to tell clients they would have to take care of the final trademark phase themselves; knowing that just that phase of the project would cost the client a few thousand dollars helped justify at least such a price for the creative services preceding it.

But what, really, was the value of the services we would provide? As in any transaction, ultimately the buyer would determine the value of what was purchased. Our services were worth whatever we were paid for them. At first this was just a few hundred dollars, even when we were our own company. In the course of two years, from the fall of 1998 to the fall of 2000, we learned how to bill quite a bit more. In retrospect I know we were underbilling even when we charged our highest prices, at the peak of the Internet bubble. Often the client team had been banging their heads against fresh drywall for weeks by the time we got to them, and in all that time they would have come up with just a dozen unworkable solutions to the problem of what to call the thing they had just been given a million dollars, or a few million dollars, to start. They would have paid us in blood.

Lest these naming shenanigans sound entirely like a joke, in the context of the late nineties business environment, they were not. Frankel used to get incredibly pissed off at me when after a stressful conference call conducted between ourselves, the end client, the interactive developer, the mark designer, and the consultant hired to manage the rest of us consultants, I would helplessly start laughing. But I wasn't laughing at what was happening so much as that I was a part of it.

The concept of *brand equity* is a useful one in determining the value of the services we provided at the time we provided them. The term, which is also used in a very general way to mean "recognizability," actually has a very specific meaning. A publicly traded company's brand equity can be calculated quite simply by subtracting the value of the company as determined by any normal assets- or earnings-based measurement from the market value of the company. The difference, positive or negative, is the company's brand equity.

Few of the companies that rose highest and fell hardest during and after the New Economy bubble had much in the way of tangible assets or earnings. In fact, few of them had a recognizable product or anything resembling a reasonable plan for making money. They were simply ideas. Nevertheless, many of these ideas progressed through tiered rounds of financing underwritten by the most prestigious venture capital firms and investment banking houses in the world, and a few at their peaks achieved values of over a billion dollars. Those values were composed almost entirely of brand equity.

At the time we were naming start-ups, the sights of all their managements were set firmly on the "liquidity event" known as the initial public offering, after which pieces of the idea could be converted into cash. In order to go through the process of becoming a publicly traded company—in order to be financed, written about, discussed by analysts on cable, and sold—the idea had to be called something. Without a name, it could hardly even be said to exist. So in a sense, Alex and I were providing the single most valuable asset our clients could hope to obtain: the magic word that might be converted into millions, possibly billions, of dollars.

2

In the fall of 1998 Jason, Dian, and I were evicted from the beach apartment in Playa. The eviction was the result of a small film festival event we held there called Tiki 2000, which marked the end of CRAP's carefree beginnings. Dress for Tiki 2000 was specified as "tiki of the future," which resulted in a mixed lot of helmets, goggles, grass skirts, moon boots, coconut bikinis, capes, ray guns, codpieces, and jungle prints, along with some seriously groundbreaking shit cobbled together from band uniforms, plastic breastplates, foliage, and rattan furniture. John Frank wore an authentic *Dr. Who* costume from his collection, and I looked fantastic in a silver banana hammock.

The party started in the afternoon, with Money D running the barbecue for a manageable crowd of forty or so:

Tiki 2000 art direction and construction volunteers, film geeks from Sundance and Cannes You Dig It?, rappers from Inglewood, and associates like Larry laBeouf and Bridget the seven-foot transsexual. At sunset the crowd swelled to maybe a hundred, manageable but getting unruly. Vinyl, the band Tony Mindel managed, made up of our friends from Marin, played on the back patio. The noise drew the denizens of the Jungle, who depended on events like this for free liquor on weekends, and then it got dark, and the bonfire started, and people really started to arrive.

It was ugly even before we started showing dirty puppet movies on a screen built from flats out on the sand. In addition to several kegs of beer, we had purchased a dozen gallons of cheap vodka and rum for icky fruit punches that we dispensed from Sparkletts water jugs, but at midnight I had to drive to Sav-On to get a dozen gallons more. Eventually, the movie screen was destroyed and set aflame, and partygoers ran and screamed and barfed and had sex in the firelight, keeping dogs and families along the strand up all night. There were still a couple of dozen people around the apartment the next morning, stinky and hungover or finishing out acid trips in the tatters of their costumes. Jason was still going strong.

Because the downstairs neighbors already hated us, we had taken the steps of notifying them beforehand about the party and providing them a room at a nearby Embassy Suites. They took the room but complained to our blue-haired old bat of a landlady anyway. Her attorney, a round and incredibly tan little man in tight tennis whites, with brown-tinted sunglasses and a gold chain coiled on his breast, arrived in a red Rolls Royce convertible a few mornings later and delivered a Notice to Quit, the aptly named prelude to an actual eviction notice.

So ended our time at the beach, in the triplex the color of a doll's flesh, under the sun and thrumming jets. Jason and I moved about a mile up Culver Boulevard, into the apartment contiguous to Jolon and Martha's in Mar Vista. The new place was only a two-bedroom, so Dian slept on the couch until he moved in with Heather's friend Shana and her boyfriend, Marcus, who was Dian's best friend, in Echo Park. The move to Mar Vista was inconvenient for Jason and me, but it proved to be a good thing for our company. Jolon drilled a hole in the wall between the apartments and networked us all into their cable modem, and he and Martha began to work in earnest on the first real CRAP Web site.

At the same time, Quiddity was gaining a little momentum, which led to some mild disagreements between Alex and me. Alex had read in some business book that the definition of a perfect business was a post office box to which checks were mailed. This definition was in line with his naturally conservative hunter-gatherer instincts, but I didn't see how we were going to get the big checks started if we didn't give a more convincing appearance of being a real company.

Jane's boyfriend, Gerhard, had joined her in her new design firm, which she was calling PlusOne. PlusOne leased a few hundred feet of warehouse space in San Francisco's design district, and Quiddity chipped in a few hundred dollars a month for Alex to have a desk there. The place was sparsely but elegantly furnished, with a wall of windows that let in milky light. It was an excellent place to meet with clients.

I had no similar arrangement in Los Angeles. I convinced Alex that for Quiddity to develop new business down there, I would have to have an office, too. Corporate identity clients could not be wooed on the Cum Couch, the vile, absorbent, and indestructible oatmeal-textured sofa that had followed Jason and me from the beach to Mar Vista. Alex argued strenuously and sensibly against the idea of my leasing space, but as my forty thousand dollars was put in as an uncollateralized, interest-free loan for developing our business, I finally had my way.

I found a space for lease on Abbot Kinney Boulevard in Venice. The street's northern tip tucked into Main Street, which entered the City of Santa Monica a few blocks farther north, at the huge upended binoculars Frank Gehry had designed as the gateway to Chiat Day's headquarters. The Web services firm Razorfish now occupied the binoculars and the building they fronted. This patch of Venice had been a grim ghetto only ten years earlier, but now it was the part of LA's Westside that most resembled San Francisco's SOMA in character. Bums still napped in doorways and crackheads still dodged down alleys, but they had to watch out for assholes parallel-parking Range Rovers.

The office was a long tunnel of a room lit by skylights, with a right turn in back to a bathroom. It was part of an old, converted warehouse, with nice exposed wood ceilings and a massive aluminum HVAC duct running along the top of one wall. At nine hundred square feet, the unit was a lot bigger than necessary—Quiddity south was just me. And at fifteen hundred a month, it wasn't exactly a bargain. But we had the cushion of the loan, and one good job, I reasoned with Alex, would pay a whole year's rent.

My friend Dave Hardy came down from San Francisco for a month and remodeled it. Dave was another friend from Brown, where he was without question the most talented artist enrolled—not that I knew anything about art, but you could just tell. During our last year he spent most of his time in the studio basement of List Hall, the Brutalist building where Art was imprisoned. His drawings and etchings were pranks on his talent, pigs and meat and old toothless geezers flying through landscapes of broken wheelchairs and washer-dryers, ugly stuff joked into gorgeousness. He glorified American grotesqueries in a way that reminded me of Robert Crumb or Ralph Steadman. His work was always funny, or made gross stuff glow, or brought out the hidden creepiness in things you had thought were cute or pretty—kittens, flowers, baby dolls. Part of his final show at school was a sweeping set of angel wings made from varnished latex gloves. When you stood on a pedestal in front of them, they made you into an angel.

Now he was living in San Francisco and working as a set builder on *Nash Bridges*. The show was on hiatus, and I figured we could keep the cost of the Quiddity remodel reasonable by salvaging most of what we needed. Dave was the duke of Dumpster diving. The San Francisco Unified School District was emptying its warehouse, so from there we got some institutional furniture; from a condemned hospital in Marin, where a friend of mine was the caretaker, we looted hardwood drawers, huge matching doors for desktops, and heavy industrial hardware. Dave drove it all down to Los Angeles in his truck.

At the office we demolished an ugly conference igloo and installed a shower in back. Dave had brought along extra materials from his own warehouse, including a roll of black rubber sheeting that he used to floor the bathroom and as a laminate on a huge oval conference table that he made for us. He built cabinets from birch ply to house the looted drawers, and topped them with brushed aluminum to match the pulls. David Goodman, a *South Park* writer with whom I had formed an informal two-person book club, came over and spent days deciphering the building's circuitry so we could hang antique overhead lamps in place of the ugly track lights. I bought an iMac, a two-line phone, and a fax machine. I had the Quiddity brand mark cut from white vinyl and applied to the glass outside the front door, and my business suite was complete.

Strictly speaking, none of this was necessary. I could have just had a phone line installed and started doing something in there. But the remodel of the office on Abbot Kinney cost only a month of work and five thousand dollars to Dave Hardy for his taste, work, and materials; and the office meant much more to me than a place where I could meet clients, make phone calls, and conduct correspondence. It was at the center of the fantasy I was developing of myself as a person of business, a person who got up in the morning and went somewhere, a person who would transform his opportunites and patrimony into something of substance.

"Quiddity."

"Yeah hi . . . so, you guys name things?"

"That's right. Our methodology focuses on discovering the innate character of the client company and expressing that character through language. Are you familiar with the field of mimetics?"

"Dianetics?"

"No, mi—"

"Are you guys like, Scientologists?"

"No, not . . . but Scientology is a great example of meme theory at work."

"What theory?"

"Meme theory, or mimetics, is an idea developed by a geneticist named Richard Dawkins. The idea is that ideas themselves, or memes, replicate through communication, just as genes replicate through reproduction. A powerful meme is an idea that's easily transmitted from one person to another. We at Quiddity think of ourselves as genetic engineers of language, and a soundly engineered name is the foundation of effective marketing. But honestly, this isn't just about marketing. This is about *who you are*."

"I don't get it."

"For instance, when I say *chair,* what do you think of?"

"Stool."

"Okay, no, what I meant was just *chair,* like the thing with four legs that you sit on, but it has a back you can lean against. What you did there was take the extra step of association to another form of seating. But what I meant was, when I said *chair,* did a picture of the thing you sit on, with four legs and a back, come into your head?"

"No. I thought *stool,* because that's what I'm calling to see if you'll name for me."

"You're a furniture company?"

"No. I just laid a huge turd! Ahahahahaah!"

After fielding a few more calls from old friends, I begged Julie Martini, a freelance journalist friend who had recently moved down from San Francisco, to join us as a salesperson.

Julie protested that she didn't know anything about sales; but she was smart as a whip and cute as a button, and I figured I'd buy anything she tried to sell me. Julie agreed to spend a couple of months with me in the Quiddity office.

Frankel and I had talked a lot about the idea of developing a special niche in the naming market. My genius concept was that the Quiddity office in Los Angeles would develop a niche in entertainment naming, developing titles for movies and television shows. Entertainment was the only business down here into which I had made any inroads, and I was sure a market existed in this area. My main reason for being so sure about it was that a competing firm listed the title of the film *Monkey Trouble* as one of its achievements.

Also, at the first meeting on the set of *Life,* Ted Demme had been interested in the naming thing. A Dennis Leary movie he was about to release, a Boston crime drama that had been titled *Snitch* throughout production, couldn't be released as *Snitch* because some other movie was being released with that name around the same time. I volunteered Quiddity to come up with some possibilities. This was not a paid job. Jason and I were just hoping to get in better with Teddy by coming up with a name for his movie. Frankel stayed up in San Francisco, while Jason and I went to the screening room at Creative Artists Agency to watch a print of the film.

I. M. Pei had designed the CAA building for Michael Ovitz at the peak of his imperial might—it was like a satellite office of the Death Star, done in snowy marble. The lobby was an immense conservatory with railings around it from which agents could look down to see who was waiting, and a Roy Lichtenstein painting that must have been forty feet tall hung on the wall facing the entrance. The screening room was awesome. There were little microphones next to the seats so you could chat with the projectionist. Ted Demme's movie was good, a gritty drama with some funny parts—which also was good, because that was how we were thinking of *The Jockey*. Afterward we came up with a list of potential new names for his movie, but Teddy ended up not using any of them, and the movie was released as *Monument Avenue*.

Julie and I cooked up a little marketing pamphlet about Quiddity's unique expertise in entertainment naming and mailed a copy to every company listed in the *Creative Directory*. Most of the executives Julie and I followed up with after sending out the pamphlet—we both hated making the calls and negotiated an every-other-call arrangement—met us with the telephonic equivalent of a blank stare.

In deciding there was a significant naming niche open in the entertainment industry, I had failed to take two basic factors into account. The first of these was market size. There just weren't that many new studio movies or network shows each year. The second was the prevalence of franchise properties. A big percentage of new projects were adaptations, sequels, or spin-offs, whose real value lay in the titles they already had. You could replace actors, directors, and screenwriters—think of the *Batman* movie series—but whatever you did, the next one was still going to have "Batman" in the title.

Trying to develop a niche in entertainment naming may have been one of the worst business ideas anyone has ever had. Nevertheless, Quiddity did get three small entertainment naming jobs aside from the freebie for Teddy, two through people I knew, and one from the mailing Julie and I sent out.

Nickelbag Records was the independent record label that belonged to the Dust Brothers, Mike Simpson and John King, who had produced the *Orgazmo* sound track. *The Sound of One Hand Clapping* had been a hit at Nickelbag—that was how I got to know them, so I guess it did lead to one job. Mitchell Frank, the label's general manager, called me and said they were having to come up with a new name for the label fast, as part of a transaction with Mammoth Records—and wasn't that what I said I did? I replied that it was, trying to sound really professional about it. But they already knew me as the dick trick guy, so I'm not sure who I thought I was kidding.

The Nickelbag recording studio was the living room of a house up in the Hollywood hills—ratty couches in a semicircle looking across the room onto a pool in the backyard, and a whole lot of recording equipment. It was an extremely mellow situation, especially right then, because nobody was recording. They had an intern named Chiba whose sole responsibility seemed to be bong maintenance. The transaction in progress was a joint venture, really an investment in Nickelbag by Mammoth Records, which in turn was majority-owned by Disney. Late in negotiations the principals of Nickelbag had learned that if Nickelbag were to become a part of the Disney family, Nickelbag could no longer be called Nickelbag—never mind that a name change would significantly weaken the asset in which Disney was investing.

Nickelbag's value did not lie in its library or roster. The label carried only a handful of bands, and of these only one, an alternative band called Creeper Lagoon, looked like it might break into the charts. Nickelbag's value resided in the credibility that obtained because it was the Dust Brothers' label—in other words, in the talent and reputation of its producing team. The Dust Brothers weren't going to change their own name as a producing team and start calling themselves the Fun Brothers or something. Even if the label's name were changed, it would still be known and marketed as the Dust Brothers' label, and therefore the brand would still implicitly reference illegal drugs. That was precisely what Disney was buying: a piece of the youth market in which hip-hop and indie rock mixed in a cloud of pot smoke. That was what kids wanted. Such were the conundrums faced by the conservative late-twentieth-century media conglomerate.

I started out trying to run a normal naming group along the semistructured lines Alex and I had sketched out—they were paying me, after all—but it was too embarrassing for me and everyone else. We ended up just sitting around on the couches and giggling possibilities. I pulled hard for *Hi Ho,* which I felt rang the right bells: fun to answer the phone with ("Hi, Ho!") and a tip of the hat to the Seven Dwarfs. In the end they decided to call the label Ideal Records, and they got the investment.

The second entertainment-naming engagement Quiddity undertook was for a new film production company formed by three guys from Chicago, which was represented by the same law firm as CRAP. The first person I spoke with was Dan, a really nice guy who seemed like he belonged in a suit. He was wearing a button-down dress shirt, pleated khaki shorts held up with a braided leather belt, and topsiders—the weekend outfit of a person who had a real job. But this was his real job now. He had just left commodities trading or investment banking to try out this entertainment thing, and they needed a name for their company.

He said they wanted a name that would refer to the partners' Chicago heritage. He was really into that, and they wanted the name to be cool and edgy, too. By now when someone said "edgy," I knew just to nod along, but the production company name he liked best and held up as an example of regional identity and edginess was the Shooting Gallery. That said "New York," it said "independent," it said "film," and there was the double entendre—although, now that I think of it, I'm not positive Dan was hip to "shooting gallery" as a term for the place where you shoot dope. He may have been thinking only of the place where you do target practice. But that didn't occur to me at the time, and the Shooting Gallery really was a pretty edgy name.

For a small fee Quiddity came up with some possibilities for the company. My favorite of these was the Rendering Plant, which seemed to me exactly the Chicago version of the Shooting Gallery. They didn't like it. They wound up using none of our suggestions and went with their own dismally generic Next Generation, which bummed me out not only because it didn't have anything to do with Chicago or have an edgy turn to it—I think it was imposed by their financing partner—but also because it seemed to Frankel and me that we were missing our marks repeatedly. People were paying us, but almost nobody was using our suggestions.

The one job that resulted from the mailing Julie and I sent out was another job for a Disney subsidiary, this one for Buena Vista Television. An executive from the company called us and inquired about our services. She was hesitant on the phone, as though concerned she might be on the wrong end of an elaborate practical joke, but I assured her that we did in fact name things and set a meeting to hear about the project and close the deal.

Buena Vista was housed in a massive classical structure whose roof was held up by giant caryatids in the shape of the Seven Dwarfs. The executive herself did not look like a television executive; she looked like someone who played a television executive on an extremely hot television drama about television executives. Despite clear amusement at my claimed profession, she acknowledged that Buena Vista did need some naming services. Dick Clark Productions had brought Buena Vista a format that had been wildly successful overseas, but no one was too excited about the proposed title, *Your Big Break*. She explained the format and gave me a copy of the sales reel.

The sales reel started out with old Dick himself seated in a studio, extolling the charms of the show, then transitioned into subtitled interviews with regular foreign people talking animatedly about how much they loved this star or that star. The most memorable guy was an excited Pakistani rug salesman: "Urdu Urdu Urdu, Michael Jackson Thriller!" The show allowed each selected contestant the opportunity to "be" the star he or she loved, either in a shot-for-shot reproduction of a famous music video or in an authentic concert setting with a big live audience. The rug salesman—and I realize that this character's being both Pakistani and a rug salesman seems like the worst type of Hollywood stereotyping, but he was from Pakistan and he was photographed in front of a rug store, where he seemed to work—went with the concert setting, and he rocked it stupendously: makeup, hair, outfit, moonwalk, nut-grabs, everything. The guy was unstoppable. In another segment of the reel there was a Celine

Dion lady who went with the music video option and trailed gauze around a moonlit set while lip-synching the *Titanic* theme song. It was the funniest fifteen minutes I'd ever seen, but that was part of the problem. Dick wasn't kidding. The show was supposed to be *magical, glamorous, fabulous.*

Quiddity came up with a long list of candidate titles for the hot executive, but I will be first to admit that none of the candidates was great. *Your Big Break* was the only project that ever truly stumped us. The problem was that the title had to be descriptive enough that viewers would know what the show was about—which *Your Big Break* wasn't, quite, because being on the show was pretty much the end of the road for amateur celebrity impersonators—without violating the *magical, glamorous, fabulous* directive. The obvious possibilities, Karaoke Something or Something Karaoke, were impermissible, because while karaoke was fun, the hot executive freely acknowledged that taking it too seriously was pathetic, and the show wasn't supposed to be pathetic. It was supposed to be awesome. The art of celebrity impersonation was honored among drag queens, but this gayest of all shows wasn't supposed to sound gay, either. I defy the reader to come up with a truly great name for this tragicomic extravaganza that describes it concisely but doesn't make it sound funny or gay. It's too late, in any case. A couple of years after we worked on *Your Big Break,* I saw its premiere advertised. It was still called *Your Big Break.*

During this early period of corporate identity consulting, some of our suggestions were good and some of them were bad. What we didn't understand yet—and this was one of the places where Alex and I would diverge—was that whether they were good or bad had nothing to do with whether they would be used. The reason nobody was using our suggestions was that we weren't charging enough for our services and doing a number of other counterintuitive things that would make us quite a bit of money later on. It would be months before we began to really grasp the psychology of consulting, though, and in the meantime we were becoming glum about our prospects.

3

In the early months of 1999 we had our first chance to pitch Quiddity's services to a seriously huge client, the pharmaceutical giant Glaxo Wellcome. Glaxo Wellcome was combining two HIV therapies into a single pill. Those therapies were already being prescribed as a "cocktail," but that made for a complicated marketing message, and because recent changes in legislation allowed it, the "new" compound would be marketed directly to consumers as a new drug.

Alex and I flew out to North Carolina and drove to company headquarters, a corporate megaplex in the woods of the Research Triangle. Clearly, it was supposed to be nice, having the headquarters out in the forest, but it felt like something out of the bad future—a secret, sterile hive in the middle of nowhere. Our "capabilities presentation" was a disaster that in Alex's view reached its nadir when I spaced out and started sniffing markers at the whiteboard. We didn't get the job, but it was our first taste of the big time.

We got our first actual *bite* of the big time on a subcontracting job for a branding company in New York. This was also the first occasion we had to really take a look at what we were doing and wonder if it was maybe a bad thing. The

end client was Columbia HCA, the Nashville-based hospital corporation that had just been nailed for defrauding the
Medicare system to the tune of about a billion dollars. The
top management had escaped implication—they were busy
running a fifty-billion-dollar health services company, so how
could they be expected to know about a little one-billion-
dollar fraud? Despite the total innocence of the upper management of any wrongdoing, or of any knowledge of it
whatsoever—they were shocked, horrified, appalled—
Columbia HCA was thinking that right then might be a good
time for a little rebranding. Quiddity was paid to come up
with a list of potential new names for Columbia HCA, though
once again none of our suggestions was used. The fraud had
been conducted at hospitals still branded as Columbia—five
years earlier, the Columbia system of hospitals had been
merged with the Hospital Corporation of America to make
Columbia HCA—so in the end they just dropped the Columbia part of their name and became HCA The Healthcare
Company.[1]

Still no one was using our suggestions—which we had
learned to call "solutions"—but we were starting to make
money. And for a while there, we were making plenty of it.
This was due almost entirely to Frankel and the desk he had
at PlusOne. Jane and Gerhard by now had taken some investment from a shadowy New Economy figure whose name
they spoke in hushed tones, and they had moved into a new

---

1. The chairman of the board of Columbia HCA at that time
was Tommy Frist, brother of Senator Bill Frist. At this writing
Senator Frist is the Senate Majority Leader spearheading "reform"
of our national health-care system, at the same time as he is being
investigated for insider trading of HCA stock.

office right next door to the San Francisco office of Razorfish, the highest flying of the interactive services firms. Gerhard became our guru of consulting doublespeak, and he brought us along on job after job.

One afternoon Frankel and Gerhard got hold of me on the phone and asked if I could come up to the Bay Area the following day. Gerhard couldn't even tell us what the job was, only that it was a "category-killing" Internet venture, meaning it aimed to rapidly gain hegemony over a whole sector of commerce, as Amazon.com had done with books. He said it would be a short engagement. The client had to have a name for the venture fast, like in a few days. Could we do that? Sure we could. Gerhard intended to book the job through PlusOne. What did Quiddity want to charge? We didn't care. What did he think was reasonable? He thought nine thousand dollars was reasonable. That sounded like a lot of money for a few days' work, but if he thought he could get it, it was fine with us.

Frankel booked me a ticket on Southwest. The next morning Frankel, Gerhard, and Jane picked me up at SFO in a black stretch limousine, which seemed a little ridiculous, but Gerhard pointed out that we needed to talk on the way. As the limousine merged onto 101 South toward Silicon Valley, I decided that if this was what being a consultant was all about—getting sudden calls, jumping on airplanes, having limousines whisk you off to secret complexes—it was okay with me.

Gerhard and Jane explained the job as we rolled along. The Internet Shopping Network was a sister company to the Home Shopping Network, itself a part of Barry Diller's USA Networks. ISN was putting together an online jewelry superstore—that was the top-secret part, that they were going to sell jewelry—and they were in a race to market against one or more competitors with equally deep pockets. Organic, the company whose brand mark Jane had designed, was on as the interactive developer. Organic had retained PlusOne to execute the identity component of the project and maybe the user interface. The online jewelry superstore had not been named, no URL had been secured, and therefore no announcement could be made about the venture. We arrived around midday at the company headquarters, a mirrored glass block in an office park in the South Bay.

Inside everybody was freaking out. ISN was operating its normal business in the building, and the new company was being put together at the same time, so the management was trying to do ten things at once. A whole team from Organic, maybe eight or ten people, was waiting for us. Gerhard introduced Alex and me as some kind of ultimate naming tag team. We shook some hands, and everybody was hustled into a conference room, maybe twenty people, the Organic group and the ISN project team. Everybody was young, from early twenties to early thirties, except for the guys in charge at ISN, who seemed like they were in their forties or fifties—regular Dilbert types with cell phones clipped to their belts, not Internet hipsters. There was no chance for Alex and me to get everybody straight, but the Organic people had more interesting hair and shoes.

The head ISN guy was going out of his mind. There in the conference room he ran me and Alex through what Gerhard had said in the car—category-killing online jewelry venture—and amplified briefly: In terms of positioning, they wanted to go up-market. They planned to carry lines like Rolex, Cartier, Omega, and Mikimoto, and those companies protected their brands by keeping them out of warehouse shopping situations. So the new venture had to differentiate itself from ISN and HSN in order to carry those product lines and attract the right customers. The name should be unique, upscale, maybe quasi-European, like Fabergé, Escada, Bijan, Versace. You know—classy. Whatever it was, though, we had to come up with it fast. Frankel and I responded that we could do that, but just so we'd have an idea, what kind of time frame was he talking about? Three days? The guy looked at his watch and grimaced.

"Barry needs it by five."

He gave us his blessing and ran back upstairs, where something even more urgent was happening. Frankel had brought along several pads of giant newsprint Post-its, and we papered the walls and windows with them. The giant Post-its were a tremendous improvement over the whiteboards we had relied on up to that point, because we could collect them and do a transcription later, instead of before each erasing of the whiteboard, and because we could just slap blank ones on top of filled ones. Despite the lack of New Media spectacle, the effect was great—whether or not there was anything good up there, by the end of the day, the sheer number of words on the wall was impressive. By the end of a couple of hours the walls were completely covered. Creativity was in the house. Work was getting done. The manager popped back in every so often to check the progress and cheer us on.

"Are you guys thinking outside the box?!" he asked without apparent irony on the first visit back. I caught some smirks from the Organic people, but Frankel and I nodded earnestly and assured him that that was precisely what we were there to do. On the next visit he came in with some seriously weird shit, a story about some toy or kids' game he'd just remembered hearing about at some convention, that was called Boogler or Gadzoink or something. That was what he wanted! Something like that! Did we get it? Sure we did!

When evening came, Gerhard helped us explain to the ISN guy that while we had not determined the final name—and in the end, of course, that would be their decision, not ours—we now had upward of a thousand possibilities, from which we would select twenty reasonable candidates and four or five highly favored ones that we would hand over the next day. The guy thought he could take that back to Barry. As the group in the conference room dispersed, Frankel and I stacked the Post-its back together and rolled them into a huge log. We piled back into the limousine, and they dropped me at SFO for my return flight on their way back to San Francisco.

The next day I asked Julie and David Goodman, the *South Park* writer I had become friends with, who had done the wiring at Quiddity, to come into the Venice office and kick around some more possibilities. Julie had a regular job now, but she was able to drop in for an afternoon. We picked some favorites from the previous day and came up with a few more ideas, and then I decided unilaterally that the company had to be called Byzantium.

I was insane to think that the Internet Shopping Network might name a spin-off Byzantium, but my insanity turned out not to matter. We soon learned that Organic hadn't been contracted yet, officially. They had jumped in on a verbal understanding, and in the meantime ISN had decided to go with another interactive developer. But PlusOne had been officially contracted by Organic, so Quiddity was paid the nine thousand just for showing up that day, and PlusOne made whatever it made, presumably more than that. So that was probably twenty-five thousand dollars made in just a few hours. We were a little disappointed not to be naming the company, but after it sunk in, the simple larceny of the thing was thrilling enough. We had been paid not a few thousand dollars for one word, but almost ten thousand dollars for *no* words. They ended up calling the company FirstJewelry.

The Internet jobs got better and better. Some of our clients even used the names we developed, and launched with a modicum of fanfare—I would list a few, but not a single start-up we named remains in operation. The credits and small reputation we built on jobs with PlusOne helped us win more jobs on our own in both San Francisco and Los Angeles. Down in Los Angeles I was getting more and more taken up with the entertainment business, but running off every once in a while to do a Quiddity job for a few days didn't really interfere with that. Some of the contacts I developed in Los Angeles turned into work for Quiddity, and vice versa. So while the situation was imperfect, and there were arguments with both Alex and Jason—really more with Brody than with Jason—about where I was putting time and attention, I was always available when Quiddity had an engagement, and when CRAP needed to meet with someone, the Quiddity office lent us legitimacy. Alex and I really worked only a few days per month, and the two of us were making more money than we had ever made before.

It wasn't like we were turning into millionaires all of a sudden, but it was enough money that I didn't worry that much about money. Alex handled our books. Whenever my checking account started to dip below ten or fifteen thousand dollars, a check for five or ten more would arrive in the mail. Once I lost a check for seven thousand dollars and didn't even know I'd lost it. When Frankel asked about the check, I remembered receiving it and presumed I'd deposited it. He reluctantly revealed that it had gone uncashed for a couple of months, and though I was sure I could not have been such a dickhead as to simply lose a check for seven thousand dollars, my checking account showed no record of a seven-thousand-dollar deposit. Frankel considered penalizing me the full amount just for being a moron, but eventually he wrote me another check.

As the jobs got better, my chortling cynicism only increased. I was not cynical about the market. I was too innocent to have any but the most basic understanding of the market. All I knew was that it was going up and up and up, and that was why things were good for us. My cynicism pertained to the work we were doing—not that we didn't come up with some okay names, but coming up with good names turned out not to be what our work was really about.

Coming up with the names was just one tiny point on the curve between starting an engagement and finishing it. The work was first about getting the work, then about making the clients feel good about the process, and finally about ratifying whatever decisions the clients reached. Those were decisions over which we ultimately had no control. At the end of the day, they were going to call their company whatever they wanted. If we couldn't talk sense into them, it was much better to help them feel good about a poor decision than to argue against it. They didn't want the right answer or even necessarily a good answer. They wanted to feel good about an answer.

That could never be said out loud, because it ran exactly counter to the line of utter horseshit paid out by really top-flight advertising and brand strategy consulting companies, especially the really, really high-end smaller ones retained by huge corporations to redirect their brands. Every consulting company had its own way of saying it, but the essential message was that a great consulting company could not be bought or bullied. They weren't even in it for the money. They were hardly even companies. They were more like think tanks. They chose to reimagine global brands not because it was remunerative but because it was *interesting*.

My favorite part of this fiction was that in the fiction, these firms carefully chose their clients, rather than the opposite. A client had to prove its worthiness, first by anteing up substantially for services that hadn't even been outlined yet, then by prostrating itself before the genius of the think tank and implementing whatever strategies were suggested. At its most absurd extension, the client-vendor relationship looked like the relationship between a well-heeled submissive and a professional dominatrix, in which the client hands over money just for the humiliation of doing so. Like that relationship, though, the client-vendor relationship was based on a fundamental lie. The whore was the one in the thigh-high boots. She got paid for pretending to be in charge, not for actually being in charge, and it was never she who would end the relationship.

This was my point of view—Frankel didn't share it. He was a nice, smart, honest guy, and he wanted to do a good job for our clients. He treated each new project as a journalistic endeavor, compiling sheaves of notes and data toward definitions of the market area, the core characteristics of the client's enterprise, and the benefits the client would be wise to express through its brand.

I did most of the talking once we were in the room. I got the client team to tell us about themselves, wrote words up on the whiteboard or giant Post-its as fast as my little fingers would fly, and drew Venn diagrams and arrows between things to imply connectedness. It wasn't rocket science or any kind of science at all, though part of my job was conveying the impression that it was—that was the function of all the diagrams and arrows. They were illustrations to the fiction: the chaos of language spuriously ordered, lists and figures balanced to imply movement, impetus, direction. At the end of a good day, sinuses burning from the smell of the markers, I could step back and survey my work with the satisfaction I imagined Saul Steinberg to feel upon completion of a handsome fake document.

It was Gerhard who usually sold our services. The Gerhard method of bidding and delivery as I came to understand it consisted of four parts: being unavailable when first approached, charging an obscene amount of money, emphasizing process over product, and documenting that process with a stack of jargon-filled deliverables. We never perfected this method on our own. We were too small and in the end insufficiently full of shit, and even our idol Gerhard was a small-time hustler compared to the big leaguers.

The most astonishing example of the method at work was perpetrated by Landor Associates in naming a Hewlett-Packard biotech and optical research spin-off Agilent. Landor Associates was reputed to have made more than a million dollars on the engagement. Agilent? What the fuck did that mean? How did you even say it? A million dollars. After the company was named, I heard a speech by the CEO of Agilent on the radio, broadcast from the Commonwealth Club in San Francisco. He was clearly a bright man—after all, he was running one of the most advanced scientific research facilities in the world—but he had to spend ten minutes of the speech talking about the company's name, how great it was, how it represented all the company's values perfectly, and how in everything they did now, they strove to be Agilent. I almost had to pull over to stop laughing.

It was like the old adage about borrowing from the bank: Borrow a thousand, and the bank owns you; borrow a million, and you own the bank. The more we were able to charge, the more authority clients invested in us. We never reached bidding anything close to a million dollars or a meaningful fraction thereof, but in a case like Agilent, you could see the inverted logic at work. Once the million dollars was paid, the client company had to get behind the decision, or admit it had been taken like a rube at a carnival. It had to will itself into belief that the name was a good name, and then support the name with even more money in design, advertising, and public relations expenditures, the wholecloth development of a "corporate messaging system."

The nature of the companies to which we were consulting did not decrease my cynicism. The people running them were for the most part perfectly nice, and I had no doubt their ventures would succeed. Why should they not? Most of the venture concepts were so boring that you could readily believe no one else had been able to stay awake long enough to brain them out: schemes for jamming advertisements between consumers and what they wanted to see, or for shaving half a penny off each of a billion transactions. And some of the venture concepts were so sinister they seemed more like comic book plots hatched by supervillains than business plans for start-ups.

Right when Frankel and I were getting comfortable, Jane and Gerhard broke up, and Gerhard took a job at Sapient managing brand strategy projects. Sapient was a huge interactive developer like Razorfish and Organic, though it was actually better positioned for the coming crash because it had concentrated on servicing Fortune 100 companies for cash rather than start-ups in which it could take equity. When Gerhard took the Sapient job, Frankel and I blinked. We realized he must have been listening during our brand strategy babbles, and we worried we might have lost our salesperson. But it turned out to be great for us. Now Gerhard could kick us some really big gigs, working under Sapient for enterprise clients we could never have handled a year earlier.

In his book *The New New Thing*, about Netscape founder Jim Clark and a company he started called Healtheon, which proposed to centralize the health-care industry, Michael Lewis describes a business model he calls "the asshole in the middle." The basic idea of this model is to become the hub through which an entire complex market area—the bigger and more complex the better—conducts all its transactions. The hub company's supposed function is to increase price transparency and transaction speed within the network, creating efficiencies that benefit all the parties involved. According to the model, increases in efficiency will always be more than offset by increases in transaction volume; hence the hub company's motivation is always to create more transparency. The part that's not quite a secret, but doesn't go front and center on explanatory materials, is that when the hub company makes its IPO, whoever started it makes a tremendous amount of money—and that, rather than the somewhat abstract notion of increasing transparency in a market, is the real motivation for becoming an asshole in the middle.

Chevron retained Sapient to help them develop a business that would be to the multibillion-dollar oil spill cleanup industry what Healtheon had proposed to be to the multibillion-dollar health-care industry. The thinking at Chevron had gone as follows: Oil spill cleanup is costing us tons of money. Other oil companies have to clean up spills, and it's costing them tons of money, too. Why don't we spin off a company that centralizes the cleanup industry? That way we can make money on oil spills, instead of losing money on oil spills. And, that way we look like environmentalists! (Do people care? People do.) One way of thinking about it was that the more oil got spilled, the more money they would make. We were paid thirty thousand dollars for a few days' work helping the Chevron executives and Sapient project managers develop palatable language for describing the scheme. But the IPO market fell to pieces soon thereafter, and so far as I know, the cleanup hub was never launched.

In early 2000 our high school friend Carlo, a hilarious entrepreneurial tax attorney in San Francisco, got in touch with us about renaming a start-up he was helping put together. The start-up was called eOffer, and Carlo thought the name was problematic in several respects. It was too close to eOffering, a company that provided early access to IPO shares; the *e-* prefix was pretty tired by that time and might signal to investors that the company was behind the curve; and when you said "eOffer" out loud, it kind of sounded like you were barfing.

As an attorney and the youngest partner in the company, Carlo was carrying a heavy load, hammering out the company's deals in addition to running interference between high-powered partners. This meant a lot of transatlantic flying, because two of the partners lived in England some of the time and were always going back and forth between there and California on weird schedules.

One of these two was Mick Fleetwood, the drummer from Fleetwood Mac. He was an international celebrity and something like six foot seven, so he was always being gawked at— I certainly gawked the first time I saw him—but he was relaxed and sharp, with an innate sense of brand strategy. (Note that the band wasn't called Stevie Buckingham, and remember: He was the drummer.) The other main partner was Ted Owen, who had pioneered rock memorabilia auctions back in the eighties, when Ian Schrager and his partners in the Hard Rock made the first market in old guitars and used underwear.

The stateside partners were regular businesspeople who were putting the financing into place. The venture was to be an auction house with both off-line and online components, specializing in rare rock memorabilia on the one end and cheaper licensed collectibles on the other: Rock and Roll Sotheby's meets eBay. They were going to launch with a live auction of John Lennon's white piano, maybe after Elton John played it in a concert in the Canary Islands or Ibiza. Carlo was trying to keep this venture on track and at the same time put in billable hours at Howard Rice, the firm where he did tax law. His eyes were holes in his head.

I was exhausted, too, in early 2000. My business with Jason had become far more than a full-time job. The conflict between that and Quiddity was becoming real, but I didn't want to relinquish either one, and the fall and winter had been difficult in other respects. The night before the start of the Quiddity engagement with eOffer, which was to be a four-hour session with all seven or eight principal partners, which Frankel had organized to occur in a rented conference room at Fort Mason in San Francisco, one of my wisdom teeth started bugging me. It had been bugging me for a while, but that night it really started to hurt, and by morning my eye on that side was closing involuntarily.

There was no question of canceling the meeting. The partners had flown in from all over the place, Mick Fleetwood and Ted Owen from wherever they had flown in from, and a couple of the others from the East Coast. Somehow I made it through the four hours of talking them toward the solution Frankel and I had already decided would be best, Fleetwood Owen.

That may make it appear that we were lazy, but the fact was that Fleetwood Owen was the best possible name for the company. It already sounded like a venerable auction house. Fleetwood was just a cool name. It had worked for Mick and for Fleetwood Mac, and it had also worked for years for GM as the name of Cadillac's most powerful and luxurious sedan. You had speed and trusty permanence all in one. Fleet. Wood. Owen was the partner. You wanted a partner in the company name, to give it a sense of stability and heritage. Owen was a perfect partner name, simple and plain, almost a cipher. Those were reasons Fleetwood Owen was a good name for the company, even if you had no idea who the partners were.

And in this case, who the partners were was the company's strongest asset. The company had capital, and they were having a back end, the databases and stuff that made an auction site work, developed in Pakistan. But everybody had capital, and plenty of online auction companies had solid back ends. This company's real equity lay in the identities of the principals—*fame, Britain, rock and roll, money, auctions*—and the smartest thing for all the partners to do was leverage that equity as comprehensively as possible.

This was not a hard sell. Mick Fleetwood understood precisely the value he was bringing to the company. Ted Owen was happy to get top billing along with him. But because the solution was so simple, the hard part for Alex and me was moving the room to the idea slowly enough. We didn't want to endanger the decision by the appearance that we were just being lazy. All the partners had to feel they had participated in the decision and then made it themselves, as was their right. Carlo was nobody's fool, and I'm sure he divined that we'd already decided what we thought the name should be, but he thanked us afterward with a poker face.

Despite the delicacy required to extend the process into a four-hour tap dance, the main thing on my mind was the disaster taking place in my face. I would have loved to go straight to a dentist in San Francisco after the meeting, but the next day I was supposed to do some promotional baloney at the Yahoo! Internet Life Film Festival in Los Angeles for a company to which Jason and I had sold a show, and afterward I was supposed to speak on a panel on the subject of the New Media Underground. On the way to the airport, I arranged an emergency dental appointment in Los Angeles, and Frankel dropped me off for the now familiar United Express commuter flight back to LAX.

The dentist did the last thing you want to see from a dental chair, a cartoon horror take. My upper right wisdom tooth was a Cadbury egg, still mostly solid on the outside but decayed into goop in the middle. It was going to have to come out, but he was worried it would implode the second he put pliers on it. Because I had been sober for so long, I didn't want the gas, and because I had so much to do the next day, I didn't want general anesthesia. I had never gone under except by my own administrations or a sharply swung pool cue, and neither of those experiences was a pleasant memory. Plus I had no dental insurance, so I was paying for the extraction with cash.

He said he could do it with just Novocain if I could deal with the noise and mess, so he numbed me up and got out the crowbars. The wisdom tooth had roots all the way back to my brainstem. It fought extraction with gruesome cracking noises that originated behind my nose and up around my ear and eyeball, way up into the reaches of my upper sinus. I thought it was going to bring out the whole inside of my head, inner ear first, then the eyeball, then my brain shaped into a distended pudding of gristle by its egress through the narrow hole, but at least it didn't hurt. At my request the dentist showed me the tooth after he tied off the gum hole. It was nasty, but it was only about an inch long, even with the root fork. Nevertheless, I was bleeding like a pig through the stitches, and he said it was going to hurt pretty bad when the Novocain wore off, so I took a prescription for Vicodin and had it filled at the pharmacy across the street.

A Vicodin prescription was technically—not even technically, totally—against the "rules" of recovery. But those same rules, inculcated into me at sixteen, had kept me from trying the antidepressants that would literally change my life, the first time they were recommended—ten years before I did try them. I still hadn't had a drink or gotten high since teen rehab, and I wasn't laboring under the illusion that I could become a responsible recreational drug user—more than a decade sober, it still eluded me how anyone could think one beer was plenty, or twelve too many—but I had had just about enough of rules.

There were ten of them in the canister. I ate one immediately. Oh, bliss. Sweet, sweet bliss. Thirteen long years and more since I had felt you. Coat me inside with glory, let the rays of the sun shine out from my forehead, make the utterances of my lips as gold. Two would be enough to slide me on a glowing rail to bed: one when this one faded but before it was gone, and I could eat all the rest the next day.

From a responsible recovering drug addict's point of view, that would be the way to deal with the situation. Don't try to ration them out. Get rid of them as fast as possible, and when they're gone, don't try to get any more. The label recommended one or two as needed every three to four hours, so that was two every three hours tomorrow, so for eight of them that was twelve hours of unremitting joy and brilliance that would put me down gently at the end. The following day I could just sack up and take some Advil. The hole in my mouth would have started healing, and whatever pain was left would serve as penance for the binge.

The next day I woke late, groggy and throbbing. I took one to get rid of the throb and had some double espressos on the way to the office so I would be awake enough to enjoy the next. Jason, Brody, and I drove over to the Sunset Strip, where the Yahoo! Internet Life Film Festival was being held at the Standard and Chateau Marmont hotels. The Standard was a former nursing home that had recently been discovered as a perfect example of swank mod architecture and renovated for the stylish young. The Chateau was the luxurious gardened castle where John Belushi had overdosed, the place where you still were supposed to take a suite if you were a celebrity who wanted privacy and proximity to the Strip but couldn't be troubled to deal with the maintenance of a mansion you owned yourself.

This was right at the peak of the Internet frenzy, when everything seemed about to explode, and the events at the Yahoo! Internet Life Film Festival were packed. The day passed in a lambent blur. I had a big wad of bloody gauze in my cheek but felt no less eloquent or attractive for it. Jason and I wore the Hawaiian shirts and plastic leis demanded for our promotional event, and we interviewed Mike Figgis for camera about his new movie, *Timecode 2000*. WireBreak, the company to which we had sold our show, had manufactured for promotional giveaway a bushel of banana-shaped ballpoint pens with our show's title, *Backdoor Hollywood*, and the WireBreak logo printed on them. WireBreak's CEO caught us stuffing our pockets with these. I was so high that I just started laughing at getting busted with my pockets full of plastic bananas, but Jason had the good sense to point out that that was what the banana pens were for—giving away —and he was only taking them so he could give them away himself, and thereby promote the show and the company. The CEO was heartily sick of us by then anyway, so he let us leave the Standard with our pockets full of banana pens.

By that time it was dusk, and I was obliterated. We made our way across the street to the patio by the swimming pool of the Chateau Marmont. A couple of hundred people were already there, waiting under red paper lanterns to hear what we had to say. It was only a silly panel, but just a year before, we would have had to scale the fence just to be in the audience. As moderator, Jason had booked the speakers: Matt Stone, because he and Trey had closed an outrageous deal with Shockwave; Les Claypool, who was always hilarious; and a couple of New Media CEOs we thought were clowns, but that was why they were there, because we had to have somebody to disagree with.

One of these bozos put forth an opinion with which I disagreed absolutely. Even as his words floated out of him and hung in the warm night air under the redly lambent globes, the perfect response was crystallizing inside me. When he finished, Jason turned to me and in his great deadpan said it looked like I wanted to respond. The lanterns swung, the faces mooned. The CEO leaned forward, politely prepared to field my response. My mind was a perfect blank. The crowd waited patiently, but finally I had to laugh and admit the truth out loud: I had no idea what I was talking about.

Three

1

Almost two years before I made that admission at the Chateau, Jason and I were meeting Ted Demme for the first time at the Disney Ranch. Afterward I went to Palm Springs, holed up in a motel, and wrote the first draft of a screenplay for *The Jockey*. When that was completed and out to Teddy for notes in the fall in 1998, Jason and I began to plan the next steps for CRAP.

Based on the small success of Cannes You Dig It?, we wanted to throw another festival event in Park City in January 1999. This year Jason had no movies playing at Sundance or Slamdance, so the event would have to be promoted on its own merits. At the post-Undance condo party where Cannes You Dig It? had first been proposed, one of our lawyers had suggested that if we ever held another event in Utah during Sundance, it should be called Lapdance. Clearly, that idea was too good to pass up.

The dissent embodied by CRAP had not manifested as an identifiable commodity, but there was a unifying theme to the few bits of media we had made, to the media submitted by filmmakers for Cannes You Dig It?, and, following word-of-mouth solicitation, to the films and videos submitted for

Lapdance: It was all too weird or just aggressively bad for any recognized festival or broadcast outlet to be remotely interested in programming it.

We had nothing like a CRAP manifesto to delineate what constituted genuine CRAP and what did not. As Justice Potter Stewart famously said of obscenity, we knew it when we saw it, and a set of rigid criteria would have violated the internal logic of the Certified Renegade American Product proposition. In any case, it was right around that time that I first heard of the Dogma Manifesto, which underscored the necessity of our not having one.

It was Heather who introduced me to the Dogma movement; I had heard of Dogma but thought it was just a generalized rubric meaning "outsider." Once again, she was on the Slamdance Film Festival shorts programming committee. The way the Slamdance selections worked was that a programmer had to be physically present for the final voting on a submitted film, no matter what time the voting occurred, for his or her vote to be counted; and final votes on a film were not taken until discussion of the film was unanimously judged to be finished. The result of this system was that the films Slamdance programmed were not necessarily the films that were most entertaining, but rather the films championed by the programmers with the most stamina, who tended to be the people who had the stamina to appreciate the most tedious submissions. Slamdance had accidentally created a process for distilling the ultimate soporific, a short films program so stupendously boring you could sit down to watch it and be knocked out cold before the opening titles.

Heather said one of the filmmakers on the committee had sent his feature film to the Dogma people for certification, and he was all worked up about whether they would certify his film. I didn't understand. She explained that for a fee, you could send your film to the Dogma people, and they would tell you whether you had made "A Dogma Film." If they said that you had, then you could put "A Dogma Film" on your promotional materials and include a card saying "A Dogma Film" in your titles. If not, then you couldn't. So what? Well, she said, whether your film was "A Dogma Film" affected your chances of getting distribution. Did I not know anything? Dogma Films were the rage, and if your film said it was "A Dogma Film," then you were practically guaranteed distribution on video, and you had a much better shot at theatrical.

I wanted to know how there could possibly be a certification process for "outsider" filmmaking. Wasn't that like a certification process for "punk rock" music—a board of punk rock musicians, who could tell you whether you were allowed to say you were punk rock? If you were in fact punk rock, you would just tell them to fuck off. That's how they'd know. But if you asked the punk rock board of directors whether you were punk rock, then they would know for sure you weren't. This Dogma thing sounded too goofy to be true, and I immediately called bullshit.

Heather was an avid collector and disseminator of unlikely information that nevertheless had some basis in fact. That I chronically doubted her information and demanded bibliographic verification of it was a source of understandable irritation to her, and she had taken to compiling dossiers and slamming them on my desk whenever I called bullshit on another fantastic proclamation. I had already received two thick probative files on different topics.

The first file treated the subject of Williams People, persons suffering from a genetic disorder that caused them to have lower than average IQs, made them about four feet tall in maturity, gave them pointy ears and almond-shaped eyes, inclined them toward singing and dancing, and impelled them to ask what was going on all the time. It had been proposed by some scholars that perhaps Williams People abandoned in the woods of medieval Europe had found one another, danced in circles, and otherwise evinced behaviors that gave rise to myths of nosy, dancing sprites who lived in the forest, a.k.a. fairies. All true, all documented in the Williams People dossier.

The second file was on Furries and Plushies. While it is old news now that there is a league of like-minded people who practice frottage in mascot costumes and make love to stuffed animals, Heather was the first person to introduce me to the concept, and I still hold that calling bullshit was a natural response. The Furries and Plushies file was delivered in connection with the story of the creepy cousin of the guy Heather and Shana had given a ride up to Park City the year before—the cousin with the *Little Mermaid* shrines and the back room wallpapered with dead squirrels. In fairness to Heather's accepting nature, the *Little Mermaid* shrines—circumstantial indicators, as she saw it, of Furriness and/or Plushiness—were not a problem in and of themselves; it was just that when you combined those with home taxidermy, which even on its own would have earned her severe disapproval, you had something much worse than the sum of its parts.

In fairness to my reflexive skepticism about Heather's arcana, her investigative thoroughness sometimes left something to be desired. She told a story on herself in this regard, about the coal ponies. The coal ponies were little beasts of burden that were taken down into the coal mines as soon as they reached maturity, to toil forever in darkness. Down in the darkness they were stabled and watered and fed, never to see the light of day again until they were too weak to stand. Right when the coal ponies were just about to keel over, the miners brought them, blindfolded against the brightness, back to the surface, where they were fed one last carrot before being whonked on the head with a shovel.

The plight of the coal ponies had so upset Heather when she first read about it that she had slammed shut the book in which it was described. Not long afterward she was at a fancy dinner in New York, and it came up that one of the old guys at the table was the chairman of a coal company. In front of everyone at the restaurant Heather went crazy on the coal magnate about the coal ponies. He said he felt bad about them, too—but she did know that it had been a hundred years since any pony had seen the inside of a coal mine, didn't she?

It was with the coal ponies in mind that I expressed doubt about there being an official Dogma certification process. Heather's dossier on Dogma, which in due course she slammed on my desk, and my own subsequent research revealed two things: First, there really was a certification process whereby you could submit a finished film to an official Dogma certification body. Second, the Dogma people—Danish filmmakers Thomas Vinterberg and Lars von Trier—were basically joking.

Their Dogma Manifesto was a set of rules for filmmaking that took the aim of returning immediacy, intimacy, and urgency to the medium. The rules are not bad ones. Shoot everything handheld. Use real exteriors and interiors. Use only practical light. Use only available sound. The idea was that if you took away the tools required for making big shitty movies, you had a better chance of making small good ones. But the point wasn't that you had to follow their rules; it was that you should stop making shitty movies. And while they had been serious in enumerating techniques whereby making shitty movies might be avoided, setting those techniques down as rules in a "manifesto" had been at least in part a Scandinavian prank.

But the prank aspect of the manifesto seemed to have eluded the American independent filmmaker community, and a thoughtful joke about how to make movies that did not suck was turned into a marketing angle over which deadly serious ding-dongs gnawed their nails at night. If the marketing angle was why you were making "A Dogma Film," then you were paddling up the wrong fjord. Fairly or not, that was exactly the kind of glum dipshittery Jason and I associated with Slamdance.

Slamdance had been founded the year after Jason first screened *Cannibal* in Park City, by five filmmakers whose films had not gotten into Sundance the previous year, either, but who also had gone to Park City anyway. Those rejected filmmakers joined forces and held their first festival the following winter. Slamdance, to its credit, had a more coherent message than CRAP could ever hope to have, but in some ways that message was what made Slamdance such a perpetually gloomy undertaking. It was a two-part message: a) Slamdance is put on by filmmakers, for filmmakers; and b) Slamdance programs only films by directors who have never gained theatrical distribution.

The DIY thing was right on, and the distribution thing was even more right on, especially considering what Sundance had become, an auction site and promotional shouting match for movies that were going to get distribution anyway—or, in many cases, already had it lined up. There were still a lot of grimy-fingered independent filmmakers who came to Park City every year, but Sundance wasn't programming their movies. They couldn't even get into screenings, much less the real events: the parties.

The actual independent filmmakers at Sundance huddled miserably outside on the sidewalks. These peasants shunned by Sundance could get into Slamdance screenings and parties. But the Slamdance parties were, not to put too fine a point on it, kind of lame. Just as people screened their films at Slamdance when Sundance rejected them (many filmmakers applied to both and of course screened at Sundance if accepted there), people went to Slamdance parties when they couldn't get into Sundance parties. So despite the unimpeachable intentions of the Slamdance founders and the very real purpose their festival served in providing a venue for actual independent films, the Slamdance Film Festival felt like a separate prom right down the street from the real prom—this one put on by losers, for losers.

Nerd-bashing the only example of real independence in Park City demands an explanation of what kind of independence we proposed in its stead. But just as we at CRAP had developed no identifiable commodity from our dissent, we were only just beginning to identify what we were dissenting against. It was not network television or big studio movies to which we objected most strenuously. Dissenting against network television or big studio movies would be like objecting to the weather, to gravity, to the expansion of the universe. With the exceptions—maybe—of Christianity and Islam, there has never been so robust an engine of self-perpetuation as American capitalism, which has reached its apotheosis in the consolidation of media interests. The entangled monolithic mass of networks and studios was too huge for any objection to it to be effective or even audible. Imagine it: standing on the sidewalk outside a network complex or studio lot, stamping your feet and shrieking, "Quit it!"

If there was so much we *didn't* like, what was it that we *did* like? And why, instead of making things we did like, did we expend so much energy throwing an event called Lapdance, whose only real functions were to give a middle finger to Sundance and point out how dolorous and dull the truly independent Slamdance Film Festival was? It almost sounds like we hated movies. But we *loved* movies.

I was a kid in the seventies, a teenager in the eighties. MTV went on air when I was in fifth grade, but that wasn't a landmark moment for me, because there was no television in my house until seventh grade. When I was a kid, it was through the movies that my culture spoke to me, and I got to go to them a lot—of course, to the Lucas and Spielberg blockbusters, but I was also treated to grimly educational marathons and flashes of terror: Kubrick's *2001* and Cocteau's *Beauty and the Beast*, both when I was maybe five, with my dad and mom, respectively.

Bert and I saw *Jaws* when I was six, and neither of us will ever recover. A few years later, he took me to *Close Encounters*. Richard Dreyfuss in those years reminded me of my father. They even looked a little alike, but it was the manic, seeking enthusiasm of the Dreyfuss characters—the marine biologist in *Jaws,* the dad possessed by visions in *Close Encounters,* the yogic, romantic Richard Dreyfuss in *The Goodbye Girl*—that really reminded me of Bert.

In fourth grade I saw *E.T.* in a matinee double feature after *Dead Men Don't Wear Plaid.* Steve Martin was still way over my head, but *E.T.* was a revelation. Who can ever forget the little guy mewling in the drainage ditch, sad and moldy as a hock of alien ham? Or the jingly keys that were so scary at the beginning, with the flashlight beams cutting through the woods, or all the funny parts—the D&D dorks and Elliott calling his brother "penis breath?"

Those were the years in which sleeping over at other kids' houses on the weekends or having them sleep over at yours were the regular things, and going to a movie was the regular event—especially when we were at my house, since there was no television. Because I slept over at different people's houses on different weekends, sometimes I saw the same movie several weekends running. I didn't mind at all if I liked the movie. *Breaking Away* and *Time Bandits*—perfect. *The Elephant Man* demolished me—once, twice, three weekends in a row I was reduced to a jelly of snot and grief. "I am not an animal . . . I am a *human being.*"

My mom, Margaret, took four of us to a Fellini double feature in fourth grade, and if the fat lady hadn't pulled her tits out at the end of *Amarcord,* nobody would have spoken to me for a week. Then it was *Aguirre: The Wrath of God,* in which Werner Herzog lost Klaus Kinski and my carpool in the Amazon. The same crew was subjected to *Kagemusha: The Shadow Warrior,* something like five and half hours of Kurosawa.

Her efforts to manage my audiovisual inputs reached a peak in sixth grade and then collapsed spectacularly. My best friend, Dean, was sleeping over, and we really, really, *reeeeeeeally* wanted to see a new sword and sorcery movie that had skulls, blades, and steel bikinis in its newspaper ad. Somehow we both had already managed to see *Excalibur,* and that had whetted our appetites for medieval sex and gore. Margaret reluctantly shuttled us to the theater where the new medieval movie was showing. Since the movie was rated R, she had to go to the window with us and buy the tickets; the R rating was an obstacle but not a deal breaker in itself. As my mom was opening her pocketbook, she asked the teenage girl behind the counter whether, in the girl's opinion, Dean and I were mature enough to handle the film's content. The zitty bitch, all of three years older than we were, looked us over and said she didn't think so. We screeched in indignation, but Margaret now was adamant. She closed her pocketbook and grimly put us back the car. Dean and I squalled in the backseat as she piloted us to another theater, where there was a movie playing that some of the ladies at her office had said was just hysterical. Yeah, right— like they would know.

None of us, certainly not my mom, had any idea what *Porky's* was about. The title was terrible—it sounded like a little kids' movie. Dean and I griped and pouted while Margaret primly purchased tickets from the counter guy, who batted not an eyelid, and we stamped into the theater. The sustained joy of the next hour and a half was capped only by the even more transcendent pleasures of the ride home, when we got to shriekingly relate all the best parts to my mom.

After that it was pretty much open season. Soon the television came in, with a cable box and VCR. By pressing a pattern of buttons on top of the cable box, you could unscramble the signal on the Playboy Channel, which started broadcasting at five o'clock. A kid up the street had a live-in cook who had a porno collection, and Dean and I got the kid to pilfer *Deep Throat* from the cook's library. *Deep Throat* jammed the VCR halfway through our viewing, and we had to pry the cassette out with a screwdriver. The VCR was never quite the same after that, the top-loading slot a cockeyed reminder of furry deltas and long, curving dongs.

Some grown-up material was too scary, though. Bert took me to see *American Werewolf in London* in a theater—this was probably in seventh grade—and the dreams that woke into dreams, the pig-monster storm troopers killing the family and then the nurse, terrified me. I lasted until the handheld run through the woods, the low Raimi-style rush to the hospital bed in the clearing. When the dead guy opened his eyes and hissed into the lens, I ashamedly asked Bert if we could leave. My sweet dad didn't even kid me about it. We just went home.

And then, by high school, movies suddenly were different. You understood that people made them—that they were constructed and finite, not worlds extending endlessly, into which you might pass and be lost forever.

Thomas Frank, critic and unknowing author of CRAP's first slogan, cites the scene in the 1953 film *The Wild One* in which the saloon keeper asks Marlon Brando, "So, what is it you're rebelling against?" and a leather-jacketed Marlon Brando replies, "Whaddaya got?" as a key moment in American

cinema because it put a first finger on the restless antago-
nism against American plenty felt by the postwar generation, even as they wallowed in it. *Rebel Without a Cause* came
out two years later, and thousands of teenage boys my
father's age ran out to get red windbreakers like the one worn
by James Dean.

If there was a generational moment in the films of my early
teenage years, a moment that named our own generation's
fatuous, self-mutilating rage, surely it is that scene in *Repo
Man*—surely it is all of *Repo Man,* but especially the scene in
the liquor store after Otto's loser friend Duke, played by Dick
Rude, gets shot trying to rob the place. Otto bends over his
friend to hear his final words. Duke gasps, "I . . . blame . . .
society." Otto says that that's bullshit—he's just a suburban
punk. Duke bubbles blood and croaks, "It still . . . hurts."

If you agreed with Marlon Brando or James Dean, you
were rebelling against people who were telling you to con-
form. But if you agreed with Dick Rude, you were rebelling
against people who were telling you to rebel. How do you
do that? You can't just go out and get a motorcycle jacket
or a red windbreaker—that's exactly what they want you to
do. You have to think about how to rebel against a culture
of fake rebellion. And as Dick Rude says, it still hurts.

It's important to point out that even as we were trying to
express this confusing generational sentiment, we were still
trying like crazy to succeed as part of the culture machine we
despised—to be rich, to be famous. For how else could we
judge the success of our rebellion? Despite the inherent con-
tradictions of this position, it was not so purely hypocritical
as it might seem on its face. Defining yourself as an outsider—
being "edgy"—was the only path to film or television author-

ship, unless you wanted to throw in the towel at the starting bell and kiss ass up the ranks from the mailroom somewhere or take a job as a television writer's assistant. And film and television were the only types of authorship that mattered.

Finding that last sentence in a book may seem a little strange, but it explains much of what I was doing in Los Angeles in the first place, and therefore it is in some regard this book's very raison d'être. While I was at Stanford in 1995, Jonathan Franzen was doing research for a *Harper's* folio piece in which he tackled the question of whether books still mattered— not in the sense of whether one kind and thoughtful reader or another liked them, but *mattered,* like had the power to influence American culture. He interviewed everyone in the Stegner program on the subject. While the two of us had a nice lunch, he seemed dissatisfied with my answer, which was that books didn't matter and hadn't for decades, maybe since before either of us was born, but that writing them was still better than working. Instead of quoting me, he chose to quote Don DeLillo and some other important writers—go figure— who held the opposite opinion, that of his thesis, that books did still matter.

At the time of the interviews, he was working on *The Corrections*. It was a big, serious book, and he wrote in the folio piece that he was working hard on it, so when I read the folio piece, I could see why he had wanted to believe that books mattered. *The Corrections* did launch him from talented obscurity into well-deserved fame and fortune—but only, I feel compelled to point out, after it was placed, amid some awkward hemming and hawing on Franzen's part, on the Oprah's Book Club reading list. So I'm afraid I remain unconvinced. Books can matter in the big, cultural way—*if they're on television*. Or are made into movies, which is pretty much the same thing. You, reader, know who Don DeLillo is, but that dude across from you on the bus, if pressed, would probably guess that he was that fat sidekick guy in Burt Reynolds movies. Hey, I don't like it either, but QED.

The "edgy" road to film and television authorship was tightly controlled, though—not by the networks and studios, which just were what they were, but by their spoiled step-children: MTV in particular on the television side, and Sundance on the film side. Bankrolled by the stupendously huge corporations that owned them—Viacom owned MTV, and Sundance sold itself annually to different sponsors—MTV and Sundance laid vociferous claim to the territory of rebellion against corporate interests. It was ridiculous—baldly absurd. But they defended the claim vigorously with marketing dollars and maintained a thin patina of credibility by plucking a few screaming freaks each year from the outside world and putting them to work.

This was great work, if you could get it—we had only to see Matt and Trey's new houses to see that. But until you had "edgy" certification from Sundance or MTV (or Comedy Central, another Viacom company), you were hardly even going to exist. You were just another loser. So it was not the networks or studios to which we objected. They weren't full of shit. It was their fake alternative proxies—the purveyors of normative, marketable rebellion—that we felt were the real enemies of truth. That was why we had so much fun plotting Lapdance. We would throw the velvet-rope party where *they* wanted to be, but we would let the geeks, freaks, and puppet makers, the guys with pimples and the fat girls in velvet, cut the line.

One thing I am afraid I am glossing over here is the overwhelming sense of belief we had in ourselves and in what we were doing. We didn't just believe what we were doing was right or fun, but that it would *work*. The raconteur's false modesty I have adopted in order to tell this story belies a very real confidence I had in myself—confidence that I would be not just a player, but a singular, distinctive force in American media. I had spent my twenties toiling in the wrong medium—an irrelevant one in which harder work paid smaller dividends. Now we would make the world ours.

Brody went to Utah early to scout for a Lapdance location. Park City was a little gingerbread ski town; every venue with a liquor license and room for more than twenty people to stand had been booked for months, some since the year before. Up the hill from town, though, she found something interesting, a mining museum called the Park City Silver Mine Adventure.

There was room for upward of a thousand people to wander around on two levels among clumsy life-size animatronic mining dioramas and exhibits of rusty old equipment. Some hopeful nut had built the place; even in the summer it operated at a loss. It was the biggest venue in the area. But Sundance had never rented the Silver Mine for an event—it was a mile out of town, and every other party or screening venue was on a five-block stretch of Main Street. What if nobody wanted to drive up there? Jason, the eternal optimist, lobbied hard for putting down a deposit. Nothing better was going to become available. We cleaned out the bank account and secured the Silver Mine for one night, the Friday at the end of the week.

Jon Jacobs, who had underwritten Cannes You Dig It?, still hadn't found distribution for *Lucinda's Spell*. His mysterious promotional coffers weren't depleted yet, so he was in for another round. But Lapdance was a much more ambitious undertaking than Cannes You Dig It? had been. Despite having been staged in France, Cannes You Dig It? had operated out of Jason's backpack. The Silver Mine alone was a few thousand dollars; we also had to get security for the event, bring in a band or two, provide housing for whatever volunteer staff we could muster, rent some vans, buy insurance, pay for travel to and from Salt Lake City, make promotional materials, and provide enough liquor for the thousand or so attendees we hoped to attract. And this time we were going to know a lot of them. If Cannes You Dig It? hadn't come off, no one would have been the wiser, but everyone we knew went up to Sundance.

Even the barest-bones budget put the event at thirty thousand dollars, and that was about twenty-five thousand more than we had. How did people pull off events like this? Even at twenty dollars a ticket—and we wanted to throw events that were free—we'd have to sell more than capacity to make up the difference.

The obvious answer was sponsorship. The Jon Jacobs thing set a great precedent for us—we'd find independent production companies whose films hadn't gotten into Sundance, or even Slamdance, that wanted to be in Park City to promote their films but didn't quite have the cash or juice to do it by themselves. The pay-for-play aspect of this proposition raised not a single eyebrow. It was just business. Sundance would program your film if it had celebrity attachments they could convert into money through sponsorship; we were just making an already transparent process more transparent. Next Generation, the company that had hired Quiddity to come up with names, was ready to put its name out. Another company we knew through our lawyers had made a movie called *Tyrone*, starring Coolio in multiple roles. Both groups ponied up a few thousand as Lapdance sponsors.

But we were still far short of the mark. Who else wanted mainstream media attention, wanted the association with mainstream celebrities that presence at Sundance delivered, and would never in a million years be welcome at Sundance? But of course—porn companies. Sundance would be happy to program your exploitainment if it purported to be a documentary in one of two formats: either a gritty exploration of porn's devastating impact on the souls of its subjects, or, conversely, a celebration of third-wave feminist sex-positive entrepreneurship. Either of those would be "controversial" and also give people secret boners. Sundance would welcome you with open arms, and you'd get a deal at HBO. But going to Park City to promote *Cum Fiesta 43*? That wasn't happening. We could think of nothing that would be more affrontive to the studied liberality of the Sundance Film Festival or more likely to garner cheap press.

Porn companies liked the idea. Even after replacing Farrell with Jolon and Martha, we weren't completely on the outs with him, and he had finally completed his nonsensical multi-genre porno epic. Jason was still in touch with Kuki, the Japanese porn company that had provided some of the financing for *Orgazmo,* and a few other adult entertainment companies. Seth Warshawski, the CEO of IEG, the Seattle-based Internet Entertainment Group, was notorious for having released the Pam and Tommy Lee–vacation sex video, but that was just the tip of the IEG iceberg. Starting out with only a couple of phone-sex lines, Seth had created the model for Internet pornography, a multibillion-dollar business in traffic and syndication. IEG cut us a check for ten thousand. Wicked and VCA, while they were not interested in giving us money, had a busful of porn stars who were making a promotional tour of strip clubs and adult bookstores in the West at the right time. Great. They could be the Ladies of Lapdance. All they had to do was show up. We also managed to get liquor sponsorship—Jason and Brody hustled Chiat Day to give us Dos Equis, and the trick with hard-liquor sponsors was telling the marketing douchebags they'd get to meet porn stars—and some other odds and ends. We weren't all the way there, but we were close enough that we thought we could bridge the gap on ticket sales at the door and maybe even make some money.

What was it, precisely, that our sponsors were sponsoring? It wasn't a film festival, even though we were calling it the Lapdance Film Festival. We had no plans to jury it. Most of it was stuff we had made or our friends had made. In addition to a second Park City screening of *The Sound of One Hand Clapping,* we would premiere Matt and Trey's penis-marionette movie, *Le Petit Package,* which Jason had convinced them to complete. In black-and-white Gallic despair, Matt parks a Peugeot and walks into the bushes with a gun. He takes off all his clothes and puts the gun to his head, preparing to end it all. A cutaway to the shadow he casts on the ground shows a death's head. But when Matt looks down at the portent of doom, his penis starts to dance. He is amazed. Music rises. His penis dances in time. His dolor lifts and is replaced by the joy of having a dancing penis. A gendarme emerges from the underbrush to arrest him, but the gendarme's pants fall down, and his penis starts dancing, too. A clown with balloons happens on the pair; his penis joins the chorus line. Then comes a mime on a bicycle, and one or two more, and by the end of it there are six or seven idiots with their pants down and their penises dancing a cancan.

Jason decided that in addition to being obnoxious and having a good time, we would showcase more challenging avant-garde material than Sundance or anyone else in Park City: a pincer attack, to demonstrate that we were both bigger douchebags and more highbrow. What Jason had in mind as the artistic center of Lapdance was a retrospective of films by the legendary auteur Stan Brakhage.

Brakhage was one of a very few real-live, recognized American avant-garde filmmakers, deeply revered within the small circle of people who made, watched, and wrote seriously about movies that might have nothing in them but a pendulum, some seagulls, and a piston going up and down, with an incessant dog bark as the sound track. He had been Jason's favorite film professor at Boulder—a wonderful, thoughtful, encouraging man who supported the making of *Cannibal* unreservedly, while other professors begrudged time off for students who were actually making a movie instead of memorizing the names of dead cinematographers. He was in his sixties and not well. The original idea was to fly him out from Colorado and have him speak at Lapdance, but he wasn't up to it, so he kindly recorded a video message to introduce his films.

The films themselves were harder to find. Brakhage didn't even have them all himself. Several existed only as single precious 16mm prints warehoused by a company that rented them out by mail, mainly to film schools wishing to screen them. We contacted the company, made arrangements for the prints to be delivered to Park City, and found a 16mm projector we could rent there for the event. Everything but the Brakhage retrospective was on video, so we bought a few cheap TV/VCR combos to supplement the video projection facilities at the venue.

I talked Heather into posing for the poster and invitation in nothing but a pink wig, blue hot pants, and white go-go boots. Dave Stotts took the pictures. Her back is to the camera, her arms akimbo. She smiles back over her shoulder. It was saucy but within the bounds of propriety. In terms of a guest list, we gave the names and addresses of a few hundred of our nearest and dearest to the PR firm our attorneys had hooked us up with, two young publicists who had just left another firm to start their own. They also got stuck with the task of making a thousand or so pink laminates, which, like the posters and invitations, had Heather's hot-pantsed ass on them. One of the PR girls was from Utah, and she recommended some football players from Salt Lake to act as our security.

Jason went up to Utah at the beginning of Sundance, a week before our party, to get the word out on Main Street. By the time the rest of us got there, he had been awake for days, drumming up the fun and taking who knows what combinations of freaky drugs. He had the endurance of a sled dog, but at full bore he was good for only about five days of non-stop no-sleep networking, weed smoking, beer drinking, coke snorting, and psychedelic eating. We were closing in on day seven, and after a final night of emergency laminating with the PR girls, he slid into one of his torpid recuperative modes, as sometimes happened once he was satisfied events were in unstoppable chaotic motion—the party was coming up, and he needed to be in peak form. Brody and I ran around dealing with minor bullshit, keg deliveries and fire codes, and got into an insane screaming fight over the lanyards that were supposed to hold the laminates around people's necks: We didn't have any. I thought whatever idea she had for solving the problem was terrible, which she was a total bitch about hearing, so I called her a cunt and was dispatched forthwith to Salt Lake City to get some pink ribbon and a bubble machine.

In the midst of significant logistical problems and clear budgetary overruns (the venue informed us that in addition to the football players, we had to hire some of Park City's finest off-duty officers to provide security, because otherwise they would have their on-duty colleagues shut us down), Jason was petulantly insisting that nothing would be right unless we had a bubble machine. Bubble machine, bubble machine, bubble machine—it was like he had developed some kind of drug-induced Asperger's syndrome. There was only one bubble machine to be had in Utah, and it was in Salt Lake City. It was about the size of a 16mm film projector and cost two hundred dollars. The last time I saw the bubble machine, Jason was gleefully test-driving it before the press conference.

We had one of those in the early evening. Lack of substance was not a problem for the attendant media. By that time Matt and Trey were "Matt and Trey," and the porn stars were all lined up behind us for no discernible reason, so there were all kinds of cameras blinding us at the table. Most of us babbled some nonsense about free expression. Farrell was suuuuper high and launched into a cosmic monologue about porno, but he kept losing track of what he had said and looping around to say it again. We played the Stan Brakhage video message for the reporters: an old man with a white beard, standing by a tree and saying something inaudible. As the centerpiece of Lapdance, his oeuvre would be projected from the balcony onto a huge screen on the far side of the building all night long. The press conference petered out. Most of the resultant clips billed the event as Matt and Trey's, but that was no more than we deserved for using them to publicize it.

The party was a qualified success. It was the biggest party ever thrown during Sundance, including Sundance events. The line of headlights stretched down the mountain toward Park City, and probably three thousand people were in and out over the course of the night. The band and DJs were great, and we didn't run out of liquor. The porn stars had plenty of it. I recall at one point helping the aging sexbot Houston, then just off the success of *The Houston 500* (at that time, the world's largest gang bang), back out to the porn bus. She was very strange up close from all the surgeries, and she tottered like a malfunctioning droid. Several other porn stars left with Kid Rock. When the Silver Mine became a complete fire hazard around midnight, we asked the cops and farm boys to please let more people in only when others left— not very nice, because it was zero degrees out, but it was ass-to-elbow in there. They said sure, and then kept letting people in. We didn't figure out what they were doing for a couple more hours: pocketing four twenties for every one they slipped into the steel box I had padlocked to a post for their convenience. There was nothing we could do about it afterward—they all denied it, of course. It wasn't like we could search the cops, and the farm boys were calm enough when confronted that I figured they had been shuttling cash out to their pickups all night.

Nonetheless, we had fun. My most vivid memory from the evening is of being packed tightly among people I did not know on the balcony and seeing one of Stan Brakhage's films jump loose from the unmanned projector. It spooled out gaily, a falling celluloid ribbon, and was trampled to avant-garde bits beneath the feet of the crowd below.

2

Our high school friend Ward had moved down to Los Angeles a couple of months earlier. He was a drummer, and he had come down from the Bay Area with a guitarist named Dave to start getting serious about their band. Just as we had vowed back in the day, we all had stayed friends. Ward had been sober for years now, but his last bender was still the stuff of legend.

He had failed to materialize at his family's Fourth of July party one summer and was missing for two weeks. We learned later that he had driven to San Francisco, sold his practically new 4Runner to a used-car dealer for ten thousand in cash, and bought a plane ticket to Los Angeles, where he located a large amount of cocaine and two attractive female cocaine enthusiasts, who introduced him to (now sadly deceased) funk grandmaster and freebase aficionado Rick James. The four of them embarked on a tooth-shattering binge that was Ward's last hurrah. We were even more impressed when, soon afterward, Rick James was arrested and sent to prison.

By the time Ward moved down to Los Angeles, he was a healthy surfer guy with a positive attitude and the kind of stable sanity that comes to people only if they're just naturally that way or if they've really, really had to work for it. Ward was more motivated than Dave the guitarist, but even Ward couldn't practice all the time, which was how he ended up over at the Venice Quiddity office helping with the design and production of the new Cannes You Dig It? booklets and scratching his head with me about where to send them for sponsorship.

We had lost money on Lapdance, but undeniably it had been effective. We had garnered Robert Redford's personal ire—he called Lapdance "the lowest of the low" in an interview afterward, which delighted us despite our having no gripe with Robert Redford himself—and there was a thin sheaf of more favorable press. At meetings or at parties we were now sometimes introduced as "the Lapdance guys." Hey! We were the "something" guys! In order to keep up the momentum, we bent to organizing Cannes You Dig It? 99 with a will.

Unfortunately, few of the companies that had supported Lapdance were interested in sponsoring Cannes You Dig It? 99. The porn companies wished us well, but the adult industry had its own event in Nice, also timed to coincide with the festival and market in Cannes. Some of the beverage companies didn't even distribute their products in France, and those that did were divisions of international conglomerates that had separate divisions in Europe.

To make matters worse, the call for entries was going swimmingly. We had a post office box now, and every day it overflowed with padded videotape envelopes. Lapdance had made us a lightning rod for the large population of film-makers either too weird or too untalented to be accepted by anyone else. Submissions piled up in the Mar Vista apartment, and we held progressively more panicky meetings at the Quiddity office.

Compiling a clear picture of how screwed we were took us up to within a month of the event. Two weeks before it was scheduled to occur, we pulled the plug. By this time all our posters had been printed, and reams of them slid among the videotapes we would not be taking to France. Regretfully we called the filmmakers and delivered the bad news. They were nice about it and gave us permission to post their films on the Web, in a sad "virtual" festival that Jolon and Martha encoded and put up on the festival Web site.

We tried to keep our chins up, but the failure of Cannes You Dig It? 99 was a low point. Our projects to date, however ill conceived, at least had happened. This one, on which all our vague hopes had hinged for several months, simply didn't, and our financial situation was getting dire.

On the plus side, the online store was now paying for it-self, doing fifty bucks a week or so in *South Park* and *Canni-bal* garbage. It wasn't much, but it was something to build on. And there were a few hundred kids from all over the coun-try, even a handful in other countries, who used our Web site's bulletin board regularly to communicate with one another. It really was becoming a community. From time to time one of them would show up on our doorstep, making it all the more real—and, more important, demonstrating to us that what we were doing was something that people wanted—dare it be said, something that people needed.

Jason and I may have been lithe and beautiful—perfect human specimens, really, both of us—but we were irregular on the inside, and if there was anything about CRAP to which we could both point with satisfaction, it was that it was a place where difference was celebrated. Not politically correct I'm-okay-you're-okay-and-we'll-pretend-not-to-notice- that-we're-different difference, but real difference, the kind against which all the powers of American media are mobilized.

I fondly offer the first two BBS posters, two women, who came out to visit us in person in Los Angeles. They came together. One was four feet tall, got around fine on crutches, and was hilarious, totally cool, and quite attractive. If I hadn't already gotten serious with Heather, I might have tried my luck, but there it was. When a sixteen-year-old in the Midwest posted a suicide threat in the forum, it was this woman who let us know, engaged the girl directly, and coordinated contact between the girl and local counselors. The friend she visited us with was really big and sort of dowdy, with pretty much hair on her jaws. This second one, Michelle, proposed to write a beauty column for the Web site, which Jason and I thought was a great idea. Heather and Shana were appalled by Michelle's beauty tips, though. The one that offended them most was the suggestion that if you wanted to blot grease from your face, public bathroom toilet-seat covers were made of the exact same rice paper that high-fashion photographers used for blotting, and you could save money by using the seat covers instead of the rice paper. I acknowledged that it sounded a little weird, but how were Jason and I supposed to know whether it was true, or whether there was anything fucked up at all about our beauty columnist's advice? If anything, it seemed to us that since Michelle was sort of challenged in that regard, she might have done more research into the beautification field than Heather and Shana, who by comparison had it easy, so we didn't listen to them.

A couple of months into the beauty column, Martha took me aside at a party and said she had to tell me something. Two things. First, Michelle had done some wrong to another friend of CRAP, Kam (www.kamiam.com), and Michelle's services as a result were no longer welcome at CRAP. This was fine. Kam was a genius and sweetheart; I hardly knew Michelle; and I never read the beauty column myself. Second: No, Martha couldn't tell me. But now I wanted to know what it was, so I pestered her until she said, cryptically drunk: "Michelle . . . is . . . Michael." I still didn't get it, so she said it again. She had to say it like three more times before I finally understood that our erstwhile beauty columnist was a post-op transsexual, and we had had no clue. Needless to say, Heather was insufferable about it.

CRAPateers in their twenties were the ones who visited most, but on our bulletin board there were moms in their forties and teenagers stuck in bad situations, small towns and lonely suburbs where they were bullied and reviled. Jason was the one of us who spent the most time on the board, and Martha kept it civil, laying down the law on the few occasions it got weird in there. And, admittedly, it got a little weird every once in a while.

One morning I came out of my bedroom to find a fourteen-year-old in sunglasses sitting on the Cum Couch, watching dirty movies and having a Schlitz for breakfast. He looked over and said hello as I got some coffee started. I asked him what he was doing in my living room—wasn't it a school day? He said yeah, for most people, but he was taking a little time off. His big sister had started an online romance with some dude named Dian, and he had come along with her from Seattle. His name was cra5h—he said he knew Jolon, too, from an IRC channel, which I knew, vaguely, meant the kid was a fairly advanced computer user. I asked Jolon about him later, and Jolon said cra5h liked to log on to the IRC from the Mir, where he had root access. I said I didn't know what that meant, but it sounded like the kid with the Schlitz had control of the server on a Russian space station. Jolon nodded, unimpressed. What was cra5h supposed to do—go back to algebra class?

So the online thing was growing, if not actually making real money, and Lapdance had demonstrated that if we could manage a baseline level of organization, we could make money on domestic events. Not a ton, but enough to bankroll setting up each subsequent event on a slightly bigger scale.

This wasn't what I had moved out to Los Angeles to do, though—sell T-shirts, be a party promoter, and act as a camp counselor for precocious juvenile delinquents. It was hard to remember exactly what I had had in mind, but the basic idea had been to work in the entertainment business and become rich and famous. Somehow this nebulous thing, CRAP, had preempted our doing much creative work at all. All I had done in that regard was make a Super-8 movie about my penis, alienate the agent to whom I was handed off at ICM, develop a weird TV pilot (The Business) that nobody was buying, and write a star vehicle for Dian Bachar. Granted, The Jockey was in development with a big-time director, but I was starting to understand what it meant to be "in development."

Through Quiddity jobs I was getting to see what things were like at financed start-ups, but I still had only the dimmest apprehension of how venture capital worked. I still had no idea that the Internet businesses so much in the news were not actually making any money but were running at astonishing losses—and I wasn't just reading about those companies in the paper, I was consulting to some of them. I figured if companies had lots of money to spend, they must be making lots of money or at least have a really good plan for how they were going to make money.

The idea of turning CRAP into one of those places, of moving the company from the Mar Vista apartments to a big building with hundreds of people in it (doing . . . what?), just wasn't on our radar. Some financial padding would have been nice, though. Whenever there was a shortfall, and there always was, Tony had to be tapped, or I was. The sums weren't huge—a hundred dollars for printer cartridges, a few hundred for some offset printing, a plane ticket here or there. Though I could sort of afford it, the expenses were adding up—adding up to what, I didn't really want to know, so I didn't keep track. Every once in a while I gave Brody a bunch of receipts, but it was understood that there was no way the company could pay me back, and those receipts just went in a file. The rest I threw away or stuck in a drawer for tax time.

All around us was success, so much that it seemed some must come our way soon, even if just by accident. Matt and Trey's initial deal with Comedy Central had expired, and their attorney had negotiated a really good new one. The initial flare of *South Park* hype was subsiding, but the show held steady as the network's main revenue engine. Not only had it brought in huge amounts of money from advertising and merchandise licensing, it had created a demand for Comedy Central on cable networks that hadn't carried it before, expanding the channel's reach by millions of households. There was a management shake-up going on, and Matt and Trey briefly but seriously considered—and were considered for—the job of *running* Comedy Central.

But it wasn't just *South Park*—the year 1999 was a special time in Los Angeles. Cash was flooding south from Silicon Valley, and a large amount of that cash was going into Content with a capital C. A few years back, Content with a capital C had meant online textual content—basically, online magazines. But the blush had gone from online textual content as big business; even I knew that *Word, Hotwired,* and even the ballyhooed *Slate* and *Salon* were losing money and had small hope of reversing that trend unless they changed their businesses drastically. The new Content was video.

Online video wasn't really new in 1999. Many porn companies had been delivering video over the Internet for years, and we ourselves had been doing it for a full year, thanks to Jolon and Martha. Broadcast.com, a company in Canada, had been putting video online since 1995 or 1996, and by the time I am writing about, Yahoo! had already acquired Broadcast.com for the mind-boggling sum of four billion dollars. But in 1999 a whole wave of new companies was rising in Los Angleles, companies purporting to be purveyors of this "revolutionary" new kind of Content. Maybe we could catch that wave.

3

One of our first meetings with a potential financier started in the headquarters of Destination Films. Carlo the entrepreneurial tax attorney had introduced Jason and me to Spender, another attorney who appeared not to have slept for six months. Spender lived in Santa Barbara; still did business in San Francisco; and was also involved in the formation of Destination, located in Santa Monica. Destination had recently raised $100 million through a bond offering, with which it proposed to become a virtual studio. There was a lot of "virtual" stuff going on in 1999. So far as I understood this concept of the virtual studio, it was that Destination would conduct the business of producing new movies, acquiring completed ones, and dis-tributing them, without incurring the overhead of a studio lot. On top of his work at Destination, Spender was working on a new project that he envisioned as the AOL of China.

Destination occupied the top floor of the only skyscraper in Santa Monica. The conference room was occupied, so Spender took us down to a Fatburger on the Third Street Promenade. He asked us how much money we were looking for. We had no idea. How much did he think we could get? Well, he said, that depended on our projections, what we envisioned as the second round, the strategic alliances we had in place, and whatever else our business plan stipulated.

Business plan? We didn't have one of those—but if he thought having one would help, we'd be happy to write one. What should it say if we wanted people to give us money? Around this point in the conversation it became apparent to

Spender that we had absolutely no idea what he had been saying about the projections, second round, and other gobble-dygook. He gave us a funny look, but nonetheless, as he finished his soda, he took the time to deliver a primer, including a hockey-stick graph drawn on a paper napkin, on how the whole financing thing worked. It sounded amazing—some of it almost too good to be true.

Spender told us that the first thing you did was manufacture shares in your company. How many? However many you wanted. They were just abstract fractions of your company's value. Ten million was a nice round number. So you sell a million of those shares to somebody for a million dollars. That's your first round. Now your company is worth ten million dollars, right?

We nodded. Our company is worth ten million dollars, because someone has paid one million for a tenth of it. Okay. Now, said Spender, here came the good part. Your company was now actually worth *twenty* million dollars. How come? Because now you have a million dollars in cash—that makes your company worth more. It could be twenty million that your company was worth now, it could be fifty million, but let's make it twenty to keep the math easy.

Now you sell another million shares, of which there are still ten million in total, to someone else. This is your second round. Only this time you get two million dollars for the million shares, because your company is worth twenty million. And afterward your company is worth even more, because why? Because now you have between two and three million in cash. (Not a full three million, because you've spent some by now.) Okay. So let's say that after the second capital infusion your company is worth fifty million dollars.

Jason and I were starting to catch on. Now we sell another million shares for five million dollars—and because we now have five million more dollars, our company is worth a *hundred* million dollars. Excellent! I will not deceive the reader, though, and write that at this point I did not feel a surge of righteous indignation. Rapacious imaginary investors had just bamboozled me and Jason out of 30 percent of our hundred-million-dollar company for a mere eight million dollars. But that was okay, because at this point, said Spender, it was time to sell shares on the public market. We put a chunk on the market at ten dollars a share. By the end of the day the stock is up to a hundred dollars—and now we are running a billion-dollar company. Dude! We're so rich!

As Spender explained it, it didn't sound like it could possibly be legal. But apparently this was what people were doing, and of the CRAP crew I was the "writer," and so it was decided that while Jason got on with picking up the pieces of Cannes You Dig It? 99 and outlining with Jolon and Martha a new Web site that featured video even more prominently, I would educate myself with regard to these new and interesting matters and author the Business Plan that would lift us all into the sky and deposit us in candy-colored Munchkinland.

Around then I moved out of the apartment in Mar Vista. Ward took my old room, and Heather and I moved in together in Venice. This was supposed to represent a new, grown-up stage in our relationship, but we had a roommate almost as soon as we got keys. My friend Scott Mitchell—we had gone to college together, and in Austin he had been my Survival Research Laboratories tour guide—was coming out to LA for postgraduate studies at a fancy architecture school called

SCIArc. Mitchell was six-five and smelled like the trunk of an old man's car—musty, like old books, with a cleansing tang of machine oil. He was a mad mechanical genius who always had three or four complicated projects going at the same time. He tended to stay up for several days running and then conk out fully dressed, either on the floor or sitting up with his black baseball cap pulled down over his eyes, as often as not with a computer or filthy gear train disassembled around him. Heather couldn't believe I'd found us a huge, messy, slightly dangerous roommate the instant we moved in together, but then she got to know him. Mitchell liked to pretend he was the grumpy, silent type, but really he was the chatty, hilarious type, with a store of weird information equal and complementary to Heather's. The two of them sat around for hours gossiping over whiskey, gross foreign snack foods, and hand-rolled cigarettes.

In the meantime I devoted the better part of a month to the Business Plan, reading and writing late into the nights at the Quiddity office. In the small hours I climbed into bed beside Heather with a feeling of satisfaction I had not known since my last semester of college, when each day I sweated out a page or two of my little novel. Only now I was not a famous writer in my imaginings, lecturing to packed halls and getting visits to my office from attractive undergraduates, but something far grander, far mightier, the new breed of *enfant terrible:* the brash young Chief Executive Officer of a New Media Empire.

Like the text-based Content companies before them, the new video Content companies were all proposing to make money by selling ads. But the more I thought about it, the more apparent it became that Internet broadcasting was not a workable business in and of itself, for the plain and simple reason that ads couldn't support the cost of content creation and delivery. If companies couldn't make money on textual content, which cost almost nothing to produce, how could they hope to make money with video content, which cost so much more?

Their answer was that they would be selling video ads—but therein lay the problem. It wasn't just the cost of production working against you. The real killer was the cost of delivering video. A conventional broadcaster's costs don't rise if more people received its signal, but an Internet broadcaster had to pay for each stream of data it sent out, so the cost of delivery could never be amortized.

That was the glaring, obvious problem with the conventional video Content business model, but solving it still wouldn't solve the biggest problem of all. The greatest advantage a television broadcaster enjoys over the Internet webcaster is the relatively tiny number of television channels. Broadcast networks perceive themselves as being under assault by cable, and in 1999 cable viewership was indeed approaching 50 percent of the television audience. But even the hundreds of channels available on a premium cable or satellite package was an infinitesimal number compared to the number of possible Internet broadcasters, which is limited only by the number of computers connected to the Internet. Internet video enjoys a "viral" marketing advantage over cable and broadcast, but that doesn't come close to offsetting the larger marketing disadvantages of the medium.

As I mulled these issues over and talked them through with

Jason and Jolon, the basic concept for our company's next iteration took shape. In one year—several more for Jason—we were already exhausted by pitching to sleepy development executives, who we truly believed wouldn't know what was funny if it walked up and kicked them in the balls with a clown shoe. *South Park* provided the perfect example of this type of executive narcolepsy, and inadvertently it had created the case study for what we proposed to do. A pilot had not been ordered until literally thousands of homemade dubs of the original five-minute short were in circulation all over the country. Even then, plenty of executives had scoffed at the notion of putting the show on the air. MTV and Comedy Central were the only bidders.

It seemed as though to sell a new show you had to already have a hit show or at least work on one—or you had to bring your own audience, as *South Park* had done. An audience was what we proposed to develop with our new, reformulated Web site. We would continue to throw the events because they generated publicity and expanded our base of underappreciated talent. We would continue to sell junk through our store because that was already in motion, and it would put us in place to capture merchandise licenses to our own stuff in the future. But our main focus would be on developing an ongoing showcase for unusual media. With investment, we would create and produce a suite of inexpensive short-format original shows ourselves and in partnership with filmmakers we met through our events and the site. These shows would be unbelievably excellent, and with the incontrovertible evidence of their excellence in the form of our rabid online fan base, we would sell the shows to cable. If things went really well, and we managed to get three or four shows running concurrently on television, we would purchase a cable channel of our own. It would be all awesome, all the time.

Brody knew how to use Microsoft Excel, and she taught me the basics of creating sums and formulas. Somewhere I had heard that Internet companies were valued at a 20x multiple of revenues. You didn't have to worry about expenses, as long as you didn't run out of cash, was my understanding. You tallied your gross receipts for the year, multiplied the total by twenty, and that was your company's value. This was slightly different from the Spender explanation of value creation, in which value was calculated as a pure function of the amount of cash invested in the company. But like the process Spender described—whereby, I eventually realized, a company theoretically could become worth a billion dollars without doing anything but take investment, which seemed like it just couldn't possibly be right—this multiple of revenues thing seemed weird. It didn't take expenses into account, and therefore it didn't take profit or loss into account. What if you made ten dollars but spent twenty? Was your company then still worth two hundred dollars? Surely, I was missing something.

Seeking to clarify this point, I consulted an old acquaintance who now worked at an investment bank in New York. He told me I had it wrong. Revenue multiples had been the thing for a while, but now they were out. Why? Because not every great company had revenues that matched its true value. With everything in the capital markets moving so fast, now companies were being valued on a multiple of expenditures, which was called their "burn rate." I got lost for a week trying to figure out how to make a graph in which losing money faster and faster looked like a good idea. But no matter how much I fiddled with the spreadsheet, I couldn't make it happen, so I just went with the multiple of revenues concept I had started with. My New Media Empire swelled at my command, acquiring computers and camera equipment, annexing offices and stage facilities, employing cadres of young creative and tech types, and closing production and licensing deals at a breakneck pace.

Amazingly, stage one, to be accomplished with a $1 million investment, would take us all the way to a $100 million valuation in a single year. Under the 20× rule, this would be achieved by hitting $5 million in annual revenues, and we could definitely accomplish that if we had $1 million with which to work. As far as I could tell, we wouldn't need a second round at all. We could just keep growing on all the money we were making.

For the purposes of this first modest plan, a $100 million valuation was set as the end goal. The next phase, going public and reaching a $1 billion valuation, would require its own detailed plan. The infusion of cash from the IPO (if we elected to go that route, which would mean relinquishing some control of the company), would allow us to buy the cable or satellite channel. After that, I didn't know. What did people do all day when they ran billion-dollar companies? I had no idea. We'd figure it out when we got there.

In retrospect it is easy to argue that what we should have been doing was just making stuff, our own stuff, instead of doing a Pied Piper routine with all the media-making weirdos we could pull together with bizarro festivals and a dumb Web site. The normal thing to do would have been for Jason and me to partner as a writing team, get an agent, crank out some spec scripts for sitcoms, and get a job on an existing show.

But that was the whole point here. We were so much better than that. We wanted to make stuff that wasn't like what was on television. Never mind that I had no idea how television was made or even, to be perfectly honest, any idea what was on television. First of all, neither one of us had cable, but I couldn't have told you the first thing about the network schedule, either. All I knew was that every time I saw a television turned on, whatever was coming out the front of it made me feel like my eyes were going to explode.

There were opportunities to go in still other directions, aside from partnering as a comedy writing team. *The Sound of One Hand Clapping* had not resulted in any series or feature offers, but I was offered the opportunity to sign as a commercial director with a new division of a fancy production company. At the time I didn't understand how much money commercial directors made—ten to twenty thousand dollars a day, sometimes even more, for doing something that was pretty much fun. But even if I had understood, it wouldn't have mattered. I was too excited about *our* company, as it was coming together in my fevered imagination during the month of the Business Plan, to seriously consider working for anyone else. We were going to be unstoppable. We were going to build a huge network of incredibly fucked-up shit. We were going to become gabillionaires—without having to sell out.

My partners received the plan, thirty pages of clean business prose with an orderly set of financials at the back and a call for one million dollars in equity financing, with remarkable equanimity. Jason had raised a million dollars before. That was how much *Orgazmo* had cost. However broke he was at present, his boundless optimism—the tragic flaw or heroic core that had sustained him through failure and success and then through seeing his former partners borne up without him into the cool green hills of Pacific Palisades and Bel Air— overrode his doubts. For Brody it was even simpler. She thought I was smart, and here at last was her exit pass from making excuses to the bank on behalf of our company and organizing quasi-pornographic parties, both of which she rea- sonably hated. Jolon and Martha were slightly more skepti- cal. But on the other hand, they had actually seen it happen before, when Jolon worked at Strategic Interactive Group.

I had some conditions, though. I very specifically wanted a new, separate LLC called CRAPtv to be formed to operate alongside CRAP, and I wanted to be CEO of the new com- pany. Chief executive officer was a title we theretofore had not allocated to anyone. If we wanted investors to take us seriously, we had to have a CEO, and since I was the one who had authored the New Media Empire Business Plan and was the one most accustomed to dealing with corporate types—in an excess of modesty, I left out that I also considered myself the in-house "talent"—that CEO should be me.

All I really wanted from the discussion was parity with Jason going forward. He had the largest equity stake in CRAP, and as a counterpoint I wanted our stakes reversed in this new company. But instead of simply talking it over with him, I had elected to bring it up publicly as a condition of my continuing to deliver up the fruits of my genius. Brody, Jolon, and Martha heard everything I said and naturally re- alized it applied to them as well. Up until then there had been little discord around the idea that there were different levels of ownership—but if we were starting a whole new company based on a renewed commitment, then was it fair that any one piggy should be more equal than any other piggy? We should all have equal stakes and equal voices in both companies.

The situation became even more complicated when Jolon and Martha chose the occasion to reveal that they had decided to start *their* own company, Kung Fu Design, with still *other* partners, so that they could take on cash clients and service them in an orderly fashion. Jolon and Martha wanted their equity in CRAPtv to go to Kung Fu. If we all had equal stakes, then that would mean Jolon and Martha as one entity would have the single greatest stake in the new company— 40 percent of it. I thought Jason might reach over and stick a pen in my eye.

The meeting lasted three hours and ended with acrimony on all sides. A few days later Tony came down from San Francisco, and with his generous and reasonable refereeing we managed to work out an equitable structure for both companies. I was chief executive officer of both companies, Jason was president of both, and, with the new enthusiasm for titles I had introduced, Brody became chief operating officer of both, and Jolon became chief information officer of both. Martha by this time had decided it was all a bunch of bullshit and said she preferred to concentrate on Kung Fu Design.

So the New Media Empire was off to a great start. But what now? Spender, it turned out, didn't actually have the million dollars at his fingertips. Not that he had said he had it at his fingertips; we had just assumed that was the case. I had thought that all we had to do was have the Business Plan, and then somebody would give us a million dollars. We were getting sort of down in the mouth when the million dollars had not materialized in our bank account by midsummer.

But we did have a bright little moment around then. Jolon finished uploading the new site to CRAPtv.com at about three in the morning one night in early July. Among the odds and ends that made up our video offering was the pilot we had made a year earlier, *The Business,* broken into three bite-sized chunks of fun. When we woke the next day, there was a message on our answering machine from people at a company called WireBreak.

We had heard about WireBreak a few months earlier, from a guy named Michael Oliveri. Oliveri was a couple of years out of the UCLA graduate art program, where he had done some sweet shit like make a pneumatic chicken cannon that shot frozen Butterballs with enough force to blast through car windshields. His latest gig was as the lead Web designer for WireBreak. This was a bit of a hustle, because he'd just started making Web pages a few weeks before, but he had been hired at a high enough level that he was more like art directing the site than writing code for it. He said nobody over there was the wiser—they didn't seem to have much of a clue about anything. But they had venture capital to start a TV network on the Web, and wasn't that what we were doing? Yes, we admitted grumpily, immediately resentful of anyone who already had the million dollars. Oliveri said he'd mentioned us to them, and they were interested in talking to us. We should give them a call. Far from seeing this as an opportunity, we had groused and forgotten about WireBreak until we got the call the morning after our new site went live.

We called back to see what they wanted. They had seen our magazine show, *The Business,* on our site, and they wanted to know if we were interested in making a movie review show for theirs. For some reason that is now impossible for me to reconstruct—that we hoped to sell the show to cable does not seem substantive enough—I was outraged that they would think we might consider making the show for them. I suppose I thought of them as our competition; but someone was trying to give us money to make a show, and instead of being grateful, I was pissed off. We turned them down right there on the phone, without even walking down the street to talk about what a deal might look like. They must have thought we were out of our minds. Maybe it was just the rush of getting such an immediate response; I suppose I figured that if the first offer came before we even got out of bed, then the rest of the day might turn up something even better.

And things did pick up quickly, though in deciding that I should be the CEO of CRAPtv, I had failed to consider that securing financing was the primary function of a start-up's CEO. I had written the Business Plan, and I now could clearly envision myself as the potentate atop a New Media Empire, but the transitional phase wasn't coming together on its own. We decided that in addition to ourselves, we needed a fundraising kind of person, someone to connect us with the million dollars.

This being the summer of 1999 in Los Angeles, people claiming to be able to connect us with a million dollars were in no short supply. Every sketchy movie, television, or music producer in town was leaving his old business and looking for deals in Content. Content was hot. We had open-ended conversations with a few different people, but the one who talked the best game by far was a movie producer named Paul Rosenberg.

Rosenberg and Jason already had done one project together, a script called *Twelve Steps to Getting Laid*. The script in theory was highly salable, in that it set up the classic romantic comedy conflict (two people clearly meant for each other are kept apart by some small thing, in this case, both having sworn off sex), and did so in an amusing way that actually worked in the context of contemporary mores. The only problem was that the writer wouldn't make the one change they thought she ought to make. It was her own personal story, so on an artistic-integrity level they understood her reluctance to make the change, but the change was pretty crucial in terms of making the story palatable to studios. The writer wasn't the recovering sex addict; one of her parents was a recovering sex addict, and *Twelve Steps to Getting Laid* was told from the perspective of an eight-year-old girl. So that project wasn't going anywhere, but it brought Rosenberg into all our lives.

His sturdy bullet head in its cap of close dark curls was reminiscent of a Roman bust, handsome but entering the years of senatorial jowliness. He had bright blue eagle eyes and a pursed-up red little mouth. In modestly lifted shoes he stood around five foot five, but he was compactly solid rather than small, and besides, he was rarely to be seen standing. Once we were in business with him, we usually met at his house in Santa Monica, where he lay trapped like a hyperactive baby in a poofy brown sofa, too fidgety and distracted to get unstuck. In his youth he had been an athlete, a top competitor on the U.S. Freestyle Ski Team, but his knees and back were ruined, and all the fearsome energy that had made him an Olympic hopeful now emanated from his mouth in an unceasing stream that ranged from mild cajolery to screaming threat and back, surging like floodwater around anything in its path, eroding any hope of resistance.

On the glass coffee table in his living-room home office were arrayed his cell phone, his multiline phone, and two laptops, a PC for day-trading and a PowerBook for his entertainment business, all surrounded by a tangle of wires. These connected to the desktop computer, phone, fax, and printer on and around the nearby glass-topped desk and served as an outer security perimeter to his playpen. Among the phones and computers were piles of screenplays marked with notes in his illegible scribble, burger wrappers, Diet Cokes, a handful of prescription canisters, and his ancient cat, Milo, who had weird furry thumbs and would fetch wadded paper when he was in a good mood. Opposite the couch and coffee table was a huge television tuned permanently to MSNBC, and at Rosenberg's desk sat his assistant, Heinrich, a befuddled German who had been bamboozled into answering Rosenberg's phones in exchange for the privilege of doing so.

Rosenberg was a talker—which is not to say that he was not a doer, but all his doing was done through talk. He was a producer, and talk is what they do. His voice, his instrument, had a distinctive timbre similar to Joe Pesci's, a puppety tenor high in the throat that returned to trademark phrases again and again. "I'm just talking!" was one of his favorites, to which you always wanted to reply, "I know, fucking quit for a minute!" Rosenberg had a sense of humor and knew how to use it, such that he was always sort of doing a Rosenberg character, this harmless funny-guy routine that had people back on their heels when the knives came out. Over time I developed a pretty good Rosenberg impression, good enough that I could crank-call Jason and make plausible demands for cocaine, hookers, and hamburgers.

He was smart. And I really did and still do like Rosenberg, even though he drove me insane at times. He was the closest thing I had to a mentor in the entertainment business. After his knees gave out, he went to Berkeley and graduated summa cum laude in business and computer science, and after that he went to work at Goldman Sachs in the San Francisco bond division. But recalling the good times he had as a stunt double in *Hot Dog . . . The Movie* back when he was a freestyle sensation, Rosenberg left bond trading for the Peter Stark Producing Program at USC.

There he excelled and won the plum of plums upon finishing, the job of being an assistant to legendary movie monster Scott Rudin. Rudin was scary but did not actually cut off Rosenberg's head and eat it, and after that Rosenberg went to work for Ray Stark, the famous old producer who made *It's a Wonderful Life* and more than a hundred other movies. By then a journeyman executive, Rosenberg went to work at Imagine Entertainment under Brian Grazer, and he was elevated to the rank of vice president around the time of *The Addams Family* and *The Nutty Professor*. By this time Rosenberg was in his thirties and a rising star. Harvey Weinstein recruited him to go to New York and work with Bob Weinstein on the new genre film company they were starting out of Miramax, Dimension Films. After his contract term at Dimension ended, Rosenberg was ready to go out on his own. He formed his own company, Saratoga Entertainment, and put together a truly excellent movie, *Go*.

Go had the misfortune to open right after *The Matrix* in the spring of 1999, and not as many people saw the movie as might have. The critics loved it, and it was going to do well on video. Rosenberg went to Cannes to accept an award in May, but that summer he was vaguely depressed. He was almost forty. All his friends from Goldman Sachs were now millionaires several times over. He had worked hard. Where was his pie?

At the time he became chairman of CRAPtv, in the summer of 1999, he was sticking his fingers in every pie he could reach. Rosenberg was a momentum player, and the more projects he could become involved in, the more additional projects he could pull into reach through those. At the beginning, despite the sizable stake he demanded, CRAPtv was surely his longest shot. Over the next few weeks, we came to realize that he had stakes in at least four or five other start-ups, and he was continuing to seek out new ones that needed a finger stuck in them. But eventually we were won over by the logic of momentum, as he explained it. In Hollywood (and, apparently, in Internet finance) the appearance of momentum was the same thing as actual momentum. So the more projects Rosenberg had on his slate, the better off *we* would be. What we should do instead of asking him what he was doing to find our million dollars was send him more undervalued projects—ideas, companies, scripts, talent, anything— and let him figure out what to do with them. Something in this tangle of logic made sense to us, or at least we got tired of thrashing around in it, so we did start bringing new projects and prospective partners to Rosenberg, and for better or worse, they, too, quickly found themselves caught in the snares and trip wires around his poofy brown sofa.

One of the first projects we funneled to Rosenberg was the Superdudes. Jason met them at a rooftop party in Chinatown one night that summer, from which he returned with what I thought must surely be a Jason-garbled version of the whole Super thing, though it turned out Jason had imagined the only parts of the Super thing that made any sense. To be perfectly accurate, when the Superdudes first came to us they were not so much an actual project as four guys who thought they were Super and thought they should be on television.

A stab at describing them would be to say they were like homosocial frat guys who had tried ecstasy and discovered hugging but hadn't yet learned the timing of it or abandoned the weight room and cologne. There was something horrible about their constant, musky insistence on squeezing you to their hypertrophied breasts. One of them, a redheaded Kiwi who was the Outback Steakhouse pitchman for a while, turned out to be a really sweet guy. But the main Superdude, an ex–college football player who looked like the Norse god Thor, loved himself with a totality that made you uncomfortable, like watching teenagers make out in public.

They had made up Super names and personas for themselves, like Atomic, Jungle Boy, Techno, and, like, whatever. The foundation of their Super thing was that everyone is actually Super and has a Super self that can be released by smoking weed or just dealing with the Superness. They had made little Photoshop collages of themselves being Super, which they had turned into laminated badges they wore on lanyards around their necks —these were full-grown adults, mind you—and they were hoping to start a Super movement in which people all over the world would make cards of their Super Selves and trade them. Grown-up Pokémon was the closest analogy I could draw.

When they came in to meet with us, they went on endlessly about the origin of the Super species, the cosmic plasma, intergalactic colors, electricity, and so on. The main thing they wanted, though, was to be on TV being Super. Since Jason had given me the high points, the two of us had brained out a way you might sort of be able to make a business out of the Super thing or at least make it into something that worked and had some sort of point. When they were done with their babble, we told them it was Super, and then we explained how if you actually wanted to make it possible for people to make custom visual identities for themselves in a systematic way, identities they could show one another and trade around, you would want to do it like this:

You would develop, say, ten different Super Boots and Feet, ten sets of Super Legs, ten sets of Super Panties, ten Super Torsos, ten Super Capes, and ten pairs of Super Hand Appendages. These would be posted to a Web site where users could choose from menus of these elements to fill in a template, sort of like one of those kids' books where you can give the creature frog feet, a lion body, and a chicken head by rearranging split pages like Dutch doors. The combination of just six ten-element menus made for a million possible character configurations. Users could upload pictures of their heads into a blank space in the template where the face went, and they could name their own Super Selves. It would be easy to set up a chat environment for Superdudes, a bulletin board for Superdudes, and a voting function whereby the most popular Superdudes would be on a top-ten list or whatever. We doubted you could get anyone to pay for the privilege of being Super in this way, but at least you'd have all the Super People registered in one place. Then you could market Super merchandise to them or, more likely, sell the registration list and all the rest of the Super bullshit to another company that wanted to add a Super identity feature to its offering—e-mail, cell phones, whatever.

They liked the sound of that! That was way better than homemade trading cards! But if it was going to be in "cyberspace," then all the Superdudes needed to be able to interact in 3D Super Space! And smoke Super Weed together and collect Super Biscuits! And the most Super Superdudes of all would get to be on the awesome Superdudes TV show with them, the original Superdudes!

It all gave me a Super headache. But Jason was right—Rosenberg loved it. He got so into it that we worried for a bit that we were going to lose him to Superness. But we didn't, and right around that time—basically, as soon as he started working with us—he performed an extremely useful function for CRAPtv. We mentioned something about the Wire-Break call from a few weeks back. Rosenberg quizzed us. What, were we crazy? He called them back and made us listen to their proposal about our making a show for their Web site, which turned out to be entirely reasonable.

Our long-suffering attorney negotiated the deal, which took several weeks and was fairly involved for something so seemingly small. But in the end it was an incredible boon for CRAPtv—twenty-six weekly episodes of me and Jason reviewing movies at $5,000 an episode, which added up to $130,000 over six months. Under the terms of the deal, we would provide the stage and rent it to WireBreak for production of the show. What this meant was that CRAPtv would have enough cash moving through it to lease a warehouse that would double as the soundstage for that show and whatever else we might do. And the warehouse would also contain our offices. Offices! The balance would cover phones, insurance, and so on and still pay us each a few hundred dollars a week. For the first time, we were an actual business.

Like an ancient pagan, Jason marked the progress of his life by participation in seasonal orgiastic rituals. Starting in January, these were Sundance (Utah), Valentine's Day (Los Angeles), Mardi Gras (New Orleans), Jazz Festival (New Orleans), Reggae on the River (northern California), Burning Man (Nevada), Halloween (Los Angeles), Thanksgiving (northern California), Christmas (northern California), and New Year's (northern California). He had hardly finished with the last one when preparations for the next began, and each could last as long as ten days, not counting prep and recovery.

I know that Jason first met the Superdudes in Chinatown in late August of 1999, because it was right before Burning Man, and a much more significant meeting occurred at the same party. At that rooftop party Jason met an individual affiliated with the Superdudes—in fact, as it turned out, the individual who originated the idea of Superdudes, though he was no longer interested in Superness.

At that time, this individual was known to Jason only as the Woodsman. I already didn't want to go to Burning Man, where I would be expected to dissemble childish wonder and share things with strangers, but finding out that this Woodsman person would be hitching a ride in Jason's minivan sealed it that I wasn't going. There was no way in hell I was going to sit in a minivan for six hours with someone named the Woodsman.

I suppose I pictured a generically annoying hippie who might bore me on the ride with lectures about sustainable hemp farming. But the stories Jason and Ward told on their return were nothing like that, and the Woodsman's terrible actuality outstripped anything I might have imagined. Timmy the Woodsman was his complete nom de guerre, and he had been naked almost from the instant they arrived in the desert. There was an accident with warning-orange paint that got all over his hands and then in the natural course of events stained his penis, and then his hands and all the rest of him got covered in the dust that was everywhere, so that he became just a filthy imp whose distinguishing feature was a bright orange penis, somewhat outsized for his smallish frame, that bobbed like a carrot before him for the rest of his sojourn in Black Rock City.

"I have the biggest penis in the world!" he yelled at other attendees. If they looked at him funny, he would yell, "In proportion! In proportion to my body, you fuckheads!"

On the ride home after five or six days of that, Jason said they had stopped at McDonald's. It was no surprise that the Woodsman had no money, since he had no pants in which to keep it, but when Jason offered to buy him a burger, the Woodsman declined. The Woodsman's position was that food was free. He didn't pay for food, not even with other people's money. That was just how he rolled. After Jason ordered his own Happy Meal, the Woodsman, now wearing some kind of diaper-tarpaulin configuration to cover his orange penis, went up to the counter.

"I'm the king of a tribe in the desert," he told the people working there. "We don't use money, but we love chicken!" As if under a spell, the workers at McDonald's filled a bag with McNuggets for the Woodsman.

"And fries!" yelled the Woodsman. "We love fries!"

So they gave him some fries.

These stories did not make me dread meeting the Woodsman any less. When Jason promised I would love the Woodsman, when he said I would have to know the Woodsman to understand, I doubted he was right. But he was right. I did, against any better judgment that might have resided in me, come to love Timmy the Woodsman dearly. Before that, though, I had my own journey to take out into the desert, out into the dark.

Four

1

My journey into darkness had really begun seven months earlier, at the 1999 Sundance Film Festival. Lapdance was fun and everything, but the real news out of Sundance that year was *The Blair Witch Project*. The producers mounted a cleverly macabre campaign in Park City, papering telephone poles with photocopied MISSING posters of the cast members. None of us made it to a screening, but when we got home we read that the filmmakers had sold their movie to a distributor for a million dollars—a genuine win for actual independent filmmakers at Sundance.

My vicarious pleasure at the *Blair Witch* filmmakers' moxie and good fortune, a pleasure definitely leavened with jealousy, transformed in the months that followed into bemusement at the credulity of Internet users taken in by the movie's marketing site, a nicely mocked-up collection of fake police evidence concerning events in the movie. Using the same search engine you used to find the marketing site, you could find plenty of information about how the movie had actually been made. Nevertheless, a widespread belief was developing that the events in the movie had actually occurred.

The receptionist at the PlusOne office in San Francisco was positively convinced of it, spending hours a day poring over the site and shivering about witches. As weeks passed and hype built on Internet bulletin boards, bleeding over even onto our own BBS at CRAPtv, my bemusement transformed into indignation. Millions of morons were going to turn *The Blair Witch Project* into a blockbuster such as had never been seen before. Granted, even among the credulous there was debate regarding whether it was or was not "all real," but that there even was debate was driving me crazy. Reading *Blair Witch* discussions was like listening to arguments between Creationists and rational people. It was embarrassing to see the rational people bothering to argue, but just witnessing the discussion made you want to start yelling, too.

By the time the movie opened in July, there was no way I was going to go see it, if only for the crabbed satisfaction of withholding my eight dollars from the architects of this mass idiocy. The lines around the block, the full-page ads announcing the $100 million mark, the fan pilgrimages to Maryland continuing long after the cast, whose characters died in the movie, were pictured alive and well on the cover of *Time*—my response to all this was simply: No. It was not real, you stupid fucks. First of all, it was about a witch. A magical evil witch. Did there even have to be a second-of-all?

I finally caved in and went to see *The Blair Witch Project* on a rainy night nearly a year after it first screened at Sundance. The horror project—really more of a terror project—I conceived in reaction to the *Blair Witch* hype was well under way; I hadn't wanted to be unduly influenced by the film itself. Seeing the movie confirmed what I had suspected, that it wasn't scary—not really, really scary, not the kind of scary that would make me wake from nightmares in panicky recoil.

It wasn't scary to me because I didn't believe in magical evil witches. But aspects of *Blair Witch*, the documentary style in particular, did lend a reality and intimacy that were missing from most Hollywood films and even from most independent films. It was the first-person perspective that got you in the gut, to whatever extent you were got. The people operating the cameras were right there. As a viewer, you identified with the person shooting, witnessing, as much as with anyone on-screen at any given time.

The POV ("point-of-view") shot, in which the audience is privileged to see an action from the eyes of the shooter or, in the case of a fictional narrative, a character, had been in use since motion pictures were invented. At the first public showing of a motion picture, in 1895, the Lumière brothers exhibited footage they had recorded of a train pulling into a station. According to reports of the event, several theatergoers dove for the floor in fear of being run over, and so it might be said that the first film ever exhibited was a horror film that used POV to powerful effect.

Certainly, the POV shot was a mainstay of contemporary horror, practically defining the genre. Think of George Romero's *Night of the Living Dead* from 1968—instantly, you see arms battering at doors and windows, reaching implacably toward you. Two movies released even earlier, *Peeping Tom* and *Psycho*, both in 1960, marked a crucial shift in use of the POV. Before then, you, the viewer, had seen the killer through the victim's eyes. But in *Peeping Tom* and *Psycho*, you became, at moments, the killer. John Carpenter's *Halloween* (1980) took this technique to a whole new level. In Steadicam shots you mounted stairs and crept down halls, stalking Jamie Lee Curtis with your knife, a phallus of dread, wagging in the foreground. Viewers were made complicit in the violence in a way they had not been before. And viewers loved it.

There was another film, *The Last Broadcast*, from which some said the entirety of *Blair Witch* had been cribbed. But *The Last Broadcast* had been so shoddily executed that it failed to convince and thereby failed to work as a horror movie. Like most, I never even heard of *The Last Broadcast* until well after the release of *Blair Witch*. But marginally better production wasn't the main reason *The Blair Witch Project* succeeded and *The Last Broadcast* failed. It was the careful execution of the hoax that lay at the center *of Blair Witch* that made the movie travel so well by word of mouth and over the Internet to create a box office smash.

The two most effective horror hoaxes prior to *The Blair Witch Project* were Orson Welles's 1938 radio play, *The War of the Worlds*, and *Faces of Death*. Welles used the conventions of a live news broadcast to present a fictional story of alien invasion. The broadcast sparked a panic across the eastern seaboard, and afterward the Department of Defense was supposed to have used the mass hysteria that occurred as a template for planning psychological warfare. But *Faces of Death* was, to my mind, a much, much scarier thing. I remembered it being talked about when I was in grade school, and I remembered seeing its box cover at the local video store. I never rented it. It sounded too scary. It was all supposed to have been real. And I learned as an adult that indeed parts of it were real—real animal deaths and file footage of real human deaths. The filmmakers had not themselves perpetrated or recorded any human deaths in the making of *Faces of Death*;

nevertheless, there was something infinitely more horrifying than aliens and witches, to me at least, in the idea that some of the deaths in the movie were real: sad accidents, suicides, and executions. That these were intermingled with animal butchery and goofy gore effects made *Faces of Death* all the more awful.

Snuff. Ineffably onomatopoetic, like *porn.* This was the terminus, where technique and taste were null. Not that *Faces of Death* was really snuff, even with its inclusion of actual deaths. Real snuff was not supposed to exist, or it was supposed to but was traded only among a cabal of sick enthusiasts. Death on film or videotape—certainly that existed, but in the form of accidents, suicides, war, executions, political murder. A real snuff film would require the apolitical murder of someone for the explicit purpose of recording the murder. What could be more abhorrent?

But clearly America felt quite differently. For what was *The Blair Witch Project* but a fake snuff movie? The events in the movie were revealed not to be real, but the marketing and success of the movie depended on the proposition that they were real. Technically, it was a piece of shit: flimsy story, terrible camera work, terrible sound. The only differences between *Blair Witch* and a well-executed snuff hoax were the magical crap and the movie's narrative position: The shooters were being snuffed out, not doing the snuffing.

Its incredible success vindicated my belief that cryptosnuff, snuff pretending not to be snuff, was one of the dominant modes of American entertainment. How better to describe blockbusters in which dozens, hundreds, thousands, millions, even billions of people are extinguished? (These events occurred before *The Passion of the Christ* was released, but the incredible success of that horror show is a concrete illustration of one of my fundamental premises, that America is both a deeply religious nation and one obsessed with snuff, and that those national obsessions are pretty much the same thing—the central Christian myth is the apotheosis of Christ through torture and murder.)

Network drama was a subset of mainstream crypto-snuff, and this was back before it started getting really hot, with series like *Law and Order: SVU* or the *CSI* franchise, in which nearly every episode opens with a gorgeous, partially naked woman strangled, poisoned, burned, shot, mutilated, or beaten to death—though sometimes they throw in a child or a handsome young man. It's network, so there has to be something for everyone. So long as the violence is imbedded in a narrative of exogenous threat or investigation and retribution, no horror is off-limits: bludgeoned grandmas, sodomized kindergartners, tits cut off and worn like hats.

Crypto-pornography was the other dominant mode of American entertainment, romance and unfunny sexual comedy being its main expressions, and those encompassed almost everything that was not crypto-snuff. Given access through the Internet, Americans had turned regular pornography into a massive business almost overnight; by halving credible estimates, you could arrive at five billion dollars in annual revenues for distributors of regular pornography. That made it the same-size business as professional sports or Hollywood movies in theatrical release.

We will get to TV news in a moment, but the point here is that the first straight, unapologetic snuff movie to be widely released—notwithstanding the inversion of its narrative position, such that the viewer identified with the victim, not the perpetrator—was, to pun badly, killing. It was killing not because it was better than regular crypto-snuff—just as the reason regular pornography was making billions wasn't that it was "better" than crypto-pornography—but because, like regular pornography, *The Blair Witch Project* claimed authenticity. It was more *real*. *The Blair Witch Project* cost $60,000 to produce and earned close to $250 million in theatrical release, making it, on an investment-to-earnings basis, the most successful entertainment commodity in the history of the world.

In order to top the success of *Blair Witch,* two things seemed in order. The first would be to eliminate any supernatural crap, like witches, and the second would be to reverse the perspective and put the camera in the killer's hands. And one more: This was 1999, and millennial anxiety was at fever pitch. I had no personal concern that Armageddon was imminent, but according to a 1999 *Newsweek* poll, a full 45 percent of Americans (135 million people!) believed that a biblically accurate Armageddon would occur within their lifetimes.

The thing about biblical prophecy was that it scared the shit out of people like them, who believed in it, and it also scared the shit out of people like me, who saw statistics like that in magazines. For who was more capable of terrible things than the person who believed the end of the world was at hand? Only one person: the person who believed he had a role to play in its end. It was not a distant step from the insanity of belief in a literal Armageddon to the insanity of believing one had a part to play in it. There were plenty of examples in the news of otherwise apparently "normal" citizens trying to accelerate the Rapture. My favorite was a farmer in Texas, who was breeding red cows and shipping them to Israel because a verse in the Revelation said there would be red cows in the area when Christ returned to judge.

That was just a nice dairyman. Charles Manson was the scary real-world prototype in this realm of deluded dooms-day agency, and there were plenty more who came after him. When I was a kid in the seventies, the Zodiac killer stalked San Francisco. In the eighties, Richard Ramirez, the Night Stalker, terrorized Southern California with his satanic rape-and-murder spree. Those were just the headliners; there were plenty of smaller acts.

In the past decade, satanic or apocalyptically themed murders had been even more to the front of the national imagination. In June 1993, in West Memphis, Arkansas, three little boys were sexually mutilated and murdered in the woods. Three local teenagers suspected of being satanists because they read about Wicca and wore black trench coats were immediately arrested, although not a shred of real evidence linked them to the crime. An HBO documentary called *Paradise Lost: The Child Murders at Robin Hood Hills*, released in 1996, demonstrated not only that the arrested teens were probably innocent of the crime but also that the murders had almost definitely been committed by the stepfather of one of the little murdered boys, an incredibly creepy man who was a lay leader of a local evangelical congregation. Nevertheless, the teens were convicted of the murders, and, as of this writing, one of them, Damien Echols, is on death row awaiting lethal injection.[2]

---

2. In 2000 the filmmakers released a sequel called *Paradise Lost: Revelations*, which presented evidence against the stepfather

It seemed America would believe teenagers to be capable of anything, if they read the wrong things and wore black trench coats. And as it turned out, on that score America was right. On April 20, 1999, two kids in Littleton, Colorado, came to school armed with assault weapons and opened fire on their peers, killing twelve other students, a teacher, and themselves. Though the Columbine Massacre, as the news media ecstatically named the event in their broadcast graphics, had no specific ties to the end of the millennium, somehow it was wrapped into the atmosphere of thrilled fin de siècle terror our national media were doing their very best to foster.[3]

Inverting the narrative persective, such that the action would be seen from the killer's eyes, was especially important to me not just because it was effective in generating fear but because of the complicity it would force in anyone who watched it. I didn't just want to scare people, make lots of money, and have articles written about me. I wanted to be able to say in those articles, Fuck you. Fuck you, you sick,

---

so compelling as to be grimly hilarious; for instance, when during the appeals process the defense considered introducing bite-mark evidence, the stepfather had all his teeth removed and thrown away. A card placed in the film informed you that the stepfather even confessed to the crime on tape, but HBO didn't allow the confession to be included in the film for liability reasons, and the court ruled the confession inadmissible because the stepfather was drunk when he made it. If you want to join Eddie Vedder in the fight for justice: www.wm3.org.

3. Sorry about all the footnotes all of a sudden. But for a better examination of Littleton, gun violence, and the media, see Michael Moore's *Bowling for Columbine*. I know he's kind of a douche, but admit it, his movies are pretty sweet, and that one features a cameo by your good buddy Matt Stone.

disgusting fucks, for participating in that. Fuck you, America, because this is what you love: violence, fear, degradation, torture, and murder. And this time they aren't dressed up in the sanctimonious clown clothes of network news, this time they aren't sublimated into a narrative of retribution that lets you enjoy the violence without admitting it was all you came for, and this time they can't be fetishized into a make-believe afterlife. You love everything you so strenuously pretend to abhor. You just paid to watch a snuff movie.

2

My concept was to make a feature-length home movie that purported to be the work of someone who believed he was the Antichrist. The fictional author of the film would have come to that belief by recognizing similarities between himself and the Antichrist in the Revelation, and between events prophesied in those verses and events that were now occurring, and he would slaughter an innocent to announce his arrival. The movie would be titled *Human Number,* the last two words of chapter 13 of the Revelation (New Revised Edition), which was the richest repository in the book of familiar phrase and imagery.

This obviously was not new material in either fact or fiction. Francis Dolarhyde, the killer in Thomas Harris's novel *Red Dragon,* which was adapted into two movies, *Manhunter* (1986) and *Red Dragon* (2002), was in part based on the real serial killer Ed Gein. Dolarhyde also believed himself to be one of the beasts introduced in chapter 12 of the Revelation, a great red dragon who, likewise having lots of head and horns and crowns, was similar to the beasts in chapter 13 with whom my Antichrist would identify. This project being just a shitty horror hoax, I tried to set aside worries about influence, and I did feel I had an original premise. So far as I knew, this would be the first feature film shot, edited, and broadcast by its antagonist.

My Antichrist would be a creature of the New Millennium. The Internet and current media technology in general were ideal, both as production and communications tools and as corollaries to markers in the text of the Revelation. In the tradition of great prophecy, the Revelation could be interpreted to mean pretty much whatever you wanted. And in the tradition of truly great prophecy, it could be interpreted, with a sufficiently elastic sense of metaphor, to describe events that were happening right now and thus provide its own solipsistic proof.

He had been a missile targeter in Desert Storm. That would give him technological fluency, a believable background for some off-kilter hacker, which for other purposes of the project the Antichrist would have to be. And it would make him about thirty, my age, right in the middle of the curve for adult-onset schizophrenia. I clearly recalled the video-game images of that first Iraq war (we hadn't started the second yet): the skyline lighting up in green-tinged night-vision blossoms, buildings placed in crosshairs and vaporized. It almost seemed as though no violence were occurring at all—until afterward, when you thought about it. The sensory and cognitive disconnect enabled by such remote-control slaughter could easily, if the truth of what had been done ever snapped into place, cause a person who had been a part of it to ask big questions. The Bible was understood to be a repository of answers to big questions. As I have outlined, it was only a small step from being a Christian literalist to believing one had a part to play in Armageddon; and it was just one more nudge from reading about the way it would happen to looking down at the page and saying: "Wait a minute—that's *me!*"

I sketched out an outline for a film ninety minutes or so in length, just long and barely cogent enough for theatrical release, to be shot on Mini DV and edited on consumer equipment. In order to give it the familiar narrative structure necessary for mainstream snuff, I broke it into three acts.

The first act would be composed of a Spalding Gray kind of monologue by the masked, voice-disguised Antichrist, in which he would announce his ascendance and provide evidence, in the exegetical manner of a deranged cable evangelist, that he and his time had arrived. The monologue would be interspersed with a *Koyaanisqatsi* pastiche: crowds, machines, suburban sprawl, traffic, war footage, airports, homeless encampments, communications equipment, mushroom clouds, NASA space video, riots, executions, retail environments, pornography, etc., all of which was footage that could be collected driving around Los Angeles, licensed inexpensively, or collected from the Internet. A webcam sex site that allowed the viewer to direct and record the actions of a solitary performer would provide the perfect environment for victim selection. A girl on one of those sites, our protagonist, would be gradually drawn during the video collage toward meeting the Antichrist face-to-face.

In the second act of *Human Number,* the victim would be present in the broadcast environment—the familiar stuff of every stalker movie, the part where the hunted befriends the hunter without realizing who he is. In this act we wouldn't see much of the Antichrist, because he would operate the camera. I didn't have the second act clearly mapped, but essentially it would be made up of a series of spliced-up conversations with the unknowing victim, conversations indicating a gradual submission to the interviewer. The Antichrist's broadcast facility would be a sealed, windowless room, a basement that was his dungeon workshop and art studio. Artwork in progress and on the walls, for which I did have a plan, would provide a rich production environment and conversation subjects leading toward the victim allowing herself to be restrained.

Act three was when it would get bad, when he would put on the mask from the first act and show her the webcam footage that the audience had already seen, mixed with some of the other weird shit, all projected on the wall, with her restrained and watching it *Clockwork Orange*–style. Once she was seriously terrified, the Antichrist would start making her recite chapter 13 of the Revelation while he prompted her with a cattle prod. After she finally got it right, the Antichrist would excise her tongue with a scalpel, and then, as she bled out the hole in her face, he would string her up in a crucifixion pose and slit her throat while the projector splashed apocalyptic slides and video over the messy tableau.

In short, a nasty little snuff movie that could be mistaken for the work of a single anonymous madman with a basement and a few thousand dollars' worth of untraceable consumer electronics equipment. It hit me for the first time, as I completed my outline, that a single anonymous madman really could make a nasty little snuff movie like this. Exactly like this. That was the idea. But actually plotting the whole thing out, figuring out how I would commit and record a murder and announce my arrival if indeed I were someone who thought he was the Antichrist, made me feel a little funny.

There was no way in the world not to know that blame for real violence was being assigned to violence in entertainment. Ritual flagellation of violent popular entertainment was a favorite activity of the violent popular news media that was just another mouth of the same seven-headed beast. Most of the criticism was vague enough not to threaten the revenue streams of the companies that made and distributed both the entertainment and the news: "Is violence in entertainment bad? Find out at eleven, after exclusive tape of a convenience-store robbery gone wrong!"

The nonprofit research and policy organization Media-scope, using articles in national journals for source material, compiled a list of thirty-two instances of verifiable copycat violence—violence in which a specific entertainment product was cited by the perpetrator(s) or someone close to the investigation—that occurred between 1992 and 1999. (Mediascope was financed from within the entertainment industry, with the purported mission of encouraging responsible portrayals of sex, drugs, and violence in the media. It closed its doors for lack of funding in 2004, and all the data generated in its twelve years of operation were taken off-line in 2005.)

Many of the crimes on the Mediascope list were especially horrible: multiple murders, child murders, child suicides. And some of the blame was pointed pretty close to home. Two child suicides had been blamed on *South Park*—though if you looked closely, the tragic story of eleven-year-old Bryce Kilduff was quite strange. Kilduff had hanged himself in supposed imitation of the character Kenny from *South Park,* who died a weekly animated death on television. What was weird was that Bryce Kilduff wasn't allowed to watch *South Park.* He based his ideas of what happened in the show on descriptions provided by his schoolmates. Should everyone, then, have been forbidden to watch it, so that poor Bryce Kilduff would never have had the opportunity even to hear of the show? Or, conversely, would watching *South Park* have saved Bryce Kilduff's life? These were weird questions I didn't see taken up anywhere, but they certainly opened the door on how difficult it would be to assign blame for violence to any individual piece of entertainment or even to violence in entertainment in general.

At the time I am writing about, Oliver Stone was defending himself against appeal of a wrongful-death lawsuit in which the plaintiffs alleged that *Natural Born Killers,* which was released in 1994, had inspired the murder of a man named William Savage and the disabling of a woman, Patsy Ann Byers, in 1995. The shooters, Sarah Edmondson and Ben Darras, spent the night of March 5 high on acid in a cabin, watching *Natural Born Killers* over and over again. The shootings occurred on March 7 and were similar in many particulars to killings in the movie. The nature of the complaint, specifically, was that "*Natural Born Killers* [fell] within the incitement exception to the First Amendment protection of free speech." The exception states that when speech "advocates the use of imminent force or unlawful action, and is likely to produce such conduct, the state may indeed forbid such speech." Here are more grim details about actions attributed to the film: In 1994 a fourteen-year-old boy in Texas was accused of decapitating a thirteen-year-old girl and told police that he "wanted to be famous like the natural born killers." In 1995, in Georgia, four people in their twenties watched *Natural Born Killers* nineteen times and were accused of killing a truck driver soon afterward. In 1995 in Massachusetts, a killing made big news when one of the accused reportedly boasted to his girlfriend that he and his codefendants were "natural born killers."

Oliver Stone and his codefendant, Time Warner, had been held blameless in the Savage murder and Byers maiming, and it looked like that decision would be upheld against appeal. In the wake of the decision, a group of senators and policy groups released a "public admonition" of Time Warner. Boy, that must have stung—I'll bet Time Warner cried all the way home. But notwithstanding that a public admonition was at best buffoonish grandstanding on the part of the senators and an opportunity to vent for the policy prudes, it was the strongest action that should have been taken. *Natural Born Killers* did not come close to meeting the criteria for the incitement exception.

On top of that, it was easy to forget, in all the hysteria, what *Natural Born Killers* had been *about*—media amplification of violence. The news media in the film glom onto nihilistic losers on a killing spree, glorifying their crimes and turning them into celebrities. While an argument could be made that Tarantino, Stone, et al., were jacking themselves off with blood for lube under the aegis of delivering a social critique, the movie was a pretty straightforward indictment of the very thing of which it was now being accused. If *Natural Born Killers* was too refined a take on what was right and wrong in America, then we had bigger problems.

And indeed we did.

In a late journal entry Eric Harris, one of the Littleton killers, inveighed against the temptation to blame anyone but him and vodka for what he planned to do.[4] Harris and his partner, Dylan Klebold, wanted credit for their crime. They wanted to be talked about. They wanted fame, legend, and a postmortem following; the apportioning of influence would mitigate the significance of their actions. Nevertheless, in the wake of the Littleton killings, parents and pundits leapt to point at the usual suspects: music, video games, television, and movies, the products of a decadent culture. And you did have to wonder—not whether specific cultural artifacts were to blame for the actions taken by Harris and Klebold, because even if they had survived the event, that could never really be known, but whether the news media's relentless coverage of violence did not lead to more violence. Especially among kids.

Because Harris and Klebold did get what they wanted, didn't they? They were talked about. And talked about, and talked about, and talked about. And despite their desire to be known, after their crimes, for having acted without the influence of their peers, they made that point a bit too strenuously. "Harris' writings contained statements like, 'When you [the media] write about this . . . When you read about this . . . We were planning this before the kids in Jonesboro, and we're going to die in there.'"[5] Harris was referring to two children in Jonesboro, Arkansas, ages eleven and thirteen, who had shot and killed four young girls and a teacher in 1998.

---

4. Dave Cullen's thoughtful article in *Salon* (http://www. salon.com/news/feature/1999/09/23/journal/index1.html) looks into possible causes for the killings and was a key source for this whole section.

5. *Ibid.*

School killings of the nineties: In 1997, in Paducah, Kentucky, a high school boy fired seven shots into his peers, killing three and wounding five. A sixteen-year-old in Pearl, Mississippi, killed his mother and then went to school and shot nine students, two of whom died. And in Bethel, Alaska, another sixteen-year-old shot and killed his principal and another student. In 1996 in Moses Lake, Washington, a fourteen-year-old turned an assault rifle on his algebra class, killing two classmates and a teacher. Surely each of the children involved had heard about those who went before them, either directly from the television or from conversations about what had been on the television.

But what was the news media supposed to do? Not report school slayings? Well, maybe not with such pounding repetition and thinly masked delight. It looked to me like the only reason they wore those tan journalist raincoats on location spots was to hide the hard nipples. But there was no getting around it: Kids killing kids was news.

And before I spun myself completely out of control, I reminded myself that I wasn't advocating killing, and I certainly wasn't actually going to kill anybody. I was making a horror movie. That was all I was doing, and I knew exactly where I stood on speech issues. I would say exactly whatever I wanted, and I would welcome any attempt to silence me, because any attempt to stifle speech was, not to put too fine a point on it, total fucking bullshit. Pornography and violence now, because they were easy targets, and political speech later. That was how it went.

I reminded myself that the right to free expression was already under a more effective assault than could ever be accomplished by pure legislation. The real threat to speech was the lock of an oligopoly on supposedly public radio and television broadcast frequencies and the fictive diversity of cable and satellite systems. I worked myself up on this subject to the extent that I was positively obliged to make *Human Number*, just for the opportunity of defending it—not as something of artistic merit, necessarily, though accolades to my artistic genius would certainly appear in all the magazines if *Human Number* made enough money, but simply as the expression of a threatened right. Making it would be irresponsible? On the contrary, *not* making it would be irresponsible. Was I afraid of standing up for something I believed?

No. I had the courage of my convictions.

3

I planned to perform the killing at midnight on New Year's Eve, at the first tick of the New Millennium (PST), and I planned to broadcast it live. Not actually live, because the messy and elaborate killing I planned could not convincingly be faked live. It was so messy and elaborate precisely for that reason.

A basic characteristic of broadcast media is that the viewer can't tell whether it's live or recorded. Nevertheless, simply informing an audience that something is live is usually sufficient to convince them that it is. For instance, when the LIVE bug is placed in the corner of our television screens, we generally believe the video behind it is live. Why shouldn't we? Experience has trained us to believe that the LIVE bug means what it purports to mean. From the living room sofa it seems almost like part of the hardware: an objective ratification that what we are seeing is real and happening right now. If we stop to think about it, we immediately realize that the bug has no connection with temporal reality other than the connection we assign it, but that's precisely the point. We don't stop to think about it, because in order to move through the world without being paralyzed by skepticism, we have to accept most signs at face value. We don't stand outside a closed door that features an equilateral triangle and the stylized image of a man, and wonder if behind that door there really is a men's room. We simply enter.

The final "live" section of *Human Number* would require very careful effects work and postproduction, because I intended this final section to run without any visible cuts. The excision of the victim's tongue and the slitting of her throat would require separate blood prostheses, and the victim would have to be moved across the room between the two actions so it could be seen that no tubes or prostheses were attached. This would be accomplished by having her freeze at certain points, at which points the handheld camera's position would also be fixed. The necessary parts would be attached or detached, and when everything was in place again, the action would resume. When the edited tape ran, it should look as though the tape had never stopped. It was a simple and primitive technique but a perfectly effective one if executed correctly.

Despite what I hoped to accomplish with the "live" broadcast, I anticipated plenty of skepticism. *Blair Witch* had just happened, and this thing would have every outward appearance of being the derivative hoax it was. Nonetheless, I was confident that at least a few hundred people would interrupt their celebrations of the New Millennium to see a pretty girl slaughtered in real time by the Antichrist or someone who thought he was the Antichrist. It seemed reasonable to anticipate that some of those viewers would record the broadcast in addition to viewing it. Recording streaming media wasn't a perfectly simple process, but it wasn't that hard, either. For the hoax to really work, the media recorded on hard drives would have to hold up to frame-by-frame examination.

One group I knew I could count on to record the broadcast, if I gave them the right amount of lead time, was the news media. None of them would simulcast the killing, but every place I contacted would put an intern on the feed. The intern would get the shit scared out of him, and then producers would be called in to examine the recording. In each newsroom, debate would ensue about whether to report the event on television, since it could so easily be a hoax and news producers would know better than anyone that it could have been recorded earlier, reconstructed, and broadcast from tape.

But as frame-by-frame examinations proceeded concurrently, and provided no actual Armageddon occurred that night, one channel wanting to win the night might go with the story, emphasizing with a great show of journalistic integrity that they didn't know whether it was real. The other channels would then have to report it, too—or, to distance themselves from the possibility that it was a hoax but not miss out on the orgy of somber head-wagging, some of which might now be directed at the first channel, report that the first outlet was reporting it.

Regardless of how the clusterfuck went down, and even if it didn't go down—in the unlikely event that every single cable news channel had the good judgment not to report on the story at all until they found out whether it was a hoax— the Drudge Report or some other online news outlet would put up an item on the broadcast and start the ball rolling.

Back at the newsroom, the intern would dub off a copy and show it to his friends. One of them would copy it or steal it, and at some point soon thereafter it would go up on the Web somewhere else. And then it was game on.

In what I thought was the extremely unlikely event that none of these things happened in any of their many possible forms, I could distribute the file myself to some high-traffic sites that would host it without any regard at all for whether it was real, because that was what they did: Stileproject, Rotten, maybe Disinformation, though the last was moving toward more nuanced material. The site from which the clip originated, meanwhile, would have been taken offline immediately after the broadcast. Taking the original site down would complicate the project of locating the server from which the original broadcast had emanated, which would be the first material step in disproving the broadcast's authenticity.

While the use of the Internet as the broadcast medium for the live-event component of *Human Number* would drastically limit the number of people who might see it, from my point of view that was not a bad thing. I wanted to start a rumor, not a riot. If it could be avoided, I hoped not to have the FBI descend on my apartment. Use of the Internet would also impeach the broadcast's credibility right off the bat, in what I thought was a good way. No matter how good a job I did with it, it would still be going out over the Internet and therefore would be taken with a grain of salt by most viewers.

On the other hand, it was unlikely that some basement Antichrist would have access to broadcast frequencies or a cable channel of his own. In that regard, broadcasting over the Internet would buttress the clip's credibility rather than undermine it. The heavy compression required for Internet broadcast would fuzz the facts more. Both the frame rate and resolution of the video would be significantly lower than the NTSC standard—10 frames per second as opposed to 29.9, and whatever resolution I wanted as opposed to 740×580. The ceiling on quality that compression imposed, usually the main liability of Internet broadcasting, would be an asset. The broadcast could be real. Or it could be faked. There would simply be no way to tell.

By now our attorneys were a bit leery of our shenanigans. Five percent was great if you were negotiating a movie star's compensation, but five percent of yet another sketchy LLC proposed by Jason or Glasgow—we had just formed CRAPtv to operate alongside CRAP—was a dubious proposition at best. Our own attorney, who wasn't yet a partner in the firm himself, was buried under deals from the partners' desks. He said to talk to one of them.

Barney was the most openly entrepreneurial of the partners, working with start-ups and helping regular entertainment clients put together their Internet deals. Some of those deals did involve actual money, but Barney was not averse to risk. Though the final product of *Human Number* would be a feature film, the project's success would hinge on Internet publicity, and that was in his wheelhouse. I also knew him a little better than I knew the other partners. No doubt he went to the same fancy industry parties and premieres they did, but he was by no means above slumming it with us and the firm's other charity clients. Despite an outward appearance of corn-fed normalcy, he was a friend of the unusual.

He heard me out on the snuff project and said it was pretty fucked up, but it did sound like it might work, and if I was determined to do it, he could help with the paperwork—not under the law partnership's card but under another he used for outside projects. He also told me the firm had taken on a new partner who was a First Amendment expert, and from what I was saying, I should probably talk to him, too.

So I met the First Amendment guy, and we hit it off okay. We knew someone in common, a talented young writer in New York with whom I had corresponded back when I was a talented young writer. First Amendment gave me the news that the talented young writer had just died of a heroin overdose. This meeting of the intellectual and the illicit moved me to go highbrow with the pitch—this project was about pushing the boundaries of artistic expression, questioning media amplification of violence, placing a mirror to the prurient gaze, blah, blah, bullshit. First Amendment raised his eyebrows, but he conceded that as I had outlined the project, it did not appear that I would be breaking any laws in executing it. The potentially tricky part, he said, was that I planned to publicize the event beforehand and perform the killing "live," but he would do some research and get back to me on that subject.

Presumably, the tricky part was that claiming you intend to commit a murder, even if you are a fictional person proposing the death of another fictional person, is different from claiming already to have committed a murder, which, if you haven't, is just a lie. Claiming you intend to commit a murder could set a panic in motion and thereby incur the famous limitation of the First Amendment established in the opinion of Justice Oliver Wendell Holmes, Jr., in 1919: "The most stringent protection of free speech would not protect a man falsely shouting fire in a theater and causing a panic." In 2000 it might still have been successfully argued that if no actual person was threatened, the threat was no more serious than a threat to kill Bugs Bunny, and if no one was threatened, no one should panic. Today? Forget it.

In my view, the actual circumstances that had resulted in the "falsely shouting fire in a theater" opinion supported my free-speech rationalizations for *Human Number*. The circumstances had nothing to do with a theater—that was merely the hypothetical action Justice Holmes used to support the conviction of a man named Schenck. Schenck and his associates had made and distributed pamphlets. On one page of the pamphlets was printed section 1 of the Thirteenth Amendment to the Constitution: "Neither slavery nor involuntary servitude, except as a punishment for crime whereof the party shall have been duly convicted, shall exist within the United States, or any place subject to their jurisdiction." On the other side of the pamphlets were printed phrases encouraging recipients to exercise their right to assert opposition to the draft. Setting aside whether a draft for World War I was a good or bad thing, this often-quoted and reasonable-sounding "falsely shouting fire" limitation of the First Amendment was created specifically and quite tortuously to stifle speech against executive policy. Schenck's crime was informing people of their constitutional rights.

At this point, late in the summer of 1999, we were several weeks into the thing with Rosenberg, but he had not yet secured our million dollars. This troubled me. Had I not written an excellent Business Plan? Were my spreadsheets not lovely? Were much less reasonable propositions not being financed daily? What was Rosenberg's problem?

I kept my ire from spiking too sharply, though, because right then Rosenberg was working out the series deal with WireBreak. Even though he and our attorney were supposed to be on the same side of that negotiation, our attorney already wanted to strangle him. Rosenberg had been with us for only a couple of months, and he was already telling us to fire our attorneys—the ones who were smart and funny, who had plenty of legitimate clients yet still returned our calls and did all this ridiculous, utterly unremunerative shit for us. Fire them? They would have laughed and thanked us. We told him it wasn't happening.

The WireBreak negotiations were actually pissing me off precisely because they *were* moving along so smoothly, because that demonstrated that CRAPtv deserved financing immediately. In the first round of negotiations, without a blink, WireBreak had acceded to our only substantive demand with regard to series rights, that we retain all television rights for the show we made with them. They wanted only the exclusive right to exploit the show on the Internet.

I had determined that the Internet rights to a property had absolutely no value except in their ability to create value for a property on other platforms, so, basically, they wanted to cover our development and marketing costs and get nothing in exchange. In the next round of negotiations, they did come back with the demand that we split television rights up the middle with them, but clearly it was an afterthought. They never would have thought of the television rights if we hadn't specifically demanded to keep them. In light of this demonstration that a comfortably capitalized company had no readily apparent plan for recouping its investors' money, I thought Rosenberg should be getting me my million dollars, pronto.

Not wanting to saddle him with another load, and also because I wished to keep knowledge of this project to as small a circle as possible, I determined to raise financing for *Human Number* independently of Rosenberg. Brody put together a rough budget for it, and it looked like the project could be done for fifty thousand dollars. That included purchase of all the equipment and tape stock; art direction, set, and props; professional makeup and prosthetic effects; a sound guy and editor working cheap but not free; some Web design; a dedicated server, co-location, and bandwidth; rent on a production space; insurance; and even some pay for me, the victim, and Brody if she were producing it. Bringing the production in that cheaply would mean pulling favors, but we were always pulling favors. Plus, in my largesse, I planned to cut in everybody involved on a few points of back end. In addition to the fifty thousand for production and post, I thought it would be smart to have another fifty thousand set aside for marketing—for hiring a PR agency to handle press in the aftermath, for throwing a screening and party up in Park City, whatever. So that made it an even hundred thousand dollars I had to raise in order to make my snuff movie.

It took three hours. First, I called over to Jason and Ward's place looking for Ward, and he was there. I pedaled my bike over immediately and explained the idea, proposing that he and I split a $25,000 block up the middle. Ward had come into some money recently, and his eyes came up triple-six. My half of that would be the last of my $80,000 inheritance—$40,000 had gone to start Quiddity, and the balance had dribbled through CRAP and CRAPtv. I felt tremendous relief at unloading the last of it, that money that had never really been mine.

I had pedaled over so fast because when I called, I heard Matt Stone's voice in the background. There was no way I would have pitched Matt directly, but if he were there when I made the pitch to Ward, he could make his own decisions. The main reason I didn't want to pitch Matt directly was that Jason was constantly being importuned to importune Matt and Trey to read scripts or consider investing in animated ideas that were "just like *South Park* but better." No doubt dozens of fabulous opportunities that didn't dead-end at Jason, their assistant Jennifer Howell, the law firm, or their agency were being crammed into their mailboxes and tucked under their windshield wipers.

Matt was an incredibly soft touch, which was the other reason I didn't want to pitch him directly. It wouldn't have been out of character for him to give away that much money just to be nice, and I didn't want charity for my project. He was already picking up every restaurant and bar tab left in a circle of condensation, and he was taking care of people's rent and dental problems all over the place. Dian was so far into Matt that Matt had taken to staging charity-style photo ops, the handshake over the handoff, each time Dian came for another check. The photos were supposed to be framed and put on the wall in Matt's office, but to sort of prove my point, they never were.

When I was done pitching Ward, Matt said the thing sounded horrible and he was in for $25,000, so just like that I was up to $50,000. Jason sat on the couch looking uncomfortable—and reasonably so, because this was right on the heels of my CRAPtv corporate fantasy power grab. Prior to putting *Human Number* in motion I had talked it over with him and explained my intentions. I hadn't opened them up to discussion, though, just said what they were. Jason was in for 5 percent of the creative side of the *Human Number* LLC. He didn't even have to do anything. In fact, it would be better if he didn't do anything—just mind the store at CRAPtv while I financed, wrote, directed, and sold this little feature film. The whole thing should take only a couple of months from start to finish, and during that time I would be at half-speed on other business—but it would be great for our company, and naturally he would get a producer credit.

This may not sound that terrible—or maybe it sounds really terrible—but it was pretty terrible. The *Human Number* arrangement, or more specifically the way I unilaterally engineered it, did nothing to repair the damage I had already done our partnership. But I wasn't thinking about that as I left the apartment in Mar Vista and pedaled to my next appointment, at the home of one of the partners in Next Generation, the production company I had not named the Rendering Plant.

This was Jaime Frey, the writer and director in their company, better known now as James Frey, author of *A Million Little Pieces* and *My Friend Leonard*, but he hadn't written those yet. Dan with the topsiders was the company's producer, was my understanding, and the third guy was the financier. The bland company-name decision had given me the wrong impression of Jaime, I thought since getting to know him slightly better—his stories made my adventures sound like tea parties.

On the phone that morning I had told him I had a pitch that was too good for the phone, and after I arrived at his house, I opened by letting him know that since our conversation I had raised firm commitments for half the financing of the project. When I was done explaining the proposition, he just scratched his beard and nodded—none of the horror or amazement I had gotten from everyone else I explained it to, but those weren't really in his interpersonal repertoire. He said that he had to talk to his partners before making a commitment, but he was sure Next Generation was in. He asked me not to take the project anywhere else for twenty-four hours. I said sure and asked him not to tell anyone else about it.

When I met with his partner Dan the next day, I had to pitch the project all over again—not for the usual reason, that the first person pitched was unable to rearticulate the idea, but because Jaime had declined to tell his partners a single word about the project except that they were doing it, which made me laugh. And then, I am afraid that I freaked Dan out pretty badly. He was a nice, normal guy from the suburbs of Chicago, and faking a satanic sex murder was probably not what he had had in mind when he left investment banking or whatever it was to pursue a creative career. But Next Generation was ready for a hit, and the fiscal logic of *Human Number* was compelling. Next Generation was in for $25,000.

After that I called it a day. The last $25,000 would be easy to get when I wanted it, now that the majority was in place, and especially since a third of the invested money was from Matt. Otherwise sensible people were made stupid by the opportunity of investing with celebrities. And if I never took the last $25,000, the value of the purchased blocks would remain that much greater; the LLC for *Human Number* was structured such that 50 percent of the equity lay on the creative side and 50 percent on the investment side, regardless of how many investment dollars were taken.

There were only two roles in the movie. I would play the Antichrist myself, though for a number of reasons I didn't relish the prospect. For one, I was a terrible actor. Single-handedly, I had ruined a high school production of *As You Like It*. I was the exiled king, not the lead but a key player, and I had never gotten around to memorizing my monologue. The Renaissance Faire blarney I improvised in place of it fooled no one, definitely not the director, who the next year would be both my English teacher and my AA sponsor.

But the main reason I didn't want to play the Antichrist was that when the movie became a runaway hit, I would be recognized everywhere I went. Of course, it would be okay with me if a reasonable number of people looked twice at me when I went out to dinner at a nice restaurant—if I were recognized the way, say, a successful writer would be recognized, which is to say only once in a while, except in places where he would expect to be recognized, like for instance at the National Book Awards. But I didn't want to be "the Antichrist Guy" everywhere I went. Talk about a nightmare.

And that was only when I was thinking about the fans. Far worse would be people who hated *Human Number* for religious or political reasons and hated me for making it. Not everybody thinks it's cool to pretend you're the Antichrist and butcher someone like a shoat. And, for that matter, what about the creepy fans—the ones who liked the movie a little *too* much? Big bummer right there. Nabokov used to get admiring letters from pedophiles.

But even that wasn't as bad as it could get. The creepy fans would be a minor inconvenience in comparison to *people who really thought I was the Antichrist*. Because surely there would be a few of those, nuts who just couldn't be convinced otherwise, once the notion was placed in their heads, the same kind of people who made the *Blair Witch* pilgrimages to Burkittsville. What if they wanted to worship me? Highly embarrassing, to have caped dorks convening covens in my driveway.

And, wait a minute. That was only the true believers who *liked* the Antichrist. What about the ones who believed in the Antichrist but did *not* like him? Fuck! I'd be hunted down like an animal! Salman Rushdie had it easy by comparison— at least he was in England. American evangelicals were armed to the teeth.

At least in part because it seemed unfair to expose anyone other than myself to the risk of murder by fundamentalist huntsmen, I decided I had to be the one who took the Antichrist's part. And in spite of the disadvantages, there were practical advantages to my performing the role. I could operate the camera, which would allow for more improvisation, let me watch the frame, and reduce by one the number of people I had to direct. Besides, if the Antichrist planned to terrorize the world for forty and two months, he would have to keep his identity a secret, which meant he would have to wear a mask. I would make sure it was a good one, and I would distort my voice in post.

As for casting the victim, I could hold auditions—or I could just ask Heather to do it. Her original purpose in coming out to Los Angeles had been to start acting in film and television. One thing she hadn't taken into account in making the move was the way productions were cast in film and television. While being of half-Japanese descent hadn't been much of a stumbling block in New York, where she had had pretty much as good a shot as a blonde at getting a role in *Hedda Gabler* onstage, in Los Angeles her auditions seemed to fall into one of two categories. Either she was reading with a bunch of other women of color—African Americans, Hispanics, Asians—for the one specifically nonwhite role on a show, the "funky friend" on a sitcom, or the "efficient lab tech" on a drama; or she was reading with a bunch of other women for the role of "Asian hooker." She wasn't even booking many of those last ones, because she didn't look that ethnically Asian. The one TV role she had booked was on an MTV abomination called *Undressed*. At present she was working behind the camera in music video and commercials; she was a little frustrated on the acting front, and I could give her a break.

She had turned down an offer to do a *Playboy* spread, and as this was a little more extreme than that, I wasn't sure she'd go for it, but I rehearsed my pitch. A little nudity, sure. And yes, you get tortured and mutilated. But what fantastic exposure if it became a hit! And more important in the near term, what a great opportunity to develop a real character who would be the focus of the whole piece. I pitched it when we were out at dinner somewhere, selling her hard on how punk rock the whole thing would be. She said she'd do it, but she wanted me to think a little more about whether I was sure I wanted to do it. Not work with her, because though naturally that would have its complications, it should also be fun. But was I sure I wanted to do this whole thing? Because I was acting kind of weird.

Acting weird, how? Well, the secrecy, for one. She understood it was necessary for *Human Number* to remain below the radar of the world at large in order for it to work. But my level of paranoia seemed to indicate that I thought the world was already trying to find out about it. One of my first actions had been to try to register the LLC's address as the law firm's, so that would be where the cops went first. After Barney saw their address on the paperwork and yelled at me, I had located the LLC at a post office box, paid for in cash and registered to a false name. The only other contact for the LLC was a pager number, also paid for in cash and registered to another false name. I was swearing everyone involved to secrecy and not telling them who else was involved, so that half the people I knew were walking around not knowing which of the other people they knew were also part of the project.

The wisdom of these blinds would become clear, I explained, when the FBI came looking for me. Heather rolled her eyes. It must be noted that somewhere along in here I had secretly gone off my meds, which I did about every six months when my prescription ran out. Despite the truly miraculous effect a tiny, 10mg daily dose of Paxil had on my baseline mood, after a few months of feeling okay I would have a hard time remembering how bad I had felt before, and gradually I would become more and more resentful of the medication's side effect of making my penis feel like it belonged to someone else.

The first signs of withdrawal were fantastic, like being fourteen again: genital responsiveness bordering on priapism and an even more overwhelming interest than usual in that most fascinating subject, myself. A few days later I would notice that my temper was getting shorter, but that would piss me off, so I wouldn't do anything about it. Over the next few days I would turn into a total asshole, subject to red flares of rage. Then the physical withdrawal symptoms would kick in, strange sensations like mild electrical shocks in my face. (These facial shocks were so bizarre that I thought at first I must be imagining them, but they were indeed listed on the manufacturer's Web site among less common Paxil withdrawal symptoms.) When the shocks abated, my libido remained at its natural state, and I wasn't seriously depressed yet, but the repetitive, tunneling thought patterns symptomatic of depression started coming back. And then, in a couple more weeks, the birds of suicide would gather under the pressing sky, and I would refill my prescription.

It was a tiresome cycle for all involved, which was the reason I had to keep it secret. But for me it was a practically irresistible cycle, because like many who take antidepressants or antipsychotics, I was subject to believing, when they were working perfectly, that I didn't need to be taking them. The simple shape of this logical loop was painfully obvious to anyone outside it. But to someone standing on the loop, arrival back at the same place each time is a source of recurring astonishment.

4

Fifty thousand dollars sounded like a lot of money, but you could spend that amount fast on a production. Heather was kind enough to go twice out into the desert with friends to scout suitable sites, peeling ranch houses stranded in toxic sand, but the cost of housing and feeding even a skeleton crew on-location turned out to be more than we could afford. Best would be something right in Los Angeles, so everyone could go home at night. Brody and I looked into a few light industrial units, but it soon became clear that the sensible thing would be to shoot in the Quiddity office right there in Venice.

Down its narrow length it had no windows, and though there was no structure above it, the ductwork and heavy beams suggested one. If we blacked out the skylights and put up flats at each end, the office could easily stand in for a basement. Nobody could complain that I was making a mess, it was secure, and there was a shower and industrial sink in back for dealing with the prop blood. Shooting loud scenes in the daytime wouldn't work because of the other tenants in the building, but we could shoot at night.

Frankel naturally wasn't wild about the idea, but the location line in the *Human Number* budget was sufficient to cover a month's rent on the office and a little more, so using the office as a location at least offset my taking time away from developing business for Quiddity. The Los Angeles Quiddity office was proving to be an unnecessary luxury, anyway. Since my entertainment-naming fantasy had crashed and burned, almost all our work was coming out of San Francisco, and we were conducting most of our jobs on-site at our clients' offices.

Dave Hardy agreed to build and dress the room on a tiny budget, and with characteristic ingenuity he determined how to do it without ruining the room he had already built. I went over the physical requirements and asked that he use chapter 13 as a reference. He hauled down most of what he would need from his own warehouse—some old furniture, a hydraulic dental chair, and a futon mattress—and with his girlfriend, Jen, who was a scenic painter, he salvaged the rest in Los Angeles. I knew they would come up with something better than anything I might design myself, but their work exceeded my hopes. My office looked like the home-mutilation chamber of somebody with serious fucking problems.

Dave and Jen had taken me to see the Henry Darger exhibit at SFMOMA—I didn't know who Darger was, so Dave proposed the field trip prior to starting work. Darger was a solitary ragpicker and devout Catholic who had died in 1973, leaving behind his ten-thousand-page magnum opus, *The Story of the Vivian Girls, in what is known as the Realm of the Unreal, of the Glandeco-Angelinnian War Storm, as caused by the Child Slave Rebellion*. Neither the manuscript nor the hundreds of mixed-media illustrations Darger had made for it were discovered until after his death.

The Vivian Girls were preadolescents, often pictured naked and perfectly formed but for the addition of immature male genitalia. Many of the paintings were violent, depicting strangulations, eviscerations, and tortures of the children, which naturally led some critics, perhaps those most uncomfortably stimulated by the undeniable eroticism of Darger's paintings, to speculate that he may have been a sexual predator or serial killer. In likelihood he was neither of those, just a lonely man typing and painting away his lifetime in service of an audience of one, himself.

The set Dave and Jen built for *Human Number* drew on Darger's spooky, repetitive, hermaphroditic style but had none of its whimsical innocence. Among the raw materials I had handed over to them were piles of remaindered porn magazines, many of them duplicate issues, left over from something to do with *Orgazmo*. On the walls of my office naked women now sprouted purple cocks and had their faces replaced with surgical diagrams cut from medical textbooks. The entire back wall of the room was a four-panel mural, sixteen feet by ten, a richly textured narrative painting depicting key events of the Revelation. It looked like the product of a long obsession, but the two of them banged it out in just a few days, painting the flats in Jen's backyard before installing them as a false wall in the office.

For the floor they rolled old linoleum over the carpet. It looked like damaged cement, and afterward we could just roll up the mess and throw it away. Onto the wall opposite the mural they screwed what had once been a futon but for the last few years had been the wall padding under the basketball hoop in Dave's warehouse in San Francisco. It looked already to have been the site of several grimy strangulations, but it was still pale enough to serve as a deforming projection screen. Through its dimples they secured wrist, leg, and neck restraints, and they hung a series of heavy pulleys from the beams. The hydraulic dental chair took prominence of place under the mantis arm of a surgical light in the middle of the room. The dental chair turned on bearings to face either the mural or the wall with the futon projection screen, where the crucifixion would occur. The rest of the room was furnished with thrift store junk, old computer hardware Jolon donated, and the recording and computer equipment we were actually using. I rigged some nasty torture implements out of rubber pipes and scrap metal, and we rented a cattle prod from a prop house. For more traditional hardware Heather and I went shopping at the Pleasure Chest in West Hollywood.

What should have been a lighthearted trip to the sex shop was shadowed by a growing feeling that maybe this project wasn't the good clean fun it had seemed at first. Not that I wondered whether I really wanted to mutilate or murder anyone, or whether—as some people seemed to think—this project was just a poorly sublimated fantasy. It was unpleasant to realize that even some people who knew me really, really well were shocked by the brutality of what I had imagined. It was *supposed* to be scary. That was the idea of a horror movie, right? You weren't supposed to get scared just hearing about it—much less working on it. It was pretend! To whom should it be clearer that it was all just pretend than to people working to put the illusion in place?

Heather wasn't having that many problems with the project, but Brody was getting more and more freaked out as the shoot date approached. My hands were more than full, though, and for me now there was no backing out. Money had been taken in, and money now was quickly being spent. I had other problems. I had to figure out how to cut Heather's tongue out of her head.

Among its whips and chains and chaps and dongs, the Pleasure Chest offered a gag that would keep the wearer's mouth levered open, presumably so a penis could be stuck in and out of it. The gag was a stainless-steel ring with straps affixed to either side that buckled at the back of the wearer's neck. Heather couldn't even open her mouth wide enough to admit the ring, but it could be cut and crimped to fit, and then wrapped in leather so it wouldn't grate against her teeth. The wrapping would narrow the hole still further, but all I had to get through it was a set of forceps. The straps could conceal a tube that wrapped around her jaw and then down her back to connect to a vat of prop blood.

For the prosthetics and blood effects we would need professional help. This came from SOTA Effects, a business in the Valley that kept alive the dying technologies of creature construction. More and more, computer-generated effects were displacing the kind of work they did, and visiting their offices was like a trip back into *Creature Feature,* the Friday night monster show that had terrified me as a kid. Aliens and mummy dummies populated the halls, and rows of skulls and werewolf heads in varying states of real and simulated disrepair goggled from the shelves. It seemed like a fun place to work, and the effects technicians were interested by the challenge of doing something that looked completely real. Most of their contracts were for creature work. They thought the ring-gag prop would work, and they said they would make some fake tongues. With a ribbon-flat tube and a smear of latex they could simulate a cut jugular for the killing at the end. To make the blood spurt right, they would pump it out by hand.

The week before Halloween, Heather and I did a few nights of loosely scripted second-act takes by ourselves, gathering footage for the edit. Then on two consecutive nights, with a tiny crew, we shot the third act—the long, single shot culminating in the sacrifice. Those nights were sleepless and strange but not scary. Everything fast was done in slow motion, and we broke character all the time to figure out angles and rig all the tubes and prosthetics. Heather was a trouper, submitting to various unpleasant activities that began with my stringing her up by one of the pulleys, mummifying her in the industrial plastic wrap used to secure warehouse products on palettes, and beating her until she bled.

I hope I need not add that all this was conducted without any actual injury to her person. I had constructed a whip of absorbent foam that flapped approximately like leather, which could be dipped in prop blood and swung slowly so that it left red trails wherever it passed. We had made incisions in the plastic beforehand, and these were invisible until the blood sluiced into them, so it looked like the whip was making them. If I do say so, it was a clever effect, much better than what could have been achieved without the plastic; and the plastic made a spooky, translucent cocoon. Heather had to spend a lot of time wrapped up in it, breathing through a blowhole, and that she didn't complain was one of many testaments to her fortitude.

The latex tongues looked and felt exactly like real tongues, squishy and meaty with a delicate pebbled texture on top, and like real tongues, each enclosed two chambers that vented at the rear. The vents connected to tubing that came out the side of Heather's mouth and wrapped beneath the gag's strap, as I have described. There were two separate ring gags, one for when the gag was put into her mouth and fastened, and the other, which was integrated with the latex tongue and apparatus, for when I cut her tongue out.

The tongue excision was to occur after I cut her out of the cocoon; duct-taped her at the ankles, wrists, throat, and forehead to the dental chair; and tortured her through a recitation of chapter 13. When her recitation was finished, we froze with the camera in place, angled on a platform situated midway through a handheld tracking shot. Heather's gag was quickly swapped, and the tracking shot resumed.

Now the camera was placed, still rolling, on a nearby shelf, and I stepped into the frame to take the forceps and a scalpel from a surgical stand beside the dental chair.

I was scared I would cut her real tongue by accident. That was impossible, as it was crammed safely back behind a huge blob of latex, but making the cut was kind of freaky, because she couldn't talk. Using the forceps, I reached into her mouth and grabbed the latex tongue, stretching it out past her teeth before slicing through it with a scalpel. I held the severed lump up to the lens as blood gushed from her open mouth.

I called a cut, and we froze. The prop gag came out, and the original gag went back in, so it could be removed on-camera. The next parts had to happen fast, so that blood would appear to continue bubbling from her mouth while she wasn't connected to any tubes. We filled her mouth with blood and restarted the tape; I unbuckled the gag, pulled it out, cut her loose from the chair with the scalpel, dragged her over to the wall with the restraints, and strapped her up.

The excision had been conducted under the spot of the surgical lamp, but ambient lighting was provided by slides projected digitally across the room against the mattress. I hadn't had time to put together my *Koyaanisqatsi* home video, so Scott Mitchell had kindly scanned plates of Satan and the Apocalypse from the Middle Ages to the present out of an art book and made them into a digital slideshow. The dental chair and our figures occluded the projections during the tongue excision, so the action was echoed in silhouette behind us, and Heather wound up crucified in the center of the projector's beam. In addition to providing Old Master production value, the slides by their juxtaposition created intermittent changes in lighting, which would help disguise any jumpiness in the transitions.

Now Heather froze again to be fitted with the flat tube and latex flap that would let me slice her jugular. The blood would start pumping as soon as I passed the dulled scalpel over the right area. It wasn't necessary that I even touch her with the scalpel, and I didn't want to touch her with it. This scalpel was dull as a butter knife, but Heather's throat was scarred from a surgery for thyroid cancer several years earlier, and it was acutely sensitive to pressure. Worried about bumping her scar, I passed the blade too far away from her skin, and the blood jumped from the wrong place in her throat.

I knew the shot was ruined. I was holding the camera in my left hand as I moved the scalpel with my right, so I saw it happening in the viewfinder, but in the hope I was wrong I didn't cut, and we went through the rest of the scene. Quarts poured out of her, gallons, covering the floor in a sticky mess and splashing all over the mattress, glazing us both in gore. She died. I turned the lens into the beam of the projector, the viewfinder flared white, and I stopped tape.

Unfortunately, the tape did show the error. This was the one shot that had to be perfect, so I asked everyone if we could reshoot the next night. By now it was nearly dawn. Heather and the crew acceded wearily but gamely; there was no getting around it—the shot was no good. The crew packed it in for what sleep they could get during the daylight, and Heather and I stayed to clean up.

The chair could be left as it was, but the crucifixion area had to be restored to its presanguinary state. This was professional prop blood, water based and relatively easy to clean up. But the ingredient that made it congeal was sugar, so it was incredibly sticky, and the water solubility meant that while it swabbed cleanly from nonporous surfaces, it tended to spread through fabric when water touched it. The stains on the futon, to which we turned after we finished mopping the floor, blossomed as soon as we dabbed them. We pressed moist towels against the stains, and they swelled and bled to join one another, tinting the fabric all the way to its edges. With each sponging press the volume increased, as though we weren't absorbing the blood at all, but hopelessly mashing at the ebbing arteries of a huge heart dying behind the wall.

By late November the edit was under way in the back room of the Quiddity office. Todd Benson, one of the *South Park* editors, was cutting it on nights and weekends. I could barely stand to join him for long enough to review the cuts. The thing was an absolute horror. I had taped forty-five minutes of sequential torture, which Todd was cutting down to twenty. He made the transitions so seamless that I couldn't see them myself. Heather sobbed and gagged and bled and died. I looked awful, a hulking torso going to fat, spattered with gore, faceless in a black hood. There was no blink, no wink, no smile, just a bad, bad thing happening in a basement room where nobody could hear it and no hope was ever going to come. It literally nauseated me. But by this time I was unable to separate the components of my nausea—the sickness I felt any time something I made was about to leave my hands from the sickness of this particular thing. Todd adjusted some colors, and we laid it off to tape.

My father and stepmother, Bert and Happy, were coming out to California for Thanksgiving. Happy's sister, Corinne, and Corinne's husband, Rick, lived down in Laguna Beach. My stepsiblings, Michael and Halle, were flying in from Atlanta and Dallas. Corinne and Rick's next-door neighbors were leaving for the weekend; all of us from out of town would be staying at the neighbors' house. I hadn't told either of my parents about what I was doing yet, and since there was a distinct possibility it was going to get ugly, I felt I owed them at least a little warning. I planned to tell my father about the project in person when we were down in Laguna.

Heather was excited about the trip because of the animals. Corinne and Rick shared a bungalow with something like thirty birds, cats, and rabbits cordoned into a maze of indoor-outdoor predator-prey safety zones by cages, doors, baby gates, and mobile knee-high enclosures that were rearranged according to schedules known only to Corinne, Rick, and the more hopeful cats. At night, parts of the house were left open to the outside so that families of raccoons and possums would have access to food and water left out for them. The only being in the household with any measure of privacy was an incontinent cat that had a basement shower stall all to himself.

The close quarters were one reason we were all staying at the neighbors' house, but there was also a concern that the preparation of a turkey at Corinne and Rick's might upset the larger parrots. Since we were going to be at the neighbors', we figured it would be okay to bring Nemo, the skinny big-eared black dog we had recently adopted. But the neighbors turned out to have special-needs cats, so we had to keep

Nemo in the yard during the day, and that night he had to sleep out in the car.

The morning after Thanksgiving, as we were having coffee on the porch, I told my dad about my project. I knew my mom would hate it, but I wasn't entirely sure what reaction to expect from my father. He had leapt to my defense when members of his parents' generation had sniped at the racier parts of my little book. He had howled with glee when I sent him my penis movie, and he had entered into a feud with the director of the Crested Butte Reel Fest when they declined to screen it. Throughout my life Bert had been my unflagging advocate, in everything I undertook but especially in creative matters. It was he who had inspired me to want to be a writer in the first place, as far back as when I was learning how to shape letters with a pencil.

But when I told him about the snuff project, he shrank visibly, both away from me and, it seemed to me, in relation to the concrete world. In the morning light that slanted through the neighbor people's flowered trellis, he looked frail and confused, old and frightened. He was in fact getting old. He was pushing sixty.

While the child in me quailed in fear at seeing my own father frightened, at the same time I felt a bloom of dark power, a connectedness with and participation in a future too terrible for him to face. He asked me not to do the thing. He didn't forbid it, either because forbidding something for the first time now, when I was thirty and in the flush of strength, would have been far too strange a moment to have between us, or because he knew forbidding it would only impel me forward. Instead, he talked about evil. He thought this thing I planned to do was *evil*—that was his word—and he hoped I wouldn't do it. Evil: a weird subject and one we didn't often discuss, because it lay so clearly between his faith and my apostasy.

While my father had no doubt my plan would succeed, would even make money, which I admitted was my prime objective with it, not because I wanted money itself or anything money could buy but because money was the only currency of success—I gave him my whole spiel—he only shrank farther from me as I went on: America would be gulled by the hoax because America was stupid, the news media would report it because the news media were bloodthirsty and irresponsible, and people would want to see it because they were disgusting. Whatever America might say about itself, this was what it wanted. Read the papers, go to the movies, turn on the television. Afterward, from the pulpit of my money, I would tell them all they made me fucking sick—because that, really, was what the hoax was about. Not faking a murder, because anyone could do that, but making people clap for it.

I told my father that while I respected his view that the project was evil, I didn't share it—and anyway, events were now in motion that I was powerless to stop. The rest of our visit was quiet. Nemo, though he had seemed only reproachful when placed in the car at bedtime the night before, had been struck by terrors in the darkness. In his panic he had coated the entire inside of the vehicle with vomit. I glumly swabbed it up as he huddled against Heather's legs.

5

One reason I couldn't stop now was that I had spent very close to fifty thousand dollars, and I now had a fiduciary responsibility to my investors. But even aside from the money and all the work put in by other people, Heather and Dave Hardy especially (Brody had quit in the middle of the shoot), there was the article that would be coming out in *Spin*.

The lead time for a monthly magazine is about three months. While small articles can be slipped in a little later, most of the purportedly hot, fresh content that fills the pages of *Rolling Stone, Spin, Details, Esquire, Premiere, Vanity Fair*, and so on is anything but hot and fresh. Monthly cultural journalism is outsourced public relations, planned a fiscal quarter in advance, marching in lockstep with the publicity departments of the same companies that underwrite the publications. I wanted to have an article about the project on the stands when I was up at Sundance selling the movie, and I knew there was one route, other than having an immense PR budget, to getting some ink: knowing an editor who acknowledged the situation above and didn't like it.

Dave Moodie had been one of the editors at *Might*, the hopeful independent magazine for which I had written a few years back. When it went out of business, he took a job as a features editor at *Spin*, which seemed like the right magazine for a placement. Its circulation was around 500,000, and it was in the alternative-mainstream sweet spot. Moodie had already been so kind as to do a little drumming for CRAPtv, placing us on a "Hot List" in *Spin* without even telling me about it beforehand. So I had called him up before I started taping *Human Number* and given him the pitch. Dan from Next Generation was on the phone with me on our second call; by coincidence the two of them had gone to the same high school in Chicago.

Moodie made me swear on all that was unholy that if he pitched the piece to his boss, I would do the millennial broadcast I described. Not that he approved of the undertaking, he made clear. But if I was going to do it, I was going to do it, and he acknowledged that it was likely to make news whether or not they did a piece on it, so having the exclusive option of timely coverage was not a bad thing.

The hitch came back to the lead-time problem. The magazine would be distributed in January, after the broadcast, but the presses would run in December. This meant the text had to be locked by late November, meaning nothing that would be described in it as having happened would have occurred at the time of its writing. I wanted to write the piece myself under a pseudonym, but he wasn't having any of that. The upshot was that by the time I went down to Laguna for Thanksgiving, I had already sent a tape of the last few minutes of the broadcast to *Spin*. And even before the taping, I had done an interview with the guy Moodie assigned to the piece.

I conducted that conversation on my cell phone, standing in the center of the baseball diamond in Playa del Rey while Nemo ran in crazy circles around the edge of the field. It was a gorgeous Southern California fall day, with a bright wind off the bay. I was as full of myself as I had ever been. Quiddity was chugging along despite my time off; jobs were lining up. Even CRAPtv was gaining traction. Rosenberg was setting up meetings for us with bigwigs all over town, and my first feature film was in production. To the south silver jets angled up over the ocean, scratching white contrails against the sky. I felt I was hovering on a bubble of possibility. I had taken a five-year tumble, but I was back.

Despite my giddiness, I was more and more certain the FBI would come looking for me when any part of the project became public. Regardless of whether I broke the law in conducting the hoax—which I was determined not to do, because to do so could cause huge liability if a judgment were rendered afterward that held the LLC or me personally responsible for costs incurred in the investigation—it would appear that crimes were being committed. Big crimes: murder and kidnapping. The latter was a federal offense, and that combined with the interstate aspect of an Internet hoax inclined me to believe that the Department of Justice, not state or local authorities, would pursue the case if it were pursued. I thought it would be okay if the FBI questioned me—provided I had broken no laws and provided it happened after the broadcast. But if it happened before the broadcast, there was no way I would be allowed to go ahead with it.

Everything would hang on what happened the week or two before New Year's Eve. I had to get the word out within that time but without intimating precisely what would happen during the broadcast. If the Antichrist announced exactly what he planned to do at such and such a URL, law enforcement agencies would track down the server's IP address and prevent the broadcast from happening, whether it was real or not.

CRAPtv and other clients were demanding most of Jolon's resources, so I had to find someone else to build the site that would house the video online. Mitchell hooked me up with some guys from SciArc who had just started a design business called Low Country Guidance. There were four of them, Clancy, Paul, Will, and Mark, and making the Antichrist's Web site was right up their dirt road. Clancy's graduate thesis had been a huge architectural model for Satan's summer house. We made a deal, and they got to work. They designed a Mark of the Beast, a biohazard-looking thing made from three conjoined sixes, and animated the mark to rotate unsteadily on the index page to a scary grinding noise. They set the site up to roll out verses of chapter 13 and end with a jump to a video window.

I needed a secure server to house it. Jolon and one of his Internet gangsters, Push, talked it over with me. Efforts to track the IP and thus me could be stymied by hosting the site offshore, but that seemed like it might be asking for worse trouble when it arrived. Spoofing the site through a vulnerable server, like one at a college, was an untenable solution because it was against the law. Any measure clearly intended solely to frustrate law enforcement was likely to torpedo *Human Number* after the fact.

We decided that the best choice was to co-locate a server in a nearby facility that had unlimited bandwidth and a policy of protecting housed servers against anything but a court order. If it got to the point of a court order, the party was over anyway. Push could secure the site against anything but a massive denial-of-service attack, which I did think was a distinct possibility: that the site would be attacked by Christian computer geeks or even nice, regular computer geeks who thought the broadcast of a murder, whether real or faked, was a bad thing. Push and I drove to Beverly Hills with a CPU and worked things out at a facility that had the right policies.

In order to reach as many people as possible and at the same time limit the potential for the site to be brought down by either a DOS attack or the authorities, I wanted an Internet marketing partner that operated or had access to high-traffic sites. In a perfect scenario, information about the broadcast would go online just hours before it occurred, and the site would come down right after it occurred.

The Internet Entertainment Group, one of our Lapdance sponsors, syndicated content to hundreds of other sites, which in turn syndicated to thousands more. Through the IEG network I would be able to reach a couple of hundred thousand people at a minimum on an extremely short time frame. IEG specialized in the distribution of pornography, but there was an element of tabloid to their offering. It was IEG that had released the Pam and Tommy sex tape, after all. I still had CEO Seth Warshawski's number, and I arranged to meet with him at their company headquarters in Seattle. I flew up on a commuter flight and took a taxi from SeaTac into town. Seattle, with its air of decaying new technology, always reminded me of the bad future. It was cold and sleeting out, the sky a steely gray. The taxi dropped me in front of an office tower downtown.

Seth's corner office on the top floor looked out over the Port of Seattle. He sat behind a dark wood executive desk, his back to the view. The desk and shelves were populated with Sharper Image and airplane catalog items, as though he had researched the accoutrements necessary to furnishing an executive suite and ordered accordingly. There was nothing pornographic about the office and nothing ostentatious, just something infinitely depressing. It could easily have been the executive suite of an insurance company or auditing firm.

Seth was my age but gave the appearance of being either much younger or, I realized as I examined him at close range, much older. He was as small and soft as a boy of twelve, and there was a boyish cast to his features, but his hair had gone completely gray, and the skin around his eyes had the delicate parchment texture of a very old person's. His voice was a papery, tired whisper, and while speaking to him I was reminded of children afflicted with progeria, that terrible disease that dwarfs its sufferers and rushes them through life. He wore downsized slacks and an elegant dress shirt open at the collar, an expensive watch on his wrist—as with the décor, giving the impression of accoutrements assumed, the correct costume for a person in his position.

He called in a handful of underlings, pale men mostly older than himself. One came in pitching a Web site application he had just been pitched on the phone, software that let you stick dildos and stuff into an apparently real and reactive girl on your computer screen. Seth was noncommittal. The assembled group sat down in chairs or leaned against the desk and bookcase. I stuck my videotape into the VCR opposite Seth's desk.

They watched as Heather was taped down and made to recite chapter 13. I hadn't given it a preamble, and I don't think any of them realized it was me in the mask. A few of them left the office when the gag went in and the scalpel came out, a few more after I cut out her tongue. By the time she was dead, it was just Seth, me, and one freaked-out underling. The underling stood with his arms tightly crossed and his eyes flitting back and forth between me and Seth. Seth looked at him and nodded, and he left.

"I can't touch that," said Seth.

I said of course he couldn't—not if it was real. But it was fake. That was me on the screen, that was my girlfriend. No one had been hurt. I explained how I proposed to use it to market the horror movie of which it was a part, offering him a percentage of the deal I would make in January. He shook his head. There was no way he could get involved, he said, even if he wanted to get involved—which he didn't, because frankly it scared the shit out of him. As it was, he received death threats with gloomy regularity. They had shot Larry Flynt, and if he put anything to do with that monstrosity up on any of his Web sites, they would shoot him, too. First in line would be his own lawyers. So thanks for thinking of IEG, and best of luck with the project, but no way.

After Seth declined to become involved with *Human Number*, I stayed and chatted for a while, allowing the realization to settle in that my proposition had frightened and even morally disturbed one of the most reviled traffickers of information on the planet.

"You do know that you're going to hell for that," said Seth as we parted.

I could not help but think, as I made my way through the hallway to the elevator down, past the eyes and whispers of those who had fled my presentation in horror, that he was in a position to know.

In the meantime Rosenberg had heard that I had a secret, spooky project in the works, and he wanted to know what it was. After my return from Seattle, it seemed like it was time to start thinking seriously about how sale of the completed film would be accomplished, so I went over to Rosenberg's house and explained it. Seth's reaction had had a significant impact on my own perspective. Perhaps it was because I hadn't prefaced the presentation with the caveat that it was faked, but Seth's reaction had upset me. So I didn't show Rosenberg the tape, just explained what was on it. He had the same interested reaction to the pitch that most people had when I explained it. Yes, it was fucked up, but in a way that was provocative, not *evil*.

But by this time I was starting to move over to the other side, to revulsion at what I had made, and so while it was nice to have yet another person respond with excitement, I wanted to hold it against him that he was interested in something so awful. Where was his humanity? I tried to explain that it really was an abomination. Rosenberg assured me I would get over that feeling, it was just jitters at having something hot in my hands, and he could definitely help me get the hot thing out of them by acting as a sales agent or producer's rep. The standard fee was 10 percent.

On the advance-publicity side, IEG was not my only contact in Internet entertainment. I was pretty sure I could make a deal with one or more of the operators of disturbing or simply weird high-traffic content sites if I wanted, but something more promising was in the works. Scott Mitchell was friends with one of two journalists ghostwriting the autobiography of Harry Knowles, the movie gossip maven who ran the Web site Ain't It Cool News. Mitchell had put the ghostwriter and me in touch with one another, and the ghostwriter thought it might be possible to talk Knowles into putting some kind of teaser for my project up on his site. I sent the ghostwriter a précis, not text from the broadcast itself but a description of it. He said he'd pass it on, and I assumed that if Knowles were interested, he would contact me to discuss the particulars.

Placing my advance information about the broadcast on Ain't It Cool News, and maybe only there, was starting to seem like a good idea. It was an online, alternative companion to *Variety* and the *Hollywood Reporter*. Almost everyone in the film industry had the Web site bookmarked. While an audience of entertainment end users was important for CRAPtv, the key audience for the *Human Number* broadcast was actually quite focused: potential buyers and distributors of the film. It didn't matter so much whether lots of people actually saw the broadcast. It mattered only that buyers had that impression when the film went up for sale in Utah, and they would get that impression if they came to the broadcast via a link from Ain't It Cool. The article in *Spin*—which, since it was coming out after the fact, would have zero impact on actual viewership—would buttress the impression of a national reach.

On December 16, 1999, a teenager in Florida threatened one of the survivors of the Columbine High School massacre in an Internet chat room, typing that he planned to come to Colorado and "finish the job." Columbine High School was closed for the day of December 17, and the FBI descended on the home of the boy who had made the threat. The attorney general went on national television and stated that it was his agency's responsibility to take every threat seriously and respond to each with the assumption that it was real. Idle threats would not be taken lightly, and the Florida teen would be punished to the fullest extent allowable by law. If grounds for it could be established, his punishment would include repayment of the expenses incurred in dealing with him, which were considerable. The attorney general reasonably added that resources expended in pursuit of malicious pranksters were resources not available to pursuing real threats, and in that respect malicious pranks, even idle ones, posed a serious danger to public safety.

By this time I wasn't sleeping very well. In truth I hadn't slept very well since the taping seven weeks earlier. I was back on my meds, but they weren't kicking in as fast as they had before, and I was experiencing a sense of dislocation and impending doom as pointedly and unremittingly as I had ever felt it. Whereas in the past I had been able to comfort myself with the psychopharmacological argument that my feeling of alienation was at least partly the result of misfiring circuitry, which could be repaired with medicine, now I wondered if the circuitry was permanently damaged.

Late on the night of December 20, I got a voice mail from the ghostwriter, letting me know something had gone up on Ain't It Cool several hours earlier. My stomach turned. This was it, then. The information was going out. But I hadn't had a conversation with Knowles to decide the shape of it. I logged on to the site and found the material immediately, at the top of the front page.

My précis had been cut up and edited into "quotations" from a "threatening letter" that purportedly had been sent to Knowles. The letter was not in the voice of the Antichrist as I had imagined him, but in my own. The editing job had garbled my words into something that was way too explicit, something that sounded like it had been written by some sick, pathetic, attention-seeking sociopath in a basement somewhere—which was exactly what my Antichrist was supposed to be.

And, I wondered belatedly, what I was? Out of nothing but a spirit of fun and mischief all these people were trying to help me, but this wasn't what I had wanted. I had wanted to control the information, to place a simple link at Ain't It Cool and then let the project Web site speak for itself. Now my words were cut up and glued wrongly together, an ugly, uncontrollable golem.

To make matters much worse, Knowles or his webmaster had opened a discussion forum for the topic. This was a possibility that hadn't even occurred to me, and it was bad, bad news. Already there were dozens of comments and threads. One or two posters seemed to like the idea, but to call the general response unfavorable would be a disservice to the eloquence of the posters: page after page of disgust and vituperation; promises to find me and kill me; derision for the stupid, baldly derivative nature of the hoax, if it was a hoax; a listing of the URL's IP number and physical location, along with information that both had been forwarded to the FBI.

The postings were coming faster and faster. There was a new one there each time I refreshed the page. It was a disaster, and I wanted it to stop, to never have happened. But by now it was one in the morning in California, and there was no way I could reach Knowles or his administrator, if he even had one, in Austin, where it was three in the morning. I didn't have a number for them, and there wasn't one on the site. I wrote an e-mail to the general mailbox asking for the "quotations" and forum to please be taken down immediately, and left a voice mail with the ghostwriter asking him to call me back the moment he received it. I set my alarm for six so I could keep trying to stop the fiasco as soon as anyone might be taking calls in Texas and tried to go to sleep.

From a position of pure self-loathing, that night was perhaps the worst of my life. Twice I drifted off and woke in our freezing bedroom so wet with sweat that I had to change my shirt and shorts before climbing back into the puddle of sheets. Both times I dreamed that I was coming to murder Heather and myself. I was mute and silhouetted, climbing in a window to cross the room and kill us both in our bed.

We held up our hands and begged and wept, but I would not listen, and I made no sound behind my mask.

Early the next day the ghostwriter called me back and said that Knowles was in Chicago taping with Roger Ebert—Gene Siskel had died fairly recently, and Ebert was taping with various guest critics. The ghostwriter said Knowles was unreachable, but he gave me the e-mail address of a person called Father Geek, Knowles's webmaster. When I reached Father Geek, he would make no changes to the site without a directive from Knowles, and he didn't want to give me Knowles's cell number. But finally I got him to give it to me, and I reached Knowles in a car as he was leaving his taping. He said in his weird high voice that he'd have the article and forum removed. Later in the day I checked, and they were gone.

Nothing bad had actually happened, and the death threats on the forum were only grumpy typing, but my imagination was opened to what it would really be like to have faceless people want to kill me. Worst of all would be if some nut latched on to what I had done and decided he had to mutilate and murder Heather, in a gruesome reenactment of my project. An incredibly remote possibility, but these things happened. My nightmares haunted me, the masked figure at the foot of the bed.

Even if I wasn't responsible in the abstract or before the law, what if a copycat killing actually happened? What if just one kid killed another kid and videotaped it, exactly as I had done? How would I feel then? Justified? Vindicated? Like I had been right? Sure. And then I'd have to blow my head off. There would be no coming back from something like that. Casting about for reassurance that legally, at least, I couldn't be held responsible in such an event, I placed a call to First Amendment. I was secretly hoping that he would either forbid me to do the broadcast in order to protect the investors—Matt and Next Generation were clients at the same firm—or reiterate his assurance that my position was legally unassailable and that that assurance would help me reconstruct my flimsy moral framework that now was flying to pieces.

Neither of those two things happened. First Amendment said he'd been meaning to get in touch with me—had I seen the news about the kid in Florida? Yes, I had seen it. Well, that didn't look good, did it? No, I agreed, it didn't. But wait a minute—he was the lawyer. Did it not look good? Was that what he was saying? He wasn't saying that, precisely. He was just saying that he wasn't as sure as he had been that the actions I proposed would qualify as protected speech. Things were getting kind of weird. People were nervous about Y2K and terrorism and everything. I said I knew that. That was the idea—remember? Sure, he remembered, he was just saying he wasn't as confident as he had been about the speech protection. What about his research? Well, actually, he hadn't had time to do the research. But he was going to get right on it after the new year. After what? Yeah, sorry about that. Going skiing, had this trip planned for a while, the family. Back in January, though.

After that conversation I wanted nothing more than to crawl into a hole and pretend the last few months simply had not happened. I didn't want to call Barney, mainly because I thought he was still pissed about me trying to register his firm's address as that of the LLC, and I didn't want to call my attorney and put him in the awkward position of helping me make a moral decision. That wasn't his job, helping me with moral decisions, but at this point, that was the kind of decision I faced.

Rosenberg helped me make it—by accident, but still, he helped. True to his word, he was already at work on the sales end of things, and he had set up a meeting at one of the big agencies. We drove to Beverly Hills and met with two guys in sharp suits at one of those endless tables they put in their conference rooms. It was late afternoon, pale winter light slanting in sideways. I glumly pitched the project. The agents looked at each other and nodded. If it were half as scary as *Blair Witch,* getting distribution would be a piece of cake. And if it had cost under a hundred grand, as I had said, the deal hardly mattered. No problem. Done.

Slumped in my chair with my eyeballs sunk four inches back into my head, I knew that now was when I was supposed to feel great. But all I could think about was hunting myself in my dreams, Heather mutilated and murdered, emotionally retarded children killing each other in basements. At the end of the meeting I brought up this last concern, the one about kids killing each other. One of the hotshots shrugged.

"Collateral damage," he said.

It wasn't his fault, and he wasn't a bad person for saying it. He was precisely right. That was a perfectly accurate assessment of how I would have to think of it if something bad did happen; and as soon as he said it, I knew I was pulling the broadcast. I didn't know whether I'd complete photography and editing and still try to sell the nasty thing as just a movie, which I supposed was still possible. But there was no way I was going to try to pass off *Human Number* as real. I wasn't going to cause any collateral damage.

It was a choice between two levels of disgust at myself, and I simply chose the level where I already knew I was comfortable. Failed novelist and now failed film director. It was pathetic, but I wouldn't have to commit suicide over it. I called Moodie to let him know. He reasonably went crazy at me. There was no way to pull the *Spin* article now, a full page with pictures. The January issue was already at the printer's. He told me he might get fired over it. I said I was sorry, and he hung up on me, and I couldn't blame him for not calling me back when I left more apologetic messages.

The money was a problem. I had spent fifty thousand dollars, and only a quarter of it was my own. I didn't have any other money. Quiddity had work on the horizon, but we hadn't worked for a couple of months, and my personal checking account was nearly empty for the first time in quite a while.

My investors weren't too happy to hear I was canceling the broadcast. The production account still held the $25,000 and change I had held back for marketing. Dan from Next Generation was the first to ask for his money back, so he got it. I wrote Next Generation a check for $25,000, leaving just enough to keep the account open, which meant I owed Ward and Matt $37,500. Technically, I didn't owe it to them, the LLC owed it to them, limitation of liability being the whole idea of forming a limited liability company—but I owed it to them. I told them that either I would finish the movie and try to sell it, or I would pay them back over time. They gave me a little shit, but neither one of them was really a dick about it, which made me feel even worse.

I slid into a deep depression for the holidays, watching them transpire dully at the other end of a long gray tunnel. Heather and I spent Christmas up in Marin with my mom. I had told her nothing about the project. The first she heard about it was when I asked if I could borrow $37,500, an idea she didn't find very interesting. The whole thing made her so sad and confused she couldn't even get mad at me. I had been doing *what?*

I made a conscious decision not to let self-loathing about the money pull me apart. If I let myself feel too sorry for myself, nobody was going to get paid back. The thing to do was just keep my shit together, table *Human Number* for the time being, and concentrate on Quiddity and CRAPtv. Alex and I had seen some good checks. Rosenberg was hustling. Internet business seemed, if anything, to be getting even more insane. I was sure an extra forty grand would tumble my way in the next year. These rationalizations didn't keep me from jolting up in a panic every morning and hating myself all day, but they kept me from falling into a real tailspin.

We all spent New Year's Eve at Tony Mindel's father and stepmother's house in Sausalito, a huge Tuscan-style villa looking out over the San Francisco Bay. I had a cold, and I sniffled and hacked through the party. The millennium expired around the world, a meridian sliding inexorably toward us, sweeping everything it crossed into the past. Watching the fireworks over the water, I half believed that each next starburst would bring the bright blank flash of oblivion, the thermonuclear white that would turn us all to ash. But as everyone knows, the evening passed without incident.

Five

1

No Christ came with a flaming sword, the Y2K bug declined to bite, and no missiles popped their tops in Ukraine or Montana. The most exciting news on the millennial front was Ahmed Ressam, the hapless asshole who took a ferry from British Columbia into Washington State with a trunk full of nitroglycerine and timers he hoped to use for blowing up LAX, but even that was anticlimactic. Ressam was caught on December 21, and by the new year he was old news.

The stock market took a deep breath and shot for the sky. The first months of 2000 were the top of the bubble for high tech in general but especially for Content. Investments in digital print had failed to return, but rather than pulling back from digital media altogether, venture capital firms and incubators were driving more money than ever into Internet entertainment.

In the six months since Spender had explained to Jason and me how the venture pyramid worked, we had done some studying up. At the new CRAPtv warehouse office, we read or heard each week of another online entertainment venture that was getting inundated with money. Most of these companies were in Los Angeles; those most in the news were DEN and Pop.com. New companies not precisely in the Content sector but with connections to it were the Artists Management Group, or AMG; Hollywood Stock Exchange, or HSX; and ArtistDirect. In the first weeks of 2000 Jason and I, often with Rosenberg as our shepherd, met with people at all these companies and at many others less ballyhooed. The object of these meetings was to get CRAPtv its million dollars, either directly or in the form of development or production deals that would make the prospect of direct investment in CRAPtv more appealing.

DEN, the Digital Entertainment Network, was rumored to have tens of millions of dollars in cash, and it was also rumored to have something even more impressive, because it was revenue, not financing: a sixty-million-dollar advertising commitment from Ford. We found these rumors both perplexing and encouraging. According to the press and its own Web site, DEN's stated mission was to cover the entire spectrum of youth-oriented entertainment online, with channels devoted to punk rock culture, hip-hop culture, extreme sports culture, and various other youth market segments. They had a show that seemed to be a teen soap for Latinos—it was hard to get a handle on what it was, sort of an East L.A. *90210*—and another targeted toward evangelical Christian youth.

What perplexed us was the central proposition, that each separate segment of a notoriously fractured youth market would simultaneously embrace a single online entertainment brand. It was the kind of idea that looked okay on a whiteboard but in practice just looked silly. MTV had accomplished hegemony over the entire youth market on television, but that was different. There really were no alternatives to MTV on television, and there wouldn't be. Viacom controlled a huge swath of the spectrum, and Viacom would protect that swath by swallowing or demolishing anything that began to resemble competition. Internet entertainment was going to be different. As a consumer you had actual choice, and you would naturally gravitate toward the authentic, the option specifically not available to you on television. We thought it was extremely unlikely that if you were a hard-core punk rocker (and I will not go off on a tangent here about the comedy inherent in the category "hard-core punk rocker" as a consuming subgroup in the year 2000), you were going to believe that the same online entertainment brand that spoke to evangelical Christian youth spoke to you.

But this analysis is far too labored—DEN just felt fake. Jason and I were no more expert in "youth marketing" than anyone else in our business environment, but that was sort of the point. We weren't doing youth marketing. We were having fun and inviting other people to have fun. Lots of the material on our site was terrible, just awful, our own material definitely included. But you could tell that the people making it had wanted to make it and that they had had a good time making it. The DEN shows were transparently the product of an artificial development and production process in which nobody was having any actual fun. Some forty-five-year-old guy with stock options and a facial peel was ordering his minions to go out there and make some authentic youth market entertainment for a precategorized splinter demo. The same thing that was perplexing was encouraging—next to DEN, CRAPtv looked almost like a sensible proposition.

Pop.com was a company that had been announced the previous spring, a joint venture between DreamWorks SKG and Imagine Entertainment, underwritten by Paul Allen's

Vulcan Ventures. Spielberg, Katzenberg, Geffen, Grazer, and Howard—an entertainment Dream Team backed by the Microsoft dollar. The Pop.com site was still just the single page from almost a year earlier that displayed the logo and original press release, but Pop.com was supposedly going to be for real, and Rosenberg had an entrée.

Before leaving to work at Dimension, he had worked under Brian Grazer, one of the heads of Imagine Entertainment. Rosenberg's exit from Imagine, as with most of his exits, had been complicated. His version of it was that he had been too good an executive, and Grazer hadn't liked having him headhunted away by Harvey Weinstein, but everything was basically okay.

Rosenberg harbored a resentment pertaining to *The Nutty Professor,* an Imagine movie, which he held up to us as an example of Hollywood's nefarious operations. He said the movie had been completely off the rails in development, and it would never have been made had not he, Rosenberg, superseded his authority as a junior executive and commissioned a test of Eddie Murphy in the fat suit. Had the test turned out poorly, Rosenberg would have been in trouble, because it was expensive. But it was so great that it put *The Nutty Professor* back on the rails it rolled down to the tune of $250 million. Rosenberg's contention was that the fat suit test he risked his job to commission was the watershed moment that had tipped Grazer toward a quarter of a billion dollars, and he, Rosenberg, had received neither credit nor reward. Which was part of the reason he had left. But he could still get us a meeting.

The first meeting we had at Pop.com, in late 1999, was with its entire staff: at that point, a skinny kid who just a few weeks earlier had been Grazer's assistant. We met with him at night in the break room at Imagine's offices in Beverly Hills. Grazer's new assistant wasn't trained yet, and this guy was still spending normal business hours getting the new guy up to speed. The break room meeting was followed by another meeting in early 2000, in the Imagine bungalow on the Universal lot.

That was only the second or third time I had been on a studio lot. The first time also had been to the Universal lot, to visit the set of Ted Demme's *Life*—another Brian Grazer project. My impression of visiting a studio lot was that it was just like it was in the movies: The guard at the gate had to have you on his list, and then the striped bar went up and you could drive in. The Universal lot especially met your expectations of what a studio lot should be, because while it was a working lot, it was also a theme park exhibit. You might see a posse of cowboys jingling past, or a bunch of art department guys blocking traffic with a huge foam Sphinx, and then from time to time a little train of linked golf carts would roll by larded down with tourists.

Grazer was a skinny dude who looked kind of like Keith Richards—he was wearing a black shirt and, you know, the hair—and I recall little of the meeting except that he was totally nice to us, and near the end of it his masseuse came in and gave him a shoulder rub at the table as we spoke. He defused the weirdness somewhat, or maybe increased it, by offering to have her massage all of us, too. We politely declined, and a couple of weeks later we were invited back to Universal, this time to meet with Ron Howard.

The Grinch was in production, and after parking we walked over to Whoville, a soundstage where it was winter forever: a curving snowscape of Seussian mounds and bridges, beneath which nestled the warmly lighted homes of all the Whos whose Christmas Jim Carrey was fucking up. Whos were everywhere, milling around the craft service table in tunics and scary prosthetic snouts. The crew was setting up a shot in which a basket containing a swaddled robot baby Who would be lowered from the sky into the middle of town. Jason and I clomped around the upper reaches of Whoville, kicking up puffs of fake snow.

After the shot went off, we met Ron Howard down where the Christmas tree would have been if Jim Carrey hadn't stolen it. He was incredibly gracious and welcoming, but there was something weirdly sad about the conversation. Gesturing at Whoville, he told us how he liked doing this okay, it was fun, but he would rather be making little short movies and eating peanut butter sandwiches, which we presumed he presumed were the staple food of scrappy young entrepreneurs. He may simply have been apologizing indirectly for the difference between his situation and ours. But he seemed to really mean it, and that was what was sad about it, witnessing that vague dissatisfaction could survive four decades of public success. He was the mayor of Whoville! He could do anything he wanted, but he honestly seemed to envy us.

He walked us out of the soundstage and over to an editing suite to show us some rushes of the movie. As we crossed the lot, one of the tourist safari trains passed by on its painted path. The tourists' heads swiveled in silent unison as they tracked the real Ron Howard, now wrinkled at the edges of his sad blue eyes and going bald beneath a baseball hat, in his natural habitat. He didn't break his stride or make any gesture of noticing them at all, either out of continued courtesy to us, or perhaps because he truly was accustomed, by a lifetime of captivity, to their gaze.

The Artists Management Group was Mike Ovitz's new company. One of the partners at our law firm had negotiated some of the terms of AMG's formation. His wife and brother had been talent managers at a company called Industry, and their alliance with Ovitz was the basis of the new company. They brought their marquee clients into the partnership, a move that developed into a Hollywood shit storm, which in combination with a rising squall between Ovitz and his former company, Creative Artists Agency, became a genuine Category 5 fecal hurricane. These massive weather events had not the slightest effect on little barnacles like Jason and me, but having shaken hands with a few of the people involved in the drama gave me a warm feeling of inclusion and importance as we went to meet at AMG.

The offices were in several floors of a building on Wilshire Boulevard that had just been remodeled in a rich cherry that gave you the feeling of being nestled in the most expensive cruise ship in the world. We met once with a talent manager and then later, in a rosy conference room, with a guy named Peter Levin, who was tasked with evaluating potential investments for the company. His back was to a subtle door that fit almost invisibly into the paneling around it. When I remarked on it, Levin nodded and said that the door opened onto a network of back corridors used only by Ovitz. I couldn't tell if he was kidding. Levin looked kind of like Harrison Ford, though he was younger, maybe in his midthirties. He gave an impression of intelligence and solidity that ran counter to the piratical douchebaggery that characterized our business environment. This may just have been the suit and tie, and Levin gave no indication that AMG might be interested in investing in CRAPtv, but based on that meeting I decided that in the unlikely event we were privileged to choose between investors, AMG would be our first choice.

Hollywood Stock Exchange was not a content company per se, in that its site featured neither video nor animation, but it was an Internet entertainment company, in that its product featured elements of both the Internet and entertainment. Rosenberg knew someone over there—he knew someone over everywhere—and we had a couple of fast conversations at cafés with one of the principals, a harried blond guy. Later on, his partner, the financial wizard who had dreamed up the HSX concept, came over to our warehouse, and we had another meeting.

The first iteration of the HSX product was an online game that was already up and running. When you registered at the Web site, you received an allotment of Hollywood Dollars, or H$, which you could invest in a digital fantasy market. The securities in the market, MovieStocks and StarBonds, were movies titles in production and famous actors and actresses. Securities in the HSX market went up and down according to player demand for them, just as real stocks and bonds went up and down according to market demand. I didn't play the game, but it was pretty popular for a while, at least in the entertainment industry, and the partner said they had already received some nasty calls from agents and executives concerned that fluctuations in H$ value might start affecting box office and talent contracts.

I didn't quite understand the coming iteration of HSX. He said that you would be able to use your H$ to purchase coupons provided by advertisers: movie tickets, vacations, what have you. That part I understood okay, but he went on to explain how what they were really doing was creating a whole new system of actual currency. I could see how your H$ account might have actual dollar value if H$ could be traded for the coupons. If you had H$200 and there was a prize valued at that that someone else wanted, maybe you could sell that other person your H$200 for just under $200. But the idea went well past that into a realm of financial abstraction that I am unable to describe accurately, because I didn't get it when he explained it. I don't think Jason got it, either. But we nodded along like we did. HSX had just received a big capital infusion and gained permission from the city of West Hollywood to put an electronic stock ticker for their exchange all around the roofline of their new building.

Rosenberg also knew Sky Dayton, one of the founders of EarthLink, and we had a meeting—not with Dayton himself, but with an underling—at Dayton's new incubator, eCompanies. Unfortunately for CRAPtv, eCompanies had made its Content play right before we came in: several million dollars invested in a company called Icebox. The Icebox principals were just setting up their new desks in the eCompanies offices. Having just been given a commitment for several million dollars to fund their idea, they were understandably giddy. While we were waiting to meet the eCompanies guy ourselves and hear the bad news that he had just given Icebox our money, Jason and I helped the Icebox guys download and install media players on their computers so they could watch video on the Internet. For a quick snapshot of exactly how insane this period of time was in Los Angeles, reread the previous sentence.

Icebox was going to strike deals with established TV writers for no money but lots of stock, let the writers do pretty much whatever they wanted, and produce the shows in Flash for online delivery. The idea was that everybody would make actual money when the shows were sold to television or the company was taken public. This actually sounded like a pretty good idea at the time—it was very similar to the CRAPtv plan, maybe better, because the talent was established.

We also took meetings up in the Bay Area. There was one at Excite in the South Bay, where they had a network operations center that looked like the War Room in *Dr. Strangelove,* and our friend Carlo set us up with a meeting at Morgan Stanley in San Francisco, with a guy who worked in the private-wealth management division, a banking group that helped extremely rich people select high-risk investments, the rubric under which CRAPtv squarely fell.

The Morgan Stanley guy was really nice and normal and displayed no indication of incipient mental collapse, but soon it would become clear that proximity to all that money had driven him around the bend. A few months later, he came down to Los Angeles and visited CRAPtv as part of a business development tour for the company he had left Morgan Stanley to join. That company was called DigiScents, and its mission was online smell delivery. He said they had broken smell down into primary components, sort of like a color wheel for the nose, and developed a smell-delivery apparatus that could be controlled over the Internet. The idea was that entertainment would have a "smell track" in the future, and DigiScents was going to own the market. He wanted to know if we had any properties that needed a smell track. We couldn't think of any, but we did try to hook him up with

Dian and his buddy Marcus, who were making a spoof short called *The Seventh Sense* in which Dian was a little kid who smelled dead people. He said that wasn't quite what they had in mind, but he'd keep in touch. That was the last we heard of him.

During this time that Rosenberg was hustling for us, I fell comprehensively under his spell. Jason worked mainly with outside talent; I schemed with Rosenberg, learning his version of how Hollywood worked and making adjustments to the Business Plan. Rosenberg got us into tons of other places and at levels we never could have gotten meetings on our own. We suddenly were players—if not Content princes ourselves, at least on familiar terms with those who at that moment were gracing the covers of financial and entertainment magazines. It was fun to listen to Rosenberg spin his nonsense about us. He spun the fact that we had started in a shitty apartment, and had only recently moved our business into a shitty warehouse, into an asset. It was proof of authenticity. He had a wonderful way of moving the focus off himself and onto us, much like Gerhard's deferral to Jane or to me and Frankel in our branding services sales meetings. Rosenberg's line was that he was just the person who had *found* us. These crazy guys! These scrappy entrepreneurs! He presented us as the real thing in a world of bullshit.

That was great, but we had some immediate problems. Sundance 2000 was going to be out of control. Pretty much every Internet entertainment company we knew of wanted to have a presence there. We felt we had been first movers in glomming on to the Sundance media boondoggle as the time and place to get exposure for Internet entertainment, and exposure was exactly what CRAPtv needed right now to convince investors that we were a legitimate undertaking. There was nothing like a sheaf of press clips to convince people you were for real. But we didn't have the cash on hand to make Lapdance happen again, and to make matters worse, our old venue was no longer available. Sundance and Slamdance had both taken note of the Silver Mine, and it was already reserved for the entire week.

The price of all the venues in town had skyrocketed with demand. This year it was going to cost us $50,000 at a minimum to put on a little party in Park City. Luckily, a few of the other Content companies were early enough in their progress that they hadn't managed to pull their own events together yet. Our events were much more Jason's babies than mine, and he was able to leverage our experience up there into enough sponsorship to make Lapdance happen. Pop.com got it started with a $25,000 commitment, and after that we were good to go. A science fiction portal called Galaxy Online came in with $10,000, and the rest was cobbled together in $5,000 and $2,000 increments. We gave Lapdance 2000 a goofy futuristic theme. Heather posed for the poster with a bulbous ray gun in addition to the pink wig and hot pants.

This year we held our event in the central venue on Main Street, a theater managed by a local real estate cabal and rented in the daytimes to Entertaindom, the online division of Warner Brothers. I arrived in Park City too late to be briefed on all the intricacies of commitment, allegiance, collusion, and betrayal between underground festivals, Internet companies, and other sketchy affiliation groups, but essentially the problem this year was that the real estate cabal had oversold its venue. We were paying for the venue and all the entertainment, but the asshole who ran Entertaindom was claiming exclusive rights to footage of the performances.

By the time I got up there Jason was exhausted, because while his days were spent dealing with the venue fiasco, he still had to promote Lapdance and network at night, which meant that by Thursday he was winding down into recuperative mode from a five-day bender. Brody took over dealing with the venue stuff and also worked out the housing, three deluxe condos a local real estate agency was foolish enough to let us rent for a few days. My only duty was to oversee the sham Lapdance stripper auditions that Jason had arranged for E! to tape for its *Wild On* series. Jason had already hired the dancers. The auditions were just for the E! taping. Dave Goodman and some bozo who ran one of the other underground festivals—I can't recall his name; he was the obnoxious younger brother in *Sixteen Candles*—joined me on the fake judging panel as the girls "tried out" for the opportunity to be go-go dancers at Lapdance. The girls were good sports about it, since it was going to be on TV. (A few seconds of that footage, along with a clip of Jason sweaty and babbling out of his head on acid inside the Lapdance 2000 venue, made it into E!'s endlessly rerun *Wild On Sundance*. A few months later, my father called to tell me his in-laws had called him to express outrage that I was the proprietor of a "nudist night club" in Los Angeles. If only.)

To my delight, on the night of the event, the girls brought along their boyfriends, a bunch of muscled dong-dancers who stripped down to G-strings and cowboy hats and bummed everybody out. That was good, but somebody ginned up a bunch of fake wristbands, so there was a riot in the street, and many of our own guests never made it into the theater. After that the party moved back to our condos, which were destroyed, and the next morning Jolon broke his collarbone on his first run snowboarding with Matt. But minor disasters aside, Lapdance 2000 went pretty well. We had a good time and got some new press. We managed to lose five thousand dollars, but for us that wasn't that bad.

Rosenberg had a rough time up there, though. Before coming to Utah he had made a big move in the market on margin. He took a few turns in the snow on his ruined knees each morning, but he spent most of his time in Park City watching money evaporate like steam from the keyboard of his laptop. He had gone short on a stock that he knew for a fact was a total piece of shit, and it just wouldn't stop going up.

2

The new CRAPtv offices in Mar Vista, the ones made possible by our production deal with WireBreak, consisted of two light industrial units of two thousand square feet each. With the help of friends we cut new doorways between the units, built a conference room in the eastern unit, which would become the offices, and turned the western unit into a stage. Dave Goodman came over and made a lighting grid to hang from the ceiling, complete with floodlights from Home Depot that could be angled and gelled for different setups. The result wasn't quite a professional soundstage—the roll-up door rattled in the wind, and you could hear planes overhead and trucks when they idled outside—but it was sufficient to our needs. Kung Fu Design, which now was Jolon, Martha, Push, a couple of other hackers, and a girl recruited from the CRAPtv bulletin board, networked the building and moved into the back area, where the eastern unit hooked around behind the western one.

As I had during the Quiddity office build, I took great pleasure in watching the transformation of empty rooms into a place of work. For Jason, having an office was even more exciting. Until now he had been working from the Mar Vista apartment a few blocks away, which by now was a wreck. He annexed the end of the eastern unit closest to the roll-up door and began the slow process of furnishing it to his taste: purple shag carpet, beanbag chair, tangled computer equipment, the VHS hoard, stickers and rave and rock flyers papering the walls. I made myself an uptight cubicle in the opposite corner.

For each episode of *Backdoor Hollywood,* our WireBreak movie review show, Jason and I attended two press screenings, rented a movie or video game, and composed arguments about the merits and shortcomings of each into a script that was then rolled back to us for camera on teleprompters. We knew each other's prejudices well enough that it wasn't necessary for both of us to see every movie, so for those we knew we would hate, just one of us would go.

We had approached Dian to reprise the role of bitchy bartender, but he called SAG to ask them if he should take a non-union job, and naturally they said he shouldn't, even though he was broke and unemployed, so he declined. That was too bad, but our friend Dennis Gubbins, a comic and actor from up home in Marin, took the gig. Dennis turned the bartender into a bitchy Irish pirate (also named Steve, though), by attaching a stuffed parrot from the set to his shoulder, naming it Petey, and talking to it in an Irish accent. We used bananas for our rating system, as in, "I give *Deep Rising* five bananas."

Each show ended in a slapstick fight. After Jason broke our ukulele over my head, we stuck to mashing bananas.

Work on the show took up about 20 percent of our time each week. I continued to plot with Rosenberg about financing, and Jason conducted meetings with a steady stream of freaks and filmmakers, building the development pool for our company. First among the freaks and filmmakers to make that warehouse their second home was Timmy the Woodsman.

It is time now to turn my attention to that tragic clown, whom we last saw ordering free fast food in a homemade diaper. The Woodsman was not a large person, but his presence was tremendous, both in the literal sense of occupying a large volume of space with noise and chaos and in the indefinable Hollywood sense. He had that star quality that has its corollary on the battlefield, in sports, and even in comedy rooms, where it is called the goo. Like him or not, and as many as liked him hated him, it was undeniable that the Woodsman had the goo. He was a classic masculine beauty—broad forehead, piercing blue eyes, strong jaw gold with stubble, a Paul Newman, Brad Pitt kind of beauty, with that confidence and ready smile that could flit in an instant to betray a scarred vulnerability. The Woodsman's body was also beautiful in its slim, defined economy. He had a dancer's frame on which any clothing seemed to hang correctly, even the thrift store rags he rocked—loud polyester shirts open to the belly, lime green trousers tight at the hips, white patent leather loafers.

Not long before Jason had first met the Woodsman, the Woodsman had come to Los Angeles in a van, but the van had been impounded, and he was homeless. Since that Burning Man trip he had spent most of his nights at Jason and Ward's, and now on most days he came to our office to perform his work.

Over my objections the Woodsman was allowed to cobble together a cubicle from broken office furniture, and from this ramshackle bivouac he launched the first wave of his assault on Hollywood. The nature of this assault was as bewildering to me as it must have been to the Woodman's prospective business partners. Part sales pitch and part performance art, part audition and part rigorous personal interview, the Woodsman's ongoing conversation with Hollywood ranged in tone and content from throaty, whispered dirty talk to demands for and promises of tremendous sums of imaginary money. He set meetings he did not attend and attended meetings he did not set, making his way across town to the lobbies of entertainment companies by foot, bicycle, public transportation, and hitched ride.

The Woodsman made his calls and took his meetings mainly as Timmy Woodsman, using his title as a surname. The origin of his title, the Woodsman, was obscure; he said it was because he was "from the woods," but he was not. He was from Fremont, California, a blue-collar suburb just south of Oakland, forty miles and a world away from where we had grown up in Marin. The word *woodsman* was a term of art in the porn industry, used to describe a male performer capable of regular and sustainable erections, and Timmy did have a semiboner a lot of the time, with which he made fairly free, running around the office in his tight green pants or silky running shorts.

Timmy Woodsman was not his only alias. He had a pile of handsome headshots stapled to wildly fraudulent résumés that named him as Snowball T. Axeworthy. I never saw him make much use of these; they mixed and drifted with all the other garbage that was so quickly piling in our warehouse, and were mainly just good for a laugh whenever you came across one. The only formal acting job I knew he had booked was as an extra in *O Brother, Where Art Thou?*

Timmy was one of the dancing Klansmen. The choreographer taught all the extras how they were supposed to dance, and then they were put in their Klan uniforms. Once under his hood, Timmy convinced all the extras in his vicinity that they weren't supposed to dance like *that,* they were supposed to dance like *this,* and as a result, Klansmen kept colliding with one another. Because of the hoods, and because Timmy kept moving from group to group, it took two whole nights of botched shots to isolate Snowball T. Axeworthy and have him escorted from the set.

The reason Timmy didn't use his real last name, which I did eventually learn, was the warrants. The warrants, I was given to understand by Jason when I expressed concern about housing a fugitive in our place of business, weren't about anything too serious—mainly to do with the impounded van. And Timmy obviously wasn't too concerned about them, because he already had a civil proceeding of his own in progress, a slip-and-fall grievance against a grocery store. He said that was the first thing you wanted to do when you moved to a new town: Get yourself to a grocery store, throw some plums on the ground, and take some pratfalls. He had a badly healed broken back from falling drunk off a mausoleum a ways back, so his X-rays looked pretty fucked up.

Straightening out the warrants would have cost the Woodsman a lot of money, so the Woodsman perforce was postponing his accounting. In any case, he had already made a down payment on his debt to society. In his early twenties, he had done nine months in state prison on drug and weapons charges. He spoke of it rarely and obliquely, instead telling a comic story of his apprehension.

At the time, he was a crackhead in Oakland, selling rock with a crew of gangsters on blocks that had rundown houses with empty swimming pools behind them, where they could hide when police cars drove by. Timmy and four large gangster associates had ventured out to sell a couple of pounds of weed to some kids who were supposed to meet them in the parking lot of the Stonestown mall in San Francisco. Timmy and the gangsters were in a broken-down Hyundai, but even the crappiness of the Hyundai did not seem to account for how slowly it moved down the highway, the burning smell, or the trail of black smoke. They kept stopping and getting out to see what was the matter, but then the smoke would blow away so they couldn't figure out where it was coming from, and then they'd get back on the road, and it would happen again. It was only when they were almost at the mall that they figured out that their combined weight was too much for the suspension. The tires were rubbing in the wheel wells, and they were burning up. When this clown car packed with thugs groaned to a smoky stop at the mall, police cruisers surrounded it immediately. Timmy and his associates had been set up; they barely made it to their own arrest. There were drugs in the car and illegal guns in the trunk, and everybody went to jail.

However much of a pain in the ass Timmy was to have banging around the office, I hoped things would work out okay for him. But Timmy quickly becoming a serious pain in the ass. Noise and mess and craziness aside—he was always bringing in new people who were almost as crazy as he was (and sometimes crazier, as in the case of Gary, a grouchy homeless guy who lived in the marsh behind our warehouse)—the Woodsman was making business difficult on a larger scale.

In addition to the business cards we had printed up for ourselves, we had printed a run of blank ones emblazoned with the CRAPtv logo, address, and main phone number but no name or title. This practice was something I had witnessed in my New Economy travels with Quiddity. For a start-up the practice made plenty of sense. New partners or employees could use the blank cards and present them with their names penned in by hand. With these cards you could also informally deputize hustlers who thought they might be able to connect you to other hustlers. Provided the logo and the rest looked professional, such hand-lettered cards actually implied success rather than sketchiness—your company was growing too fast to keep up with such mundane stuff as printing new cards every time it brought on someone new.

The Woodsman got his hands on a stack of these blank cards and went apeshit. In no time half the incoming calls at CRAPtv were for Timmy Woodsman, the producer. Half of these calls were from people even more out to lunch than Timmy was himself, and that was no big deal except that it tied up the phones. But just as often and more problematic, the calls were official Hollywood calls from people with whom we might at some point want to do business. I couldn't deal with the Woodsman's calls, so I just quit answering the main line, and the Woodsman appointed himself our receptionist. Half the calls were for him, anyway, so he got those, but now we weren't getting our calls. The Woodsman's message-taking protocols left something to be desired. In summation, our phone situation was in disarray.

He was also using the stage side of the warehouse as the rehearsal space for something he called "Hot Hot Dancers," which so far as I could tell was him and a handful of deranged belly dancers getting incredibly wasted and developing improvisational routines on the standing *Backdoor Hollywood* set, which as a result was falling to pieces. The rattan stapled to the bar was peeling away, our pineapple lamp was smashed, the walls had some kind of sticky stuff splashed on them, and Petey the parrot was losing feathers at an alarming rate.

I couldn't wait for the Woodsman to be banned from the office. But banishment required consensus, which in our company meant everyone had to be in total agreement—I was our CEO in title, but that didn't mean anybody ever listened to me. Jason naturally was the holdout, but even his patience eventually was exhausted, and we came together and told the Woodsman the deal. He was banished. Not forever. And not because we didn't love him, because we did. But if he had shows—if he was a producer, as he said he was—then the onus was now on him to come up with something real. Go out there and make a show. Until then, we were all still friends, and Ward and Jason even said he could keep staying at their place, but he couldn't hang out at the office all day.

Timmy took it well, and I was certain this conversation marked the end of my professional relationship with the Woodsman. There was no way this lunatic could muster the resources necessary to put together even the sketchiest sketch of a one-page treatment.

My mother's birthday came in March, and to celebrate, Heather and I took her to Santa Barbara. The three of us spent the weekend at a hotel up on the hill over town, a pretty old place with bungalows scattered around the garden. Heather and I stayed in one of them, and my mother slept in a room on the far side of the garden, down a winding path and past a pool filled with lily pads. An elaborate wedding was in progress at the hotel throughout the weekend, and I woke from naps to see snatches of its advance: boys with pink cheeks and their hair gelled up greeting arrivals in the parking lot, pastel bridesmaids sneaking smokes in a courtyard, the bride bustling by in her train.

It was not unusual for me to spend most of a weekend away from Los Angeles sleeping facedown and sweating into hotel linens. I was still rebounding from the depression of my failure with *Human Number,* and on top of that I was legitimately exhausted from work. At the height of the hustle to secure investment for CRAPtv, Frankel and I were getting slammed with Quiddity engagements.

My mother also was exhausted and slept for much of the weekend, which was as uncharacteristic for her as it was normal for me. Waking hours in Santa Barbara were, I think for both of us, dreamy in the extreme. I recall moments of bright, childish sensation and the blank buzz of empty air, sitting on whitewashed boulders set into the curving lawn, looking out over the sleepy city to where the horizon smudged the sea and sky. My mother, always fair, was paler than I remembered her. The skin on the back of her hands was transparent, bones and blue veins revealed. Was she simply getting older? We all were, sliding daily closer to oblivion. But her pallor and lassitude seemed somehow more alarming than that incremental process. She was only fifty-six. Maybe she had a cold or hadn't recovered from my Christmas revelations. Or maybe there was nothing wrong at all, and the cottony membrane of unreality that seemed to shroud the weekend was over my eyes only. I tried not to think about dying as we hugged good-bye at the airport.

In any case, I was immediately immersed again in work. Frankel and I were working on the Fleetwood Owen account, and CRAPtv investment prospects were aligning. Rosenberg and I spoke practically hourly, he at home on speakerphone and I yammering loudly from wherever I was on my cell, about angel rounds and valuations—mainly valuations, because CRAPtv's valuation lay at the heart of most of these discussions. There were by now several parties interested in maybe giving us money, but they wanted to do so on terms I thought valued us too meagerly—as though we were just some guys with an idea, not a functioning enterprise that was already sustaining itself on revenues. One million dollars was sort of a standard valuation for a Content concept. In my humble opinion, we were past that and into the $5 million valuation range appropriate to a small but profitable Content company. One day Rosenberg reached me while I was taking a crap at World Wraps on Melrose. Heather and Brody were out in the main part of the restaurant, which was crowded with noontime wrap eaters. The connection wasn't great, so I felt like I had to yell.

"No! A million dollars isn't enough! Can you hear me? I'm taking a crap at World Wraps! I SAID A MILLION DOLLARS ISN'T ENOUGH!"

After that, the call was dropped, so I finished up and went back out into the restaurant. Everyone in the place looked at me in disgust. Heather and Brody shook their heads. For one brief moment, I was aware that I was turning into the kind of person whose ass I would normally want to kick just on principle.

Marc Geiger was a former record executive who had started Lollapalooza with Perry Ferrell. His new company was Artist-Direct. Lollapalooza had had its problems, but ArtistDirect was going to change the face of the music business. What Geiger had already accomplished was pretty impressive: He had brought four of the five major labels together and talked them all into investing in ArtistDirect simultaneously. In January ArtistDirect had taken $97.5 million in equity financing from Yahoo! and every label but Bertelsmann-owned BMG. (BMG was hedging its bets in the opposite direction, putting money into Napster—buying a huge stake in what it perceived to be the primary threat to its own financial health.) Even to little, unsophisticated me, it looked like the four of the five majors were colluding to deliver consumers a viable, revenue-generating alternative to file sharing. Geiger had positioned his company to be the vehicle for that collusion and at the same time guaranteed Internet-wide reach through Yahoo!

Right when Geiger was in the middle of the ramp-up to his own IPO, Rosenberg brought him to meet with us at the CRAPtv warehouse. Geiger talked over our plan with us and said that after his decks cleared in a couple of weeks—meaning after the ArtistDirect IPO, when his stock would suddenly be worth a gazillion dollars—he'd be happy to put $250,000 of his money into CRAPtv as part of a $1 million first round, at a $5 million valuation.

This was a huge moment for us. Many of the potential investors with whom I had spoken in the past few months had said to be in touch when we had the first piece in place. Securing the keystone investor for the first round was the hardest part. We could hardly believe our good luck. And then, before ArtistDirect even went public—this would have been in the last week of March 2000—Hollywood Stock Exchange, the company that made a fantasy market in MovieStocks and StarBonds, tendered us an offer of $2.5 million for a controlling 51 percent stake in CRAPtv.

Even the reader without much talent at arithmetic will calculate that this offer valued the circus sideshow of a company Jason and I had built, with $25,000 from Tony Mindel and something like that from me, at a meaningless shade under the $5 million valuation I wanted. There were important caveats to the HSX offer, though. First, the offer was not $2.5 million in cash but $2.5 million in Hollywood Stock Exchange stock. (Not H$—actual HSX stock.) HSX was still privately held, so our $2.5 million wouldn't be liquid until several months after HSX went public or was bought. Naturally, we would have preferred a cash offer; nevertheless, shares in HSX were much more real than shares in CRAPtv, as HSX stock was backed by partnerships and a large cash reserve.

We also would have preferred that the offer were for a 49 percent stake in CRAPtv rather than a 51 percent stake, so that we could maintain control of our company's future. On the other hand, the fact that the offer was in HSX stock meant that our payment might soon be worth much more than $2.5 million. Presumably, HSX planned for their stock to increase in value. Considering how inexperienced we were with real business, might something not be gained by handing that part over to people who actually understood it? We could just do the fun stuff.

The other upside of the offer was that HSX would assume our overhead after any transaction. This in itself was extremely appealing, for each month at CRAPtv was a new adventure in creative budgeting. Forget about the $2.5 million in whatever form—if we took the offer, our rent would be covered, and we'd be paid actual salaries for continuing to run CRAPtv. Those salaries would probably be around $60,000 a year, which to us was plenty. None of us was in a rush to buy a big house or fancy car. We just wanted our company to be a success.

We talked the HSX offer over with Rosenberg and even managed to get Geiger on the phone. Geiger was great about it and told us to do whatever we thought was right—no hard feelings if we wanted to take the offer. But if we didn't, and provided nothing went catastrophically wrong for him in the next two weeks, we had his support in growing our company quickly and also keeping control of it.

We took a deep breath and politely declined the HSX offer. I think our declining it surprised the shit out of them. While their offer to roll us up wasn't pure charity—they must have seen some value in CRAPtv or at least the potential for value to be created there—we were, after all, just a handful of morons in a dirty warehouse. They wished us the best.

It may seem strange that I didn't know the exact day of the ArtistDirect IPO before it occurred. Once the date was set, it was public information. But I didn't own or follow any stocks. I was able to make sense of the written part of the business section when I flipped through a newspaper at lunchtime, but I never looked at all the little symbols. I knew only that the IPO was coming up and that afterward the first quarter million of capital would be available to us.

Over the next few days I put together the list of people who had said they might be interested in investing in CRAPtv after we secured the first piece of financing. First among these was Peter Levin at AMG, who, even though he hadn't quite said that he was interested, had made such a strong impression on me.

On the afternoon of March 29, 2000, I placed a call to Levin's office. His assistant put me through immediately, and Levin asked me what was up. I was really nervous, but I tried to sound calm and professional as I brought him up to date. A week earlier we had received an offer of $2.5 million in stock for 51 percent of CRAPtv but declined it in order to maintain control of the company. We now had $250,000 in capital committed by Marc Geiger as part of a first round, which would be available to us as soon as ArtistDirect had its IPO. We were planning to use the earlier offer as a benchmark for valuation. Basically, we were looking to sell 20 percent of the company for $1 million. Did AMG remain interested in pursuing this line of discussion?

There was a long silence on the other end of the phone. Then Peter Levin told me that ArtistDirect had gone public that morning. I flushed on my end of the phone. I should have checked to see when it was happening. But I tried to cover and said that was awesome news. There was another silence. This one was really long. Then Levin told me in a weird voice that it had been the worst IPO he had seen all year. Now I was the silent one. I didn't even know what that meant. How could an IPO be bad? I thought an IPO was supposed to be good. Sensing the conversation was over, I awkwardly got off the phone.

In the course of the next couple of days I learned what it meant to have a bad IPO. A bad IPO was when you offered your stock to the public at a price, and the public decided it wasn't worth that price. Let's say you offered it at $10 a share. That didn't mean people had to pay that much for it. If nobody wanted it at $10, the price went down until people did want it, to $9, $8, $5—whatever. The market determined the price; that was what made it a market. For the last five years the demand for new stocks had almost always exceeded supply, so that a stock offered at $10 might easily be trading at $20 by the end of the day, which resulted in a doubling of the wealth of the people who had owned it at $10. It hadn't even occurred to me that the inverse was equally possible, but that was precisely what had happened with ArtistDirect.

Shares of the company had gone on the market at $12 and lost 22 percent of their value on the same day, trading down to $9.41. To compound the problem, the company had made an obscure reporting error with regard to options or shares it had granted talent, and now it might have to pay $30 million to buy those back. That wouldn't kill the company—they still had tons of cash on hand from the last private equity round—but it was pretty bad news.

The ArtistDirect IPO marked the end of the Content bubble and in fact the end of the tech bubble in general. We were way too dumb to know that, though. It took us months to get the picture. We just thought it was another dip in the road for CRAPtv and continued, like cartoon lemmings, to run long after our feet had passed the edge of the cliff.

3

Within two weeks, WireBreak put *Backdoor Hollywood* on indefinite hiatus, i.e., cancelled it. We had made only seventeen episodes of the twenty-six-episode order, but a point in the deal negotiated by our attorney, bless his heart, stipulated that even in the event WireBreak stopped production, as they just had, they would remain liable for payment of the CRAPtv production fee for each episode on the previously agreed-upon schedule. Our overall cash flow declined, but in addition to our production fee, we continued to bill them a nominal amount for storage of the set they technically owned and didn't want to have to pay for building again if production resumed, so things were not nearly as bad for us right then as they might have been.

But the cancellation of production on *Backdoor Hollywood* awakened us to the necessity of having more than one source of revenue. We were such dummies that we didn't understand that every single Content company that was operating on invested rather than earned money was now in a position similar to WireBreak's. We made calls and were warmly welcomed in to pitch. All over town companies were bleeding out, but every CEO running one of those companies knew that if he showed the slightest sign his company was in trouble, the next, now-delayed round of financing might recede far into the future, which was exactly what he couldn't afford. Things were fine!

As a result of the need to maintain appearances, Content companies weren't stopping renovation on twenty-thousand-foot warehouses they were leasing for five dollars per foot per month—and those were the practical companies, the companies that hadn't already committed to a five-year lease on a tensioned- glass ziggurat. Jason and I took a pitch meeting at Icebox, the company whose management we had met at eCompanies and helped install media players on their computers. In the intervening months, Icebox had taken $60 million in venture financing and moved into a spectacular facility in Culver City. Their headquarters was populated with pierced and dyed Flash animators so perfectly matched to the Herman Miller furniture and fun-filled paint scheme that it appeared the entire staff had been ordered wholesale from a compatible New Media HR catalog.

Jason and I pitched to a heavy, bearded guy who was that crucial half-generation older than we were that meant he actually had something at stake in all this nonsense. When we were done outlining a handful of ideas for animated shows for him, he nodded and asked us what deals we had with television companies, to which we replied, none. He shook his head. Sorry, Icebox was buying only from people who already had television deals. We groaned and left grumpy. In the car on the way back, we thought maybe that was his way of letting us down easy. Maybe our ideas sucked. But we had been given to understand while setting up the meeting that now that Icebox was up and running, they had moved past their original strategy of working only with name writers and now were really looking to make alternative content.

It was months before I realized how badly the Icebox executives must have been freaking out. No matter what Jason and I were peddling that day, and no matter what their stated mission, we weren't going to be selling anything to them unless the deal would generate a press release that could move them closer to more capital. (Icebox eventually dealt itself a pretty much fatal blow with one such press release. The company thought they had maybe sold a show to Fox, and they put out a press release that said so. Fox responded in the press that there was no deal, that essentially the Icebox press release had been a fabrication, and Icebox started handing out pink slips.)

But Pop.com was chugging up to speed. The scale of the undertaking meant it had taken a while to build steam, but from where we bobbed in our little CRAPtv coracle it still looked like Pop.com was going to swamp everything in its wake. Jason and I drove out to Glendale to pitch the new executives who had replaced Grazer's former assistant. The Pop.com facility was the size of an aircraft hangar. At the time of our first meeting there, in the spring of 2000, the building already housed a hundred employees, and it was so big inside that it still felt empty.

Making a deal with Pop.com took several weeks of back-and-forth between their attorneys and ours, but in the end the deal was a fantastic one for CRAPtv—so good, in fact, that we could hardly believe it. Over a period of four months we were to pitch Pop.com forty shows, ten per month, and for providing this service we would receive $50,000 in cash plus 100,000 shares of the privately held Pop.com. Wary after witnessing the implosion of ArtistDirect, I asked a friend in venture capital how to value the 100,000 shares. He advised that we not value them at all but consider only the cash being offered. Was it worth it to pitch forty shows for $50,000? Sure it was. We were accustomed to pitching for free, and we were about to run out of money. Okay, so take the cash, and then look at the shares as a windfall that might occur at some unspecified time in the future.

He said there was no way to guess at what value the shares might be convertible, but if anyone had a good chance of making a go of Content, it was Pop.com. DreamWorks and Imagine had access to television and big-screen distribution, and they also had access to the effectively unlimited cash supply of Vulcan Ventures. Ten dollars a share was a nice middling value at which shares might be offered to the public, so that meant, on top of the $50,000, a potential windfall to CRAPtv of something more or less than $1 million. This was just to *pitch*. It was a first-look deal, meaning we had to pitch to Pop.com before we pitched to anyone else, but we were happy to do that. Pop.com had a mere two weeks after each ten-show pitch meeting to decide whether they were buying any of the shows we had pitched and, if they were, to enter into reasonable negotiations to produce those shows. After that two-week period, complete ownership of the pitched shows reverted to CRAPtv, and we could try to sell them wherever we wanted.

The $50,000 would easily cover our overhead for the entire four months of the deal. If Pop.com picked up even one of our shows for production, we'd be in great shape, with cash flow at least similar to that of the WireBreak deal to carry us into the foreseeable future. If Pop.com went public, we'd suddenly, after a waiting period, have an absolute shit-load of cash—and all without having to give up any of our company. So, just as the WireBreak money was petering out, it looked as though we had arranged for another four months, twice as long if we were careful, of overhead and development for CRAPtv. High five.

With this deal closing, our festival events and Jason's endless stream of meetings with nut-job comics, animators, puppeteers, filmmakers, and performance artists suddenly made perfect retroactive sense. We could come up with a lot of pitches on our own, but forty distinct short-format pitches complete with talent, presentation art, and some kind of one-page treatment would stretch even our ability to mint baloney. We called everybody in for another round of meetings and started putting the materials that already existed into some semblance of order. Rosenberg continued to look for financing, and I continued to revise the Business Plan, but now we were wondering if we were going to need either one. We might be able to scale CRAPtv on revenues alone.

The terms of the Woodsman's banishment were easing. He really didn't have anywhere else to go. Since we knew he would colonize any space available, his office hut had been dismantled and replaced with a table so tiny it could hold nothing but the fax machine on top of it. The fax machine did have a phone cradle the Woodsman used, but the machine was on a second line and capable of storing received faxes in memory, so his use of it for shady calls wasn't much of an imposition.

He claimed to be in production on a show now, which he would present to us when it was finished. The Woodsman did not speak of pilots, reels, sketches, presentations, or series. Everything was a "show," and he was such a crazy fucker that I had no idea what he meant by the term. The show was being shot and edited by a character the Woodsman had found somewhere in his wanderings, a kid named Danny Diamond, who looked like a Bruce Weber boy with the face of a naughty hawk. Danny didn't say much at first, just lurked around with his hands in his pockets, so it was hard to form much of an impression. I figured he was a film school chump the Woodsman had hustled into following him around with a camera.

In due course the Woodsman delivered what I thought he would never in a million years be able to deliver: a videotape that showcased his inimitable entertainment offering to powerful effect. While not a conventional pilot, sales presentation, actor's reel, music video, or sketch packet, the tape combined elements of each. It was a show—the Woodsman show. It was rough and handheld but nicely shot, and it was cut quickly and elegantly to music. And it was super funny. There is no way to convey in prose precisely what was so funny about it. I am tempted to employ a fictional elision and simply say that it was The Funniest Tape in the Whole Wide World and leave it at that. But it wasn't The Funniest Tape in the Whole Wide World; it was just a really funny tape.

It opened on the Sunset Strip at night, with the Woodsman dancing on street corners, between lanes, and on the hoods of cars stuck in traffic. His moves infused the thrusting animality of *Thriller*-era Michael Jackson with Gene Kelly's balletic, slippered grace. He moonwalked over pavement, spun around streetlights, splayed himself on windshields. When not received warmly by the occupants of the cars he was dancing on, he humped their bumpers until they bucked him off with sudden starts and stops and tried to run him over. Spliced into this improvised dance routine were snippets of conversation with people inside the cars. His patter into the rolled-down windows was a mélange of producer hustle, audition, and prurient solicitation—a greatest hits of his phone calls to Hollywood. The final bit in this segment was his filthy propositioning of a limousine full of squealing sweet-sixteeners who had their heads and arms stuck out the sunroof and who loved every second of it. The piece ended with Timmy chasing the limousine down the street as it sped away, only to run up the trunk when the car hit a red light and dive headfirst into the pink and shrieking hole.

Next Timmy walked in daytime along Venice Beach in a fur coat, mirror shades, and one of those stupid crumply cowboy hats, talking passionately about the craft of acting. This monologue transitioned into a sketch called "Showtime in Five Minutes," in which Timmy drew a crowd for a lot longer than five minutes by continually saying that showtime was in five minutes. When he had a good audience, he dispersed them by rolling around on the cement like he was having a fit.

An indoor nighttime sketch called "Straight Fags" was a paean to the Superdudes. It was cut to a smooth and sexy Moby track, and the whole thing was just Timmy stalking around an apartment and checking himself out in mirrors while he played with his abs and nipples until he got so turned on that he had to start jacking it in his sweatpants. Then I finally got to see "Hot Hot Dancers," and that was pretty hot, and the tape ended down on the carpet in a hallway with Timmy on his hands and knees grimacing into the fish eye as he stuck both ends of a bent copper wire into an electrical socket. A spark, a shout. The screen goes black to the sound of laughter.

The Woodsman had gone and made his tape, and it was the goods. (By the way, *Jackass* hadn't premiered yet.) True to our word, we welcomed him back into the daily rhythms of

CRAPtv. We also recognized that the Woodsman had not made this tape on his own. Timmy was the talent and the originator of the sketches, but Danny Diamond had done more than simply shoot and cut under the Woodsman's direction. Danny had effectively directed and produced the tape. He was a talent in his own right, and as we began to provide resources for continuing production of the Woodsman show, whatever that might eventually turn out to be, Danny Diamond became an integral member of the CRAPtv collective, if that is the right word for the nexus of scofflaws centered at the warehouse.

Danny already had a little collective of his own going in the Valley. He was just in his early twenties, but he had an Island of the Lost Boys charisma, such that wherever he went he wound up attracting and loosely guiding the actions of a small gang. There were three or four of them now living in a dumpy apartment hard by the highway in Burbank, and among them they had a handful of DV cameras and a couple of Final Cut editing stations.

Physical production was our weakest link. Jason and Brody knew how to run a shoot, but the only cameras we had were Brody's three-chip Sony and the consumer one-chip left over from *Human Number*. Both of those were taking serious beatings, and none of us knew how to run Final Cut. Danny and his group became our de facto production and post partners.

Danny was from Ohio and had grown up mostly on a farm way out in the country, walking miles with his little brother through cornfields to get to school. His mom now ran a Christian rock and rap label back home, and his younger brother was a sensation on the Christian rap scene. Danny, like the Woodsman, was a great dancer; he and his brother had won some break-dancing contests as leaders of a b-boy ensemble, the Diamond Factory. He was smart and had a great eye, and once he opened up, he was hilarious.

Danny's charisma had gotten him into some trouble before he came to Los Angeles. He was living in Florida when he and some friends discovered a pasture a couple of hours outside the city that contained thousands of cow pies bursting with psilocybin mushrooms. Danny's organizational tendencies took over, and soon he had made arrangements for two carpools of lost boys to traipse out to the country and stay in a motel for a couple of days of harvesting. They filled a bathtub with mushrooms, went back to town, and moved the mushrooms into the local college market at a reasonable price.

After the next good rain they went out to the pasture again, and everything was going gangbusters—pick a mushroom, eat a mushroom—until a news chopper roared in low and trooper cruisers bounced in across the field from all directions to surround them. Somebody had dropped a dime, probably the motel owners. Back at the motel the bathtub was half full, so with that plus the backpacks they were wearing, it was pretty serious. Danny got off with probation and some community service, but now he had a record, and the local news put up his mug shot and said he was a teenage drug lord, which made living there kind of a bummer, so as soon as he could work it out with his parole officer, he left the state. So Danny Diamond was a hustler like ourselves and like everybody else we were dealing with, but he was unusually talented and really very sweet.

Aside from the Woodsman and Danny Diamond, dozens of other individuals and groups contributed to the CRAPtv development slate—far too many to enumerate, and those not mentioned in these pages are left out not necessarily because they were any less unique or interesting but because nothing resulted materially from our partnerships with them. Among those who cannot be left out were Ian and Beckett, whose alter egos were the entertainment and fashion reporters Misty Bay and Tawny Fall.

Our work relationship with Ian and Beckett began when Jason crashed the same Oscar party they did. The party was at a restaurant in West Hollywood that we were passing on the way back from another party; Amanda Demme had said to meet her there, but I was pretty sure we weren't on the list. It was late, and neither I nor anyone else in Jason's Windstar had the appetite for bamboozling doormen, but Jason would not be deterred. We let him out and sat in the car to watch. Jason was an expert, and he timed it perfectly. Just as Gina Gershon stepped out of a car by the entrance, he disappeared backward between some ficus trees that were blocking an open window and fell out of sight, presumably onto someone's dinner table.

The rest of us laughed and went home, but Jason stayed late and partied with Ian and Beckett, who had squalled their way in through the front door as Misty and Tawny—it takes a tough doorman to hold off two heated queens in wigs and heels—and were "reporting from" the party. The tape they got from that night didn't come out too hot, because their cameraman was just as loaded as they were, and the microphones they had were just props, so you could hear what they were saying only when they were close enough to fog the lens. But that was perfect—they were hysterical, and we could provide technical support.

Their Misty and Tawny characters were sort of a Joan and Melissa Rivers duo, though funnier and of course much more attractive. Beckett as Tawny was a bit gawky and had a nose almost as big as mine, so there were natural limitations, plus she wore Sally Jessy Raphael glasses, but Ian as Misty could have passed for an attractive older woman who'd had too much to drink and a couple of bad plastic surgeries—it was not unimaginable that you might accidentally make out with her. Ian was hilarious both in and out of character, the kind of improvisational comic who could go and go and go until you were either laughing really hard or thinking about hitting him to shut him up. Beckett played the perfect straight-man-lady, nodding along with earnest concern and redirecting elegantly when Ian started missing with his riffs. Beckett further endeared himself to me by ownership of a fluffy little white dog named Creepy, who ran straight to Jason's corner the first time he was brought to the warehouse and crapped on the purple carpet. Creepy must have enjoyed it as much as I did, because on every subsequent visit he tried to repeat his crime.

Since *Backdoor Hollywood* had been cancelled, it was now available for sale to cable. WireBreak was supportive of our desire to move the show to television. They had come up with the late-breaking idea of selling their four or five shows (all of which were now "on hiatus") to television, and they had cut a five-minute sales reel for each from existing episodes. Their editor had done a particularly good job with our show, making it look much funnier and more energetic than it was. They didn't mind if we were the ones pitching the show, as contractually they would remain attached if it sold.

Setting aside the erotic magnetism of our on-screen presence and the scorching brilliance of our critical insight, we thought we might have a shot at getting *Backdoor Hollywood* on air strictly from a service and demographic perspective. Despite America's continuing obsession with the movies, there wasn't a single trustworthy source on all of television to which you could turn for movie reviews, unless your idea of a trustworthy source was a middlebrow baby boomer in a sweater vest. Considering the sheer amount of programming devoted to movies and movie stars and the supposedly savage competition among broadcasters for young viewers, this was just weird. Wasn't it? (No. Cable channels depend on the studios for advertising dollars, even when they aren't directly owned by the same companies—which most of them are, anyway. But no television executive can say that bluntly, and we were too dumb to figure it out on our own.)

We wangled a meeting with the Comedy Central executive who had fought for the purchase of *South Park* and oversaw its production for the network. Jason wisely insisted that we bring along a couple of other tapes besides the *Backdoor Hollywood* sales reel for the moment that always came in a pitch meeting, when the executives smiled wanly and said, "That's nice. Do you have anything else?"

He packed along some recent tape of Misty and Tawny and, over my objections, the latest cut of the Woodsman show. The latest cut included a couple of new sketches and footage of Timmy at the Electronic Entertainment Expo, the video game convention held annually downtown, where he had sexually assaulted Sonic the Hedgehog and staged a spectacular slip-and-fall on the linoleum before being escorted out by security guards and climbing blithely into someone else's limousine, which drove away with him. I admitted the Woodsman show was starting to look pretty good. But what if they wanted it? Then we'd be fucked.

Comedy Central was way up in a tower in Century City. We were shown in to a conference room that looked north and east over Beverly Hills. It was a gorgeous spring day in May. Wind off the water had pushed the smog inland toward the mountains. Miles below us at Beverly Hills High School, kids crept like silent ants through their afternoon sports practices. I felt pleasantly adrift up there in the sky, floating with my forehead pressed against the glass over the sunstruck idiot city.

They were a tough audience to read, but it was easy enough to see that they weren't into *Backdoor Hollywood*. No thanks. They liked *Misty and Tawny* okay, but they didn't think it was meaty enough for a whole show, more like a regular sketch for a show, which was true.

Jason was right, as he usually was in these things. We did have something else, and the team liked Timmy the Woodsman. We watched the tape once, then wound it back and watched it again. The executive asked us if he was really crazy or just acted crazy. It is only in retrospect that we can see the moments our lives tip over, when one small white lie sets an avalanche into catastrophic descent. We swore up and down that the Woodsman was no crazier than we were. His act? It was just an act! Wasn't it great?

They called our office the next day to say that they wanted to make an offer on the Untitled Timmy Woodsman Show. Rosenberg had hooked us up with an agent at CAA, and we asked them to please give him a call. It had been just over two years since we decided to start this company, and we finally had a real-live television pilot deal on the table.

To the jaded television producer who knows the odds of going all the way from script to pilot to series, a pilot deal at a cable network is no big thing. The money isn't great. Your chance of making it even to a six-episode order is only maybe one in five, and the odds of going past that are much worse. You know not to put your whole heart into a pilot deal, because most likely your heart will be broken. But to us, a Comedy Central pilot really was the brass ring. Like the close brushes we had had with financing and the Pop.com deal that had finally closed—the first $25,000 payment was now in our bank account—it seemed almost too good to be true that we were in negotiations to make a real-live television pilot with Comedy Central.

The dream of programming a whole alternative network with things we actually wanted to watch was still on our horizon, but by now we understood that a successful television series, even more than equity financing or a raft of deals with online content providers, would put our company in a position to branch out and make deals on whole new strata. We fetishized the possibility of producing the pilot to the extent that we were reluctant even to talk much about it. In the meantime, early in the summer of 2000, we serviced the Pop.com deal, shuttling over to Glendale in Jason's van once a month to present ideas from the CRAPtv development slate.

But as it turned out, Pop.com wasn't quite ready to begin production on anything. So property after property, if such a businesslike word may be applied to our material, reverted to CRAPtv with the tacit understanding on both sides that we'd still be happy to produce any or all of the shows we had pitched if Pop.com decided they wanted them. Reversion meant that our slate could be integrated into the Comedy Central pilot, which, in creative discussions with the executives there, was transforming into a variety hour featuring a range of our content, hosted by Timmy the Woodsman.

This was not a good direction to be heading in, and we knew it, because we knew Timmy the Woodsman, but we didn't have the balls to argue against it. The paperwork wasn't finished—in fact, their business affairs department had yet to generate a formal memo—so we just smiled and nodded enthusiastically at every suggestion. Ideas for the show's format ranged from a seated-host late-night talk arrangement that threw to clips, to a kids' show for grown-ups more like *Pee Wee's Playhouse*. If it was to be a talk format—which seemed incredibly risky since Timmy was so unmanageable, and he was unlikely to transform into a glad-handing talk show host overnight—we wanted to shoot it all handheld on Mini DV at Venice Beach, with a cardboard box for Timmy's desk. That was how we were used to working. Comedy Central thought we should shoot it on a stage with a live audience and BetaCams on jib arms. That was how they were used to working. We nodded and smiled, waiting for paperwork.

This open-ended development schedule left us with lots of free time, so that summer Jason and I both drove up north with relative frequency. Sometimes we went together, and sometimes we went separately. Frankel and I had some Quiddity work, and summer was the busiest season in Jason's pagan event cycle. Early August was Reggae on the River, up in Humboldt. The year before, he had passed out there in the middle of the day with his legs submerged beneath the cool, clear lens of the Eel, and a week later the whole front of his legs peeled off like chaps. I hadn't attended Reggae on the River in nearly a decade, and I wasn't going this year, either. Three days of dreadlocks, Jah, and genetically engineered weed—by the end of it they would all be speaking in Jamaican accents and calling each other brah. No, thanks.

The week following Reggae on the River, we convened in the basement of Tony's mom's house in San Francisco. Jason, Tony, Ward, both Jonathan and David Korty—it felt just like old times. Though all of us were going slack and losing hair, floundering toward middle age, a night together in that basement was a nearly pure return to childhood: the familiar smells and sounds and voices, final arguments over the best beds and blankets, and then all of us off to snore like dogs in an accustomed den. And just as I had been awakened from slumber many mornings in the past with those kickers and mumblers and foul-breathed blanket thieves, I was awakened early by a phone call from my mother.

4

She was apologetic about calling so early in the morning. And everything was fine. But she wanted to let me know, in case I was on the way over to her house, that she wasn't there. Why? Because she was at Marin General Hospital. Just for a little while, and she would be getting out later in the day. So I shouldn't bother coming to the hospital. But in case I went to the house and wondered where she was, that was where she was.

Did anybody else know? No, she hadn't wanted to bother anyone. She had driven herself in last night. I see. What was it that was wrong? Oh, nothing. Nothing, really. Maybe a little anemic. She wasn't feeling that good, and her doctor had told her she might want to go down to the hospital, just to be safe.

Coming from my mother, this information was cause for serious alarm. But more than that, it was her voice that frightened me—faint, blurred, confused, like she was talking in her sleep. I got off the phone and started waking people up at Tony's. I didn't have my car, so we piled into Jonathan's and they dropped me at the hospital. They offered to stay, but I had no idea what was going on yet and said I'd call them later.

This was the hospital to which I had come in sixth grade when Fat Pat broke my collarbone on the playground, where I was given my first and only but never forgotten dose of injected opiate when the line in the emergency room was really long and I started sniveling. This was the hospital to which I'd come after separating my shoulder, still jangling from acid taken the night before, in a lacrosse game. This was the hospital where just a few months after that I spent six weeks boxed up in the Adolescent Recovery Center, learning about sobriety with a bunch of other fuckups. And now it appeared, as I came into the infusion room on the top floor of a new wing that hadn't yet been built back in all those other times, that this was the hospital in which my mother shortly would die.

She lay pale in a bed by a window with tubes dangling into her arm. It wasn't the kind of pale that comes from staying inside out of the sun, but the kind that comes from being drained of blood, the paleness of a corpse. Her lips and gums were the wrong color, a grayish blue. She turned her head and tried to smile. Her teeth were darker than her cheek.

What I managed to put together over the next hour or so of intermittent conversation with my mother was that for several weeks she hadn't been feeling right. A few days earlier she had seen her regular doctor, who had been concerned that she was becoming seriously anemic and drawn blood. The doctor had opened the lab results while working late last night. He was so disturbed by them that he called her immediately and told her to get to an emergency room as quickly as possible. By that time she was hardly conscious. She had barely managed to answer the phone and make sense of what he was saying, and then, weak and disoriented, instead of calling an ambulance, she had driven herself to Marin General, where she had collapsed and been transfused. Her hemoglobin level was so low the staff could hardly believe she was alive, much less that she had driven herself there.

As new blood continued to drip into her veins, she grew visibly rosier, and then she drifted into what looked like a comfortable sleep. I can't recall how many units of new blood she took that day, but it was several. There was something almost vampiric about how the new blood restored her so immediately and so dramatically. It was like a children's television magic trick, a flower's life in time lapse backward. Years inverted. Decades. Watching her sleep and softly breathe, I knew I would drain strangers by the dozen if that was what it took to keep her flush. She woke in the afternoon feeling much better: warm, not dizzy, herself. I found her car where she had abandoned it cockeyed in the parking lot. She got dressed, and we went home.

The next day was filled with a desperate giddiness. My mother blinked fast and smiled tightly and insisted that she felt just fine. I grimaced along and tried to be funny as I drove her around on her errands. She kept trying to get me to go back to Los Angeles, but all the things about my life that tended to drive her crazy in normal circumstances prevented her from finding an argumentive footing—it wasn't like I had a normal job where someone was expecting me. CRAPtv was just trying not to spend money until some kind of Comedy Central deal kicked in, and the farther we stayed from our checkbook the better. I was up here to do Quiddity business with Alex, anyway. It frightened me, the way she was trying so hard to make me leave. She was acting like a cat or dog that knew it was dying and wanted to sneak off under the porch to do it. In the afternoon we did something ridiculous: went to a bicycle store, where I talked her into buying herself an expensive new mountain bike.

Margaret had been an athlete when she was young, to the extent girls were encouraged to be athletes back then. She was a beautiful swimmer, powerfully muscled on her tiny frame, and even as an adult, without practicing, she could crank out more push-ups and pull-ups than most men. When she joined a gym in her forties, she was just going about her little mom fitness routine when one of the serious weight-lifting guys challenged her to a push-up contest. She demurred at first, but when he pressed her, she let him do as many as he could, and then she did that many and one more. The owner tried to talk her into becoming a competitive bodybuilder, which embarrassed her enough that she stopped going to the gym.

After that she rode a mountain bike on weekends and took brisk walks in the mornings before it was light. But in the last few years she had stopped riding, and then, so gradually I had hardly noticed, slowed the pace and frequency of the walks. The gradual replacement of exercise with naps and her sleepiness in Santa Barbara a few months earlier—how could I not have recognized these as unnatural? I was furious at myself for not realizing she was sick.

She hemolyzed—destroyed her own red blood cells—at an alarming rate. People suffering from fairly extreme forms of hemolytic anemia require a transfusion of new blood every few weeks. Within a day my mother's blush had gone. Her urine was dark, shaded brown with dead corpuscles. In two more days she was short of breath again, dizzy and confused. Her symptoms were similar to those of severe altitude sickness or blood loss, disorientation moving toward shock, and had the same cause. It was a slow suffocation; the blood in her veins was incapable of carrying sufficient oxygen to meet the requirements of her body and brain.

We went back to the hospital. A blood draw indicated that her hematocrit, a generalized measure of blood cell count, was back down close to where it had been when she was previously admitted. She was transfused again, again with multiple units, and again she dozed off as she filled with color. The reason these sessions made her so sleepy, I learned, was that she was given an antihistamine beforehand to limit her body's immune response to someone else's blood. And, also, her body went into a kind of mild shock at the introduction of foreign fluids. But the sleep seemed full and restorative, different from the panting retreat of her anemic naps, and it was nice, not frightening, to watch her doze. She woke warm and flushed.

Though no official diagnosis had yet been rendered, an oncologist had visited her even before I arrived from San Francisco that first morning. A technician had aspirated a sample of marrow from her pelvis. The aspiration must have been a horrific experience, because my mother acknowledged that it had been "unpleasant." This marrow sample was now being analyzed down at the Stanford pathology lab. Without knowing specifically what kind of cancer she had, we both understood that it must be cancer, and that it must have reached an advanced stage.

So far she had told only a handful of people there was anything wrong. Reasonably enough, she wanted to know her diagnosis and prognosis herself and come to some sort of terms with them before opening the floodgates of sympathy and concern. But there was also an element of denial in her insistence on secrecy—if no one knew about it, perhaps it wasn't really happening. The day after her second transfusion I drove her to her office so she could return calls and push through a pile of correspondence. It was dusk, and we were back in the car to leave when she saw her oncologist walking across the parking lot. This was the doctor who had sent her marrow down to Stanford, and I had missed him on the first day. She told me I was going to love him and rolled down her window to call out. He smiled and came over to the car, greeting her warmly and shaking my hand. His name was Dr. Peter Eisenberg.

Dr. Eisenberg was a portly but vital man, maybe in his early fifties, with the red-bridged nose of a runner and a salt-and-pepper beard. In the past seventy-two hours, Dr. Eisenberg, without his knowledge, had been comprehensively vetted by my aunt Tawnie—technically, my ex-stepaunt, but we were as close with the her family as with any of our blood kin. Dr. Eisenberg was supposed to be the best, and Tawnie was in a position to know. Her research on physicians, dentists, educators, Realtors, babysitters, and any other persons who might provide support services to the job of keeping your family's lives in order and on track was so rigorous that she could have started her own credentialing service. Not that those were her only areas of interest—she was also knowledge-able in the areas of architecture, contemporary art, and glo-bal politics—but without a doctorate in fluid dynamics, you would have small hope of becoming her pool guy.

Dr. Eisenberg may have passed her vetting process with flying colors, but he struck me as far too happy to be a highly respected oncologist. Cancer was, after all, the pinnacle of seriousness—thus the saying "serious as cancer"—and this grinning man was wearing a Mr. Potato Head tie. I could not help noticing, as my eye bounced up and down between Dr. Eisenberg's face and Mr. Potato Head's, how very closely Dr. Eisenberg, with his tanned forehead, bushy eyebrows, close-set eyes, and different-colored nose, resembled Mr. Po-tato Head. If Dr. Eisenberg was as smart as he was reputed to be, he was aware that he resembled Mr. Potato Head, and therefore it followed that he knew that each solemn conversa-tion he had over the course of his day as a highly respected oncologist was punctuated by a goofy sight gag.

My mom asked Dr. Eisenberg if he knew yet whether she had lymphoma. Since she had no obvious tumors, and lym-phoma was often detected first through abnormalities in the blood, it already had come up as a strong possibility.

Dr. Eisenberg said he didn't know yet. The results would be in tomorrow. But we should keep our fingers crossed in the hopes she did have lymphoma.

"Wait," said my mom. "I thought lymphoma was bad."

"It's terrible!" he responded gleefully. "But if you have lymphoma, then you get Dr. Lucas! And she's the best!"

We bid good evening to this madman and went home. The next day we went to our appointment at Dr. Eisenberg's practice, located in a strip of seventies-era office buildings adjacent to Marin General. There we learned that she did indeed have lymphoma: an indolent Stage 4 non-Hodgkin's B-cell lymphoma, complicated by hemolytic anemia. Lymphoma was a cancer of the white blood cells—that I knew—and the rest was explained by Dr. Lucas, the hematologist of whom Dr. Eisenberg had spoken so grandly the prior evening.

Her first name was Jennifer—Jen. Like me, Jen Lucas had gone to high school in Marin County, a few towns north. She was one year older than I was. In elegant flats she was about my height, though by contrast she was attractive, clear-eyed, and serious. While I had been making an ass of myself with navel gazing, penis twisting, and branding scams, Jen Lucas had been going to college on a basketball scholarship, matriculating to Georgetown Medical School, advancing hematology research at Stanford, and being recruited as the youngest partner by twenty years at the best private oncology practice in northern California, where her job was saving people's lives.

My mother gave permission for me to remain in the room as Dr. Lucas took down her medical history. I don't remember much of the conversation except that my mother discussed her mother, who had died of cancer of the throat and neck, and her brother, who had died of a brain tumor just a year earlier, and I remember that, as a routine part of the questioning, Dr. Lucas asked my mother whether she had had any periods of sexual promiscuity in her life. That was when it hit me that my mom might die very soon. Or not simply that she might die very soon—because that already had struck me hard the second I had seen her drained gray in the hospital bed—but that in dying so soon she would miss so very much. That was such a dumb way to think of it. Miss so much. But how else to put it?

"No," my mom replied softly. "I'm afraid I haven't lived a very exciting life."

To keep from sobbing I concentrated on understanding the diagnosis: indolent Stage 4 non-Hodgkin's B-cell lymphoma complicated by hemolytic anemia.

Indolent sounded pretty good. I figured you wanted your cancer to be lazy. Unfortunately, no. *Indolent* in cancer language meant "incurable." Cancer cells were vulnerable to chemotherapy only when they were in the process of splitting. If they split rapidly, that meant chemotherapy had a chance of killing them all. If they split too slowly, the chemotherapy would kill you before it finished killing your cancer. However, it was possible that chemotherapy could be used to push my mom's disease back to tolerable levels until it grew intolerable again, when perhaps it could be pushed back again.

Stage 4. Okay, four wasn't a big number. How many stages were there? Jen Lucas smiled wryly. There were four stages. Five was dead. *Non-Hodgkin's.* I knew a couple of people who had had Hodgkin's disease, and they were fine now. So, non-

Hodgkin's, probably also bad. Correct. *B-cell.* A type of white blood cell, or lymphocyte. B-cells protect the body against bacteria or viruses by secreting antibodies, proteins that attach to the foreign organisms and attract other immune system cells that kill the bacteria or virus. You want your B-cells to work right. My mother's were producing an enzyme that, instead of attacking bacteria or viruses, attacked her own red blood cells.

Lymphoma was the cancer that all the other words described. The good news was that lymphomas as a group were better understood now than ever before, and indolent lymphomas often proved to be manageable if treated with the right chemotherapy protocols or new treatments called monoclonal antibodies. Unfortunately, it was hard to know in advance which would work better to fight the disease; the monoclonal antibody therapies were too new for adequately long studies to have been conducted. Another piece of good news was that lymphomas were Dr. Lucas's specialty, and the Stanford clinic she had just left, she told us with no false modesty, was the best lymphoma clinic in the world.

Complicated by hemolytic anemia was where it got really bad, though. The hemolysis caused by the enzyme my mother's cancerous B-cells were secreting was much worse than the cancer itself. Not only was this condition seriously life-threatening, it was quite rare. Maybe a couple of hundred cases identified per year, which meant that data would be scarce and there weren't going to be a lot of clinical trials.

The most urgent order of business was not to eliminate the cancer but to counter my mother's hemolysis. I wanted to know whether she could just keep on getting transfusions forever—

they had been so amazing. Like magic. Unfortunately, no, said Dr. Lucas, for a couple of reasons. First, there was the risk of hepatitis or HIV infection. This risk was not terribly significant: Those infections were relatively rare in the blood supply, and either was less deadly than my mom's present disease—a chilling thought, that she would have been better off with AIDS. But the real reason transfusions wouldn't work indefinitely, said Dr. Lucas, was that with each unit of new blood my mother's body absorbed, it also incorporated the donor's antibodies. My mother's body chemistry would become progressively more hostile to the introduction of foreign blood. Eventually, her allergic reaction, now suppressible with a dose of Benadryl, would become systemic shock, and her immune system would rise up in revolt and kill her. It would be best if my mother required no more transfusions at all before the cancer could be checked, because even if it could be checked—of which Dr. Lucas seemed fairly confident—it would be back. And the more transfusions she had left when that happened the better.

The two specific avenues of treatment available to my mother were a chemotherapy cocktail called CVP and Rituxan, a monoclonal antibody therapy from Genentech. Either might be effective, but each carried a significant risk of unpleasant side effects. In the case of Rituxan, there was a remote possibility that the first administration would kill her. But if one treatment didn't work and wasn't fatal, the other could be tried afterward.

A day or two later my mother received her first infusion of CVP. The protocol, or treatment regimen, called for weekly infusions of the cocktail over a period of four weeks. She would also be administered a compound called Procrit, which boosted her production of red cells. It was the same stuff professional cyclists used to dope their blood.

My mother's infusions took place in a sunny room off to the side of the oncology office. The infusion room looked westward through picture windows onto the green and black northern slopes of Mount Tamalpais. It was a lovely view, the same view enjoyed from living rooms all up and down the Ross Valley. It was the same view as that from the front porch of the Adolescent Recovery Center at MGH and, I silently noted upon entering the room, as that enjoyed by patients half a century ago in the tuberculosis ward of the condemned old Ross Hospital a mile up the road. It was a view to die by.

Four comfortable medical recliners faced the windows, and in the recliners sat patients in various states of decimation, pale fluids dripping into them from plastic bags. Some slept. Some knitted or read, some looked out the window. My memories of those patients now blend together, exhausted figures fading in and out of existence. Most were women my mother's age, in their fifties and sixties, but there were also men and a woman in her twenties we saw there from time to time.

We made friends with the nurses, the technicians, and the women who ran the front office. My mother was a model patient. Each week she told them from between gray lips that she was feeling good. Better. Definitely better this week. They weighed her and took her temperature and blood pressure, both always low, and then pulled a blood sample from reluctant little veins. The draw told the story. The test tube went into a small centrifuge right there on the counter, no bigger than a tabletop copy machine, that hummed and then printed her complete blood count: platelet, lymphocyte, and hemoglobin counts; assorted other indices of blood chemistry; and the generalized number that was her hematocrit. These numbers were entered into a binder and compared to the numbers from the week before. Tiny gains and losses. She was in bad shape. Not long into the chemo she had to be transfused again.

Caring for my mother required very little of me physically—nothing, really. I simply took up residence in the back house, the small cottage behind her home, which the original owners had built as an aviary. She hardly let me drive or cook for her, doing almost everything herself even as the chemotherapy began to take its toll. Her house was cold, which exacerbated her anemia, so I laid down weather stripping at her doors and windows and went with her to a hardware store to buy an electric heater for the kitchen.

A strange, sympathetic exhaustion overtook me that first month. My lassitude wasn't that of the overworked caretaker, but just that old familiar, daytime torpor—the tunneled vision, the muffled sky, the hissing static of the void. At night I sat awake and read or watched rented movie after rented movie, unable to sleep. By day I wanted nothing but to lie down and close my eyes. When she was transfused or infused and started to doze, the exhaustion settled on me like a lead-filled blanket, pulling me down to the floor beside her bed or chair and pressing me into dull oblivion.

Over the course of a month she gradually let her family and friends know her diagnosis. She worked on the phone from home and found a replacement for her post as head of the vestry at her church. The chemotherapy tired and nauseated her, and the prednisone, a steroid that was one of its ingredients, made her jumpy. Eating and sleeping were difficult. Soon she would be losing her hair. In anticipation of that she made an appointment with her hairdresser, who cut it to a couple of inches. But that thinned and fell out patchily, looking sadder than if there had been none at all. She let me shave her head with clippers on the patio behind her house. Tufts of my mother's hair, fine and pale as baby's down, drifted over the bricks and floated, spinning softly, in the pool.

SIX

1

Frankel dropped in often. He knew that my mom loved to cut flowers from the magnolia and camellia trees in her yard, and that normally she would clamber up to get the blooms she wanted. He brought over a pruning pole on which he had stuck letters spelling out MARGARET MCPRUNE and the injunction that she NIP IT IN THE BUD. He was as sweet as ever.

But our business was in trouble, and we both knew it. In the spring we had taken on a third partner, Aaron Gigliotti, who we hoped would drum up new business. Through no fault of Gigliotti's, nothing much was happening. PlusOne had closed up shop. Frankel had rented out a small San Francisco office for Quiddity, and that was where he and Gigliotti made their calls, but all the companies that had been operating on venture money were going broke, and no new ones were being formed.

Jason and I made plans to meet backstage at the Fillmore Theater a few days after Labor Day, a.k.a. Burning Man. Les Claypool's new band was playing there, and Jason was going straight to the Fillmore from the desert. He arrived wild and windblown, looking like he had just crossed the Sahara on a camel. Everyone asked about Margaret, and I was brought up to date on what was happening with CRAPtv, specifically with regard to Timmy the Woodsman. He had disappeared.

After Burning Man ended, there was this thing called the Afterburn—Burning Man offered something new to hate about it every time it was mentioned. The Afterburn was a week or so in which a contingent of people with nothing better to do remained in the desert. Ostensibly, Afterburners were staying the extra week to restore the area to its natural state—clean up litter, rub out tire marks, and what have you—but mixed in with the civic-minded and environmentally conscious modern primitives were plenty who just didn't want to go home. The Afterburn was to Burning Man what ugly dawn was to the all-night binge, a period of regret and repentance, or, for the truly committed, of doubled doses and really getting into the shit.

During Burning Man proper the Woodsman had gobbled up a whole lot of liquid acid from the cache of Elrond, a barge-dwelling hippie-future-medievalist associate of Jason and Tony's who split his year between Burning Man and the Renaissance Faire. The liquid acid in question was heavy, heavy metal, according to Jason, who was qualified to know, and the Woodsman, after taking his initial dose, kept sneaking back into the tent and licking up more of it until he had disposed of half the vial.

The reader who has never taken too much LSD may not be impressed by what consequences such an action may bring, but such consequences may be seriously fucking severe. Jason said the Woodsman had grabbed a pocketknife and slashed his arms to ribbons, then run around bumming the highs of Burning People by gaily spraying them with his blood. He was brought to ground and taped up by one of the volunteer EMTs who roved around Black Rock City, as Burning Man called its site, but since there was no facility in place for quarantining people so disastrously high as the Woodsman, nor anyone with authority to impose such a quarantine in any case, the Woodsman was released back into modern primitive society.

Burning Man was drawing to a close by the time of his release, and people in the camp of Jason et al.—Burning People were encouraged to call their affinity groups camps—were ready to go home. But the Woodsman wasn't ready to go home. No, indeed. He was laboring under the belief that he was part, if not wholly, a wolf, dog, coyote, or some other kind of animal that whimpered, barked, bit, and lived in the desert year-round. Jason hung around for a couple of days of the Afterburn hoping Timmy would chill out, but when the Woodsman wasn't ready to leave after those couple of days, Jason remanded him to the care of Elrond, who was staying for the whole Afterburn.

Things went okay until the Afterburn was over and Elrond was ready to go back to his barge. Elrond called Jason from a pay phone in Nevada to apologize. He had been able to coax the Woodsman into his car and start across the desert toward the road, but halfway there, the Woodsman had started yipping and biting, with the result that Elrond had been forced to kick the Woodsman out of the car—literally kick, with his feet, which luckily were encased in tooth-proof boots. Drive-along remonstration with a barking Timmy through a cracked car window proved futile, and when Timmy removed what was left of his clothing and ran for rough ground where the car couldn't follow, Elrond had regretfully made his way alone to the highway and placed the call. CRAPtv's primary entertainment asset was, as of my receiving this situation report at the Fillmore, missing in action somewhere along the California-Nevada border.

Timmy came in from the cold four or five days later with a sketchy account of what happened after he was ejected from the car. He had been "on maneuvers" up in the mountains for the first couple of days, but eventually he grew hungry and thirsty and cold, and he made his way back down to the highway. Despite realizing it would probably be best if he got a ride somewhere from someone, he retained a bit of the paranoia that had sent him into the hills in the first place, so in order to use the road as a guide but avoid being seen by passing motorists, he had uprooted a shrub and run down the asphalt with it, stopping and pretending to be a bush whenever a car hove into view. But a keen-eyed motorist had penetrated this Wile E. Coyote disguise and talked him into a car. This kind person dropped Timmy at a truck stop, where Timmy made the acquaintance of a Christian trucker, who bought him some clothing and a steak dinner. The Christian trucker was going east, and Timmy wanted to go west, so they parted ways, and Timmy made a sign out of cardboard and went to stand out by the highway, where he was picked up by an attractive volunteer Burning Man EMT (not the one who had bandaged him), a girl on her way back home to San Francisco. She dropped him off in the Haight, and from there he had made his own way back down to Los Angeles.

By mid-September my mother's condition appeared to be stabilizing, and I drove back down to take care of a few things. We had learned that Pop.com was closing its doors.

We learned this not from Pop.com itself but from multiple news outlets that were having a field day with the puns. After all the excitement, the Vulcan Ventures multimillions, and the stock option deals, Pop.com had never even launched a Web site.

It had paid CRAPtv the first half of the fifty thousand dollars, but it still owed us twenty-five. We needed the money if we were to hang on until the Comedy Central pilot came into effect—if in fact it ever would. We had yet to receive a formal deal memo. When we called Pop.com to see what was going on, nobody called us back. My tiny mother had been in charge of collecting delinquent accounts for the employment service she had managed all those years, and she advised me that if we were unable to get through to anyone on the phone, the best thing to do was go over there in clean clothes and wait politely in the lobby until the person with whom we wanted to speak came out to see us. She said I should take Brody with me, because having a nice girl there would keep it from seeming thuggish.

Brody and I drove over the hill into Glendale, where the Pop.com parking lot was pretty much empty. The front door was open, but there was no one at the receptionist's desk and no one in sight inside. Most of the furniture was already gone. We called into the emptiness. Eventually, an assistant-type girl poked her head out of one of the executive offices lining the wall to our left. She walked uncertainly to where we stood and asked what it was we wanted. I imagined a cluster of executives huddled together around the corner, shushing each other and wishing we would go away. We asked to speak with the executive on whose machine I had been leaving messages. The assistant went somewhere to find him. She returned after a while to say she was sorry, but he was unavailable. If we wanted, we could leave a message with her. It flummoxed the poor girl terribly when we said that was okay, thanks, but we'd just wait. Apparently, nobody else was using that strategy. With many a cowish glance back, she carried this second message into the cavern.

In a few minutes the executive stomped out to us with his panties in a terrible twist, squalling that he wouldn't be bullied or threatened, and he was calling the police if we didn't leave the premises immediately. But he must have realized how foolish he would look if he called the cops and had to say, when they arrived, that prim little doe-eyed Brody had been threatening him, so he heard us out. He relaxed a little when we promised we weren't threatening anything at all, just pleading our case, putting faces to a silly company name on a contract in the hope that he would put us on the list if Pop.com were able to cut a few final checks. He made no promises, but he said he'd see what he could do.

That fall I made the round-trip to Marin about once a week. I tried to be with Margaret for all her checkups and treatments, and I made it to most of them. I drove Interstate 5 in the dark after traffic had cleared, learning the Central Valley exits by heart: Buttonwillow, Coalinga, Santa Nella, Lago del Mar, specific nowheres in an endless midnight nowhere. I listened to classic rock on the radio or more often to nothing, just to the sound of my engine and tires and the wind buffeting the car, from time to time pushing in the smell of slaughterhouse. Weird gas fires burned west of the freeway, and lights twinkled at night where no buildings could be seen in the daytime.

These strange nighttime drives were errands of both filial devotion and obligation to my business partners, but they also were my secret refuge. As soon as I arrived at either destination I longed to be back on the road. The nighttime highway was the only place I really felt at peace, adrift in atemporal limbo between the worry of my mother's cancer and the disaster of my work. I nursed a persistent fantasy of checking into one of the anonymous roadside motels to stop time and sleep, sleep for days, watch cable, read trashy paperbacks, and think, living on Denny's and gas station snacks, until I was refreshed and ready to return time's arrow to motion.

The good son's choice would seem to have been simple: to stay with my mother until she got well or died. I did make an office for myself at her place, in the guest cottage out by the greenhouse. I talked her into getting DSL and strung cable out to the cottage. And as a good son, I spent many days with my dying mother—not out of obligation but greedily, having fun, storing the pleasure of making her laugh against our looming mutual loss.

But with that loss looming, I felt the weight of all her expectations of and for me—expectations I had willingly taken as my own expectations of myself, even as I resented them and deferred their achievement—bearing down with terrible urgency. On the one hand, these expectations were huge to the point of laughable hubris—that I should live up to some unspecified potential I had been credited with as a child. From the time I was able to think, rightly or wrongly, I had silently understood that it was my obligation to deliver up some great work of art, invention, theory, or institution, some measurable contribution to the human endeavor. I recalled reading a child's biography of Thomas Edison when I was ten or eleven, learning of what he had accomplished by that age, and excoriating myself to the point of tears for already having fallen so far behind. By my early thirties I had fallen comically—absurdly, pitifully—short of meeting any grand expectations. My contribution, such as it was, was an embarrassment even to myself.

But on the other hand, my mother's hopes for me were pitifully mundane. In light of the outrageous advantages I had been given over 99 percent of humanity, it was her reasonable hope that I would be up to the basic tasks of adulthood: feeding, clothing, and housing myself. I was now entering midlife, and if I didn't think of something soon, I would have to ask my dying mom for an advance on her small and carefully kept estate in order to pay my rent. Avoiding the need to present her with that final disappointment was one reason I traveled so frantically up and down the state, scheming, hustling, plotting. All my business partners were doing their best to be good about granting me time away, but both businesses were having trouble, and I was growing irritated with my partners in both.

Each time I came back from Marin, the CRAPtv office was messier and more depressing. Jason wasn't complaining about my absence, but he didn't like it that the main thing I did on each return was disparage new projects and note that the office was in worse shape than it had been when I left—not just messier, but dirtier, with dishes in the sink and cat shit in dark corners. Brody, who had been my ally in fighting for order, was getting short with both of us. She was trying to keep things together, but it was an uphill battle.

Jason was broke, and Ward had declined to pay Jason's share of the utilities at the Mar Vista apartment, so now they didn't have electricity. The gas still worked, so there was a stovetop and hot water, but basically they were camping in there. Brody hired Jason as a PA on one of her commercial jobs so he could make some cash. She gave him the easiest position, driving the agency people from their hotel to the shoot in a van, which meant he could sit around all day and make phone calls until they were ready to go back at night. All he had to do was get up on time to pick them up. Brody had been on the set for three hours and the first shot was set to go, cranes and everything in place, but the agency people weren't there yet, so the shot was being held. She called Jason to see where they were, and his cell phone woke him up in bed. Brody went behind a trailer and sobbed, then sent somebody else to the hotel.

When Quiddity had been functioning, it had demanded only that I show up from time to time and do my three-card monte. Now that the company was having trouble booking jobs, Frankel wanted me to do more. Potential clients had chipped away at our proposals all summer and then declined to engage us. The last bid we had put together was for a company in San Francisco that hoped to centralize the reservation and routing of all the shipping containers in the world and thereby shave a thin slice of profit off every single item bought or sold anywhere on the planet. But even those wishful thinkers had the sense not to give us thirty grand to tell them what to call themselves.

I gave it one burst of energy, writing up a business plan for Quiddity so we could look for venture capital, but we knew the timing was wrong, and in October, Alex and I decided to dissolve our partnership. I think he couldn't believe that when finally faced with a decision, I chose CRAPtv over Quiddity. Frankel was organized, positive, smart, and thoughtful—he was a perfect business partner. The easy pickings were gone, but there was still money to be made. It wasn't like all business was ended, everywhere, or like we were ill equipped to participate in it as a freelance consulting team. We knew the language, we had the experience, and we had the connections—if we wanted to do it.

But I just didn't want to do it. I knew that the middle-class survival, even real wealth, I could gain by a wholehearted commitment to corporate cheerleading would never satisfy me. Not because it would be boring to attain or dirty once attained but because it would never be enough. It might come with extra cars and summer homes, but it would never bring me fame. I wanted to be famous. That was it, my dirty secret, too shameful to speak aloud: I was just like everyone else.

We were worried about the Woodsman. Rampant jackassery was one thing, but slashing your arms and running naked into the mountains had the distinct ring of a cry for help. He was still spending most nights on the couch at Jason and Ward's dark apartment and his days at the CRAPtv office, where he was allowed to convert one of the lofts into a private lair. His phone privileges were wholly reinstated, and his interrupted conversation with Hollywood resumed. I wish I could write that the reembracement of the Woodsman to our bosoms was entirely charitable, and indeed by now we did feel a practically familial obligation to him. But his disappearance had reminded us that we really couldn't afford to lose him.

Certainly Timmy understood the situation, but to his credit he never once tried to use it as leverage for anything. In fact, I believe it frightened him that his fantasies of becoming a professional entertainer were in danger of coming true. He had been clowning his whole life, and no one

GLASGOW PHILLIPS

had ever offered to pay him for it. Instead, they had kicked
him out of school, out of his home, out of his job when he
could get one, and out of bars when he could not. I may
have been a grump, and Brody may have been a little snippy
sometimes, but we didn't kick him out. Jason and Ward had
ten times our patience, having custody of the Woodsman
both day and night.

The stage side of the warehouse, in disuse since WireBreak
had cancelled production of *Backdoor Hollywood*, became
the Woodsman's de facto domain. His gradual furnishing of
the loft on that side was like a clown-car gag in reverse. I
would come into the stage side from the office side and find
the Woodsman dragging a futon, carpet remnant, or large
piece of taxidermy straight up the ladder and into his hole;
it seemed impossible he could fit all that stuff in the loft,
which was only twenty feet by eight, and a low five feet from
floor to rafters. He put cardboard and fabric up around the
railings for privacy and strung bare bulbs for light.

Danny Diamond and his lost boys were around a lot now,
too, and they had made friends with Jolon and Martha's
Internet gangsters in the nether reaches of the warehouse.
Danny had a bear suit somebody had permanently borrowed
from a costume department, and from somewhere else a frog
costume had been purloined. Or it may have been a Peter
Pan or Robin Hood costume—it was just a green tunic and
tights. But the bear suit was of high quality, a six-foot teddy.
One of his saucer-sized button eyes dangled forlornly by a
hank of brown yarn. Timmy the Woodsman loved the bear
costume, and he used to wear it around the office quite a bit.
With that and the green frog outfit, he and Danny shot a few
episodes of *The Bear and Frog Show*.

For the role of Frog they recruited Gary, the crackhead who bivouacked in the wetlands behind the office. Danny and the Woodsman traded Gary beer, cigarettes, and sometimes a few dollars in exchange for playing the role of Frog in their skits. Gary's black pirate beard and crazy eyeballs sticking out of the top of the green tunic were a scary sight. He was an evil scowler and paranoid threat mutterer, and often he would break a scene to renegotiate his contract. I kept my distance from *Bear and Frog* production to the extent I was able, so the following may not be correct, but my impression was that Gary the Frog's ongoing contract negotiation was the central conflict of *The Bear and Frog Show;* it was a typically "meta" CRAPtv production. Other than fights over cigarettes, the show seemed mostly to be just Timmy running in circles and yelling incomprehensibly from inside the Bear head while Gary glared out of the CRAPtv Dumpster, or Timmy and Gary jumping up and down in the Dumpster while Danny laughed and taped.

The Woodsman was turning thirty. He expressed surprise and a measure of disappointment at having lived so long. He had always been sure he would die young, and thirty was not so young. We threw a party for him in a restaurant that had big fire pits, and everyone was there, but it was an awkward, bittersweet evening. You got the feeling that no one had thrown a party for Timmy in a long, long time. He behaved himself and didn't make a scene, not even with an open flame available. I believe that he was touched. Not that any of us was under the illusion that he was a new person now, healed of damage, but I think he genuinely understood that we accepted him as one of us, not some stranger who had tumbled in our midst, fun for now, but maybe that was all.

I know we were all surprised a few days later when he staggered into the office kitchen area stinking of solvent, naked except for a filthy comforter wrapped like a cape around his shoulders. For a second or two none of us realized anything was seriously amiss. A few days earlier he had pranced into a meeting we were having with Andy Dick sporting nothing but a boner and pair of boxer briefs I recognized as my own.

"It burns!" he yelled hoarsely now.

This was something he often yelled, usually in reference to the Rash, an ailment from which he suffered, but this wasn't about the Rash. He clutched his stomach and fell sideways against the wall. We finally got it out of him that he had drunk half a gallon of paint thinner up in his loft. We stood there idiotically for a moment as he writhed in the juncture between wall and floor, and then we entered into a discussion about what you were supposed to do when somebody drank paint thinner—whether you were supposed to make him drink milk or water or nothing; whether you were supposed to make him vomit or definitely not let him vomit—before my head cleared and I told Jason to just drive Timmy to the emergency room as fast as possible.

"My ass! My ass! It's coming out my ass!" groaned the Woodsman.

And indeed it was, a fuming spume of turpentine. He tried to get into the bathroom and start shitting it out into the toilet instead of just letting it leak down the back of his legs, but he was cramping so badly he couldn't even reach the doorknob. We hauled him up by the armpits and started for the door, but the Woodsman said he wanted a cigarette, and we were all in such shock that somebody actually gave him one and almost solicitously lit it before someone else realized that if it were lit, he would certainly catch on fire if not explode, whereupon Timmy started laughing at having almost tricked us into immolating him. We dragged him out to the Windstar and shoved him in the back, still leaking in his volatile comforter. Jason and Ward jumped in front, and they peeled out for the emergency room at Daniel Freeman Marina Hospital just a few blocks away.

Brody and I stood in the kitchen for a few minutes looking down at the puddle of paint thinner. I climbed up into Timmy's loft and took a look around—it was filthy and reeked of solvent—and then we went down to the hospital in another car. Timmy had been admitted to the ER, and Jason and Ward were in conversation with the admission lady for the psych ward, a frizzy-headed amateur comedienne in a big purple caftan who inappropriately overidentified with whomever she was checking in—because she was crazy, too! Judy, Janet—whatever her name was, something jolly—pressed her business card on us and insisted we should all hang out. Make a show! Join forces! Have fun! I knew I should find the scene amusing, a clammy stand-up joke—"Hollywood is so crazy, even the psych ward lady has a head shot!"—but I just wanted to hit her in the face.

Because the trauma to Timmy's intestinal tract was so severe, he couldn't be admitted to the psych ward yet but had to be held and monitored in the regular part of the hospital, which had the disadvantage of not being locked down. But Timmy wasn't going anywhere that night. He would be admitted to the psych ward for evaluation when he was well enough to walk over there. By visiting hours the next afternoon, when we were allowed to go see Timmy in his bed, we had all agreed it was time for a serious evaluation. Drinking a jug of paint thinner wasn't funny.

He looked awful, but by all rights he should have been dead. The doctors were amazed at his constitution. They hadn't been able to do anything but give him some stuff to coat his stomach, monitor him, and hope for the best. He was still shitting so much—or more like just steadily leaking and then from time to time blasting out a cloud of napalm—that for once it didn't even make sense for him to keep his pants on. He was wearing one of those hospital smocks that tie at the back, and that was it. Since he had been checked in wearing only the comforter, he didn't have any shoes, just the paper slippers they had given him.

The following day at the office, we discussed whether we should mention this recent development to Comedy Central—or, for that matter, to anybody. CRAPtv was being represented in the deal by a television agent we hardly knew, the guy at CAA to whom Rosenberg had introduced us. He seemed like a solid character, but we were just getting to know him. And maybe everything would be okay in a week or two, so why rock that boat? We knew our attorney wouldn't panic. He'd seen all kinds of shit. But since we already knew that, we figured it would probably be most considerate not to burden him with something he'd rather not know. Plus, we figured the Woodsman had a right to whatever privacy we could provide. He might have been publicly crazy, but he was entitled to get treatment for it privately.

We took the next day's visitation in shifts. I had the evening shift, alone. Timmy seemed markedly better than the day before. Physically he was practically back to his old self. He said his ass was still on fire, but other than that he just felt sort of weak, and now he was wearing pajama bottoms with his smock. In fact, he said, he was ready to check out of the hospital. I said I wasn't sure that was such a hot idea. It was pretty serious, what had happened. The doctors wanted him to stay a little while, at least to be evaluated in the psychiatric ward that was right there at the same hospital. Timmy said that he could understand my point of view and theirs, but what none of the rest of us was taking into account was the black helicopters.

We both laughed uneasily. The black helicopters were an old trope with the Woodsman. But as a trope they were so tired, so baldly plagiarized from pop apocrypha, that we always figured the Woodsman was kidding about them. On this occasion he tied the black helicopters in with Master P, a rapper of nefarious reputation, whom Timmy had long claimed had a hit out on him—and considering Timmy's colorful history in Oakland (Master P is famously from New Orleans, but he built his No Limit business in the East Bay), the hit part seemed entirely plausible. But was it not unlikely, I asked, that Master P had command of a black helicopter squadron? Was it not generally understood that the federal government, not a cabal of murderous gangsters, operated the black helicopters? Timmy squinted. Maybe the feds. But more likely, the helicopters had been sent by THE BIG SHE.

This was the first I had heard of HER. When I asked what he meant by THE BIG SHE, the Woodsman went silent and stared at me for a long evaluative moment—like maybe I was fucking with him or maybe he couldn't trust me. At some point in the middle of this long moment, I finally came to understand that all the funny business, the interchangeable truth and lies, the conflation of the real and the imaginary, the laughing at pain and sobbing for gags—it came down to an inability to know for certain where the dividing lines were drawn. Right there my heart broke for the Woodsman, that poor crazy asshole. But I had to hear the rest of it. I pressed him about THE BIG SHE. What the fuck was he talking about? He shook his head. I was better off not knowing. But if I insisted on knowing something about THE BIG SHE—and I did—I could know this:

SHE WAS SO BIG, SHE WAS LIKE A GANG.

Night was falling outside his narrow window. Visiting hours were long over. I told the Woodsman that I was glad he was feeling a little better and that we would all be back to visit tomorrow. Eat some pudding, let the old alimentary canal heal up a little, and there would be plenty of time to talk about checking out—or maybe about taking his doctor's advice and spending a little time over on the psych ward, which, come on, probably wasn't a bad idea, and no one would think any less of him for it. It had been a tough couple of days. At the very least he could use the rest. Right, said the Woodsman. Except he wasn't tired, and the nights here were no fun. You could still hear the helicopters at night. You heard them *more* at night. And night was when SHE was at HER strongest.

When I got up, he followed me to the door of his room, where we hugged—the Woodsman was an enthusiastic and powerful hugger. He said he'd walk me out. I told him I didn't want him to walk me out, but he followed me anyway. The hallway was empty and eerily dimmed, like an airplane cabin at night. The building seemed to have fallen asleep in the hour or so I had been visiting with Timmy. I walked backward toward the front of the hospital, admonishing him to quit messing around. A nurse spotted us as we crossed a perpendicular hallway and told the Woodsman (with whom, her tone made clear, she had already had dealings) that he wasn't supposed to be in this area. He pointed innocently at me, like it was my idea for him to be out in the halls. She rolled her eyes. We were past the intersection, and I kept telling Timmy to quit following me, and he kept insisting he was just walking me out, but now he was keeping ten feet away from me in case I made a grab for him. We were both laughing like it was some stupid game.

At the hospital's double doors I got the Woodsman to promise that he wasn't going to come outside after me. I backed up a few feet into the parking lot while he hung like a chimp from the sill, grinning at me in his goofy pajamas. Another nurse pushed a trolley up the hallway behind him and hectored him about being out in front. The Woodsman turned around to give her some double-talk, meanwhile backing outside, so that by the time he was done with what he was saying, he was outside the doors in the parking lot with me—classic Woodsman flimflam, the backward walk-and-talk. He spun back around and raised his eyebrows. We both were laughing again now. It was clear he was making a run for it, and I was edging to cut him off, when he faked left and went right, leapt over a low hedge, and ran his silly ass off up the sidewalk to freedom.

2

Timmy resurfaced twenty-four hours later, looking like a chocolate-covered monkey. He said he had run from the hospital to the marshland between the freeway and our office, where he dug a "mud hole," and since then he had been buried up to his eyeballs, monitoring the helicopters. Considering the density of LAPD chopper traffic over our neighborhood, it must have been a long night.

We tried to talk him into checking back into Freeman. The hospital administrators felt pretty bad about his escape and were prepared to admit him into the psych ward immediately. But the Woodsman expressed concerns about medical torture, and now that THE BIG SHE was wise to that place, SHE would find him in a heartbeat—if SHE weren't running it herself, which he was beginning to suspect.

None of this was good news on the mental health front, but if Timmy didn't want to check back into Freeman, there was nothing we could do about it. Legally he was an adult, and we had no authority over him. The only threat we could make was that if he didn't check himself in, we wouldn't have anything more to do with him, and we weren't prepared to make that threat. By now this had nothing to do with our business ties. The thought of him alone and on the loose, hunted by imaginary death squads, was more than any of us could bear.

A suicide attempt is embarrassing for everyone involved. The Woodsman seemed chastened, and he was more generally cheerful and cooperative than ever before. We were all eager to put it behind us. We made him do the usual bullshit thing, sign a promise that he wouldn't hurt himself—a process made doubly ridiculous by the Woodsman's fantastic propensity for fraud—and then we just tried to be kind and keep him busy with little projects around the office.

* * *

The first four-week CVP chemotherapy protocol had pushed back my mother's cancer, but it had also weakened her significantly. We were in a waiting period—waiting to see which would recover faster, my mother or her lymphoma. If enough time passed between relapses, treatment with CVP could be continued for some time. It was rough, but it could keep you alive.

Dr. Lucas hoped for a period of six months before my mother's hematocrit dropped again. The length of the period between resurgences of the disease would be an indicator of how long my mother might hope to survive. Each time the protocol was used it would be less effective, and the cancer's refractory period would be shorter. The longer the length of that first interval, the longer the time until there would be no intervals, only terrible decisions.

Two months after the first protocol ended, Margaret's hematocrit fell off a cliff. This was deeply discouraging to us, and it plainly made Dr. Lucas furious. The two of them were tough customers, my mother and Jen Lucas. My mother's quick relapse signaled a change in both their attitudes toward her treatment. Neither was accustomed to not having her way, and at this point they both seemed to roll up their sleeves. Not that my mother had been a bad patient or that Dr. Lucas had been anything but serious in treating her, but now my mother quit working, and Dr. Lucas abandoned any pretense of oncological detachment.

My mother's employer had been an absolute sweetheart, and he had insisted on paying her for working full-time even while she was being treated. But until now, my mother had declined to actually make herself unavailable to the tenants of his commercial properties, and from time to time during her first treatment or recovery I would come into the main house from the back house and find my bald little bird of a mother perched at her desk, negotiating in a whisper with a contractor who had failed to fix a leaking roof. Now she parceled out her responsibilities to others at the company.

She turned inward, taking naps when she needed them and attending workshops offered as part of the integrated care package at Marin Oncology. This being Marin, a panoply of alternative and supplemental treatments was available. She went to seminars on meditation and an Eastern practice called qigong that seemed to make her feel better, and we both got a laugh out of it when somebody sent me a JPEG of a bunch of Korean monks pulling a bus with their penises as a demonstration of qigong's power.

There was a chance that a second protocol of CVP administered immediately—essentially a continuation of the first protocol, since the interval had been so short—could push the cancer below the critical level. My lay understanding of how cancer propagated was that since new cancer cells were created by the splitting of existing cancer cells, there was a critical level below which their splitting was hardly measurable and above which it was catastrophic. Though a second CVP protocol now would be quite difficult for my mother to tolerate, it could conceivably work.

It was in this period that we became close friends with Jen Lucas and with her partner, Jenn Emberly—right, Jen and

Jenn—an adorable director of animation at Industrial Light and Magic. When my mother's hematocrit stabilized again and she began her second recovery from chemotherapy, my mother and Jen Lucas began meeting at dawn for hikes around Phoenix Lake in the dell above our town. Jen Lucas ran my mom ragged on these walks, but presumably she knew better than anybody else what my mom's body could tolerate, so I was delighted at the extra monitoring as well as at the pleasure my mother clearly took at having someone new to know and enjoy during what, I was now becoming resigned, might be the twilight of her life.

Bert came out from Colorado to visit with her, and he built a fountain in her yard. He and I drove around to hardware stores, getting the parts. He dug a little pool under her camellias and placed a teak Buddha beside it. The three of us went together to an herbalist's shop called the Pine Street Clinic, where the herbalist prescribed Chinese warming powders and fungi for my mother, and where they had a peach-colored standard poodle that was friendly and supposedly could sniff out melanoma—why not? In both my parents' houses now there is a picture taken on that visit: my mom and dad, divorced nearly thirty years by then, smiling on a sofa in her living room. Bert is tan from his life in the mountains and the summer that is only recently gone, and Margaret is pale as bone.

All these events transpired in what felt to me like muffled gloom. I was never quite awake during the day, and at night I stayed up in the back house making adjustments to the CRAPtv business plan, which now ran on past fifty pages of rambling monologue on convergent media, interspersed with bitchy case studies examining financed start-ups that had crashed and burned due to my not having conceived them, and appended with a projections spreadsheet that swelled, retracted, and exploded like a fissioned atom according to whatever Rosenberg thought would sound good to whichever person he was promising to get it to next. After noodling with the plan, each night I read thrillers and police procedurals until dawn, boring my way through through ten thousand pages of Tom Clancy, Michael Crichton, and Patricia Cornwell. I also learned from a Peachpit Press *QuickStart Guide* how to write primitive HTML.

It now was November, and the Comedy Central deal was still pending. It seemed that it would always be pending, and there was nothing we could do to stop it from pending forever save make a clean breast with regard to our star's having gone insane. Between days passed in the shadows of autumnal Marin and the chilly squalor of the CRAPtv warehouse—the place had been in even worse decline since the paint thinner incident—I drove up and down, up and down, up and down Interstate 5.

Jason and Ward decided that despite our narrowed circumstances, Lapdance should be held again this year, and it should be held in a large geodesic dome we would site in a Park City parking lot and call the Electronic Igloo. We would use the dome for screenings and panels during the days and for parties every night. They had already priced the dome. So with my newfound HTML expertise I made matching Web sites in pink and blue for Lapdance 2001 and the First Annual Electronic Igloo Media Conference. The idea of producing a festival alternative to Sundance was long past being passé, and I glumly militated against our going this year even as I completed the Web sites. Now there were at least fifteen alternative festivals competing for underground legitimacy so as to be noticed by the mainstream media and thereby become legitimately alternative, a paradox that no longer amused. We met a few more wacky filmmakers every year, but as far as I was concerned, we already knew plenty of wacky filmmakers. They were a plague on our existence.

The main thing, though, was that this year we just didn't have any money of our own to lose, and the Content companies that were foaming over with cash the year before were all gone. Then Sundance simply made a preemptive strike—they must have been really sick of all of us little fuckers who came every year to poop in the punch bowl—and reserved almost every venue in town themselves. The geodesic dome idea failed to find traction for lack of early financing, and by December, the only place we had a prayer of reserving for use as the Lapdance venue was the grimy basement bar where we had screened *The Sound of One Hand Clapping* in 1998.

This was a gloomy step down and back, but Jason remained undaunted. If there was no more Content money to finance our boondoggle, then we would go back to our early strength: porn. Renewed porn presence, which had been in short supply at the semilegitimate Lapdance 2000, would confer the benefit of pissing off Sundance and the city all over again. But all the other ghetto festivals were just as sleazy as we were, and they had already snapped up the good porn sponsors.

Our sources were tapped out. A fundraiser was what we had been wanting all along for CRAPtv, what Rosenberg had turned out not to be—at least not for us. Rosenberg had, since joining us, managed to get a couple of million dollars for a film production company he was forming with a partner who was leaving a comic book company. Rosenberg's new company had outside financing from an heiress to the Lauder cosmetics fortune and supposedly distribution through Dimension Films. His new company was going to concentrate on taking comic book and video game properties to the big screen. The migration of properties from one media platform to others was one of the many things meant by the media business buzzword *convergence,* and Rosenberg and his partner were all about convergence. They couldn't name their company Convergence because it was taken, so they ran through a list of semi-synonyms and settled on Collision Entertainment, a decision that would turn out to be apposite.

Rosenberg told us that his new company would be great for CRAPtv—momentum, synergy, etc.—and the first thing they were going to do was sponsor Lapdance. As part of our delivery to Collision in exchange for sponsoring Lapdance, I designed a brand mark for Collision to replace their crappy temporary brand mark, which was a drawing of two trains running into each other. The new mark was excellent, if I do say so myself. It looked like the rectangular yellow street sign you see at the top of a T intersection, the double-headed black arrow ←—→, only in the Collision logo the points were reversed → ←. They put it on all their business cards and stationery and on the door of their office in Beverly Hills. In fact, we contracted all the collateral and delivered it to them—before they decided that they couldn't pay for the Lapdance sponsorship. So that was off to a great start.

We were pretty much screwed in terms of having someone to raise money for Lapdance—except for this one character named Josh Younger, who worked in the LA office of a New York music management firm. Josh Younger was a classic music industry cheeseball straight out of New Jersey, still rocking that East Coast macho hustler style that on the West Coast read as gay as assless chaps: short hair spiked up with lots of gel, pecs a little puffy from lifting weights, a too-tight black-ribbed cap-sleeved T-shirt, lots of silver rings. Late 2000 was when the streamlined bondage cuff was really finding its place as a piece of mainstream haberdashery, and Josh Younger rocked the bondage cuff on not one but both wrists. He had a tattoo in Hebrew characters on his knuckles, which he told me, when I asked, read "chutzpah."

His pitch re Lapdance was compelling in the depth of its flattery. Our offering was tremendously valuable. Incredibly valuable. We were the edgy alternative festival guys. Everybody knew that. We just didn't know how to market what we had, or to whom. Josh Younger knew those things. Knowing those things was Josh Younger's business. He could easily raise a hundred thousand dollars for the event, and he was perfectly willing to work entirely on commission—just 10 percent, because he liked us and because it would be so easy. So we shook hands, and he asked for his check for ten thousand dollars.

Ha ha ha, but he wasn't joking. He wanted the $10,000 as an advance against the commissioned $10,000 and only backed off his demand when we countered that, instead, to back his guarantee, he should first give us $100,000, and then we'd give him 10 percent of it, and then when he had raised $90,000 for us, he could have the rest of it back. I thought our business with Josh Younger was concluded. We had wasted a little bit of each other's time, but no harm done, okay bye. But instead of leaving after our ridiculous counter, he appeared to take a moment to think about it. And right there I was back in: Holy shit, he really *did* think he could guarantee the money!

Where was he going to get it? Simple, he was going to get it from *Hustler*. His office was in the Flynt building on Wilshire, and Josh Younger was tight with the people at *Hustler*. Tell you what, why don't we draw up a proposal outlining the whatever, the benefits, how many clicks and impressions and stuff they would get with a sponsorship, and he would set up a meeting over there. With whom at *Hustler*? With upper management, don't worry about it.

And soon, further easing my skepticism about Josh Younger and his chutzpah, the meeting was set up, and Jason went over to the black oval LFP building to pitch Lapdance to *Hustler*. Jason returned to say the meeting had gone great. I was sorry to have missed it, because surely it would have made my own weirdest-Hollywood-meetings list. He said the *Hustler* offices were crazily ornate, with fake Sun King furniture all over the place and ten-foot nudes in gold rococo frames looking down from every wall. He and Josh Younger had been shown into a conference room like the inside of a jewelry box, and there they had pitched some big fat guy who was maybe mildly retarded or on really heavy drugs, but the guy's name was Flynt, Jimmy Flynt, and the meeting was undeniably at the *Hustler* headquarters—so it had to be legit, right? Jason said the Jimmy Flynt guy had said that he wasn't sure the magazine would cover all of the hundred grand, but definitely most of it. The only reason we didn't have payment already was that the guy had to check in with the board (that should probably be "the board") to see if they wanted to let anybody else in on the Lapdance opportunity or if they wanted to keep the whole thing for themselves.

After our first meeting with Josh Younger, Jason and I had had a snicker about his bondage cuffs, so before the *Hustler* meeting, Jason had rummaged around in the *Human Number* prop box and borrowed the big nasty padded bondage cuffs. These weren't the thin, decorative kind of cuffs you could find at Urban Outfitters but serious torture restraints designed to immobilize three-hundred-pound muscle-bottoms, and they looked absolutely ridiculous. But Jason reported that in the elevator down from their successful pitch, Josh Younger had noted his (Jason's) cuffs with some admiration and said that he was psyched to see that Jason understood the power of the cuffs, because he himself was almost superstitious about them. That very morning he had jumped in his car and made it halfway to the office before he realized he had forgotten to put on his cuffs, and he had turned right around and gone back to get them. Going back to get them obviously had been the right move—clearly, it was the power of the combined cuffs that had let him and Jason seal the deal with *Hustler*.

Since we didn't have a check from *Hustler* yet, I wasn't sure how sealed that deal was. But my mom was dying and it was almost Christmas, and since I hadn't been around enough either physically or mentally to have had much positive influence on what was happening with CRAPtv, I was making a concerted effort not to be such a controlling cock about every single thing that went down.

* * *

Just before Christmas a wonderful present arrived: a deal memo from Comedy Central, specifying a late May delivery date for *The Hot Show,* as we had entitled Timmy's pilot. We were all going north for the holidays. Normally, we all spent a good deal of them together up in Marin. Jason and Brody's mom and stepdad's house in Mill Valley was always warm and full of food and guests, and Ward's parents had a lovely annual Boxing Day party at their house in Sausalito.

This year the holidays were complicated by the issue of what to do with the Woodsman. He wanted to drop in on his parents in the East Bay, but he didn't expect to stay with them for the whole ten days or so that we were planning to be up north. We made a plan to leave him there on our way through to Marin before Christmas and collect him at some point afterward. If we collected him before New Year's, then he would stay with us at one of our parents' houses until we all went back down to Los Angeles.

We caravanned north in several cars and all drove to Timmy's childhood home, an A-frame in the semiurban flats of Fremont. The street was decorated brightly for Christmas, blinking lights hung from ranch house eaves, fiberglass reindeer cavorting in yards. The Woodsman's family's next-door neighbors had strung the redwood in their front yard, which must have been a hundred feet tall, with maypole garlands of multicolored bulbs.

Timmy's mother met us at the door and warily invited us in. We made small talk for a few minutes in the living room. If we had hoped this visit into Timmy's childhood would help us understand who the Woodsman truly was, we had hoped in vain. He seemed as much a stranger as we were to that home. His conversation with his mother was short and factual—how long he planned to stay, whether his sister would be visiting with her husband, whether they would be upset that he was home for Christmas. I think we were all glad to leave that place, where, despite stitched samplers on the walls and gilt-framed family pictures—not many of Timmy, though —sadness emanated like a gas from the brown shag wall-to-wall.

He lasted there until the day after Christmas. Jason and I negotiated on the phone regarding who should take the first shift. Despite Margaret's illness and the fact that there was more room for Timmy to bang around over at Jason and Brody's, Jason had me on significant points. He and Ward had had full-time custody of the Woodsman down south. They deserved a break, and all he was asking for was a couple more days. But more important, as I knew perfectly well, Christmas was the central annual event at their house, a six-day Old World stretch of strudel and presents. Their grandmother, Mrs. Pschorr, who was now in her eighties, came over at dawn on Christmas with her poodles and took up a fortified position in the living room, which she held until New Year's Eve. Dropping that satyr the Woodsman into the few days per year of crystal and silver and German fruitcakes that Grandma could hope for around the holidays would constitute the depth of heartlessness.

I prepped Margaret as well as possible, but I had already told her too many stories for her to be completely easy about the situation. I am ashamed to say that I played to her Christmas spirit—no room at the inn for this poor wanderer, and so on. Heather and I drove over to the East Bay in the evening and picked up the Woodsman at a BART station under an

overpass, then drove him back to my mom's house. He behaved himself admirably that first night, greeting my mom in
the front hall just before bedtime and retiring meekly with his
blankets to the cottage behind the pool. Heather and I slept
in the main house in the office that had been my bedroom.

When Heather and I woke, the Woodsman was already
in the kitchen having coffee with my mom. He was manic
and sweaty, bouncing around her little kitchen. He was doing
his best to be helpful—he kept asking for "chores"—but the
crazy was under such a thin sheet of not-crazy that I could
tell he was freaking my mom out. She was too sweet to take
me aside and say he had to go immediately, but she was still
weak from the chemo, and she already had the frozen smile
and blinking stare that signaled an interaction off the rails.
Heather knew by now how to recognize that look, so she
grabbed my car keys and drove off to visit with some of her
old friends in San Francisco.

I figured the best thing to do would be to try to wear
Timmy out. We bundled up, put Nemo on a leash, and set
off. Our path took us out my mother's short street to Shady
Lane, which ran straight down a colonnade of massive elms
between gingerbread mansions. I had no idea what the Woodsman, that scarred and addled veteran of Oakland streets and
the penitentiary, thought of this cozy fold in the hills of privilege. But he seemed to be doing okay, so we jogged up to
Phoenix Lake, and I let Nemo off the leash. He shot off into
the bushes, reappearing every hundred yards or so to look
back at us as we made the long, arduous hike up the back
slope of Mount Baldy. I was hoping to grind the wiry Woodsman down to a manageable level of manic energy, but not
a chance. He was like my demented black dog, still pop-

eyed and bouncing when we got to the top and looked out over the county and the bay's northern reaches where they spilled out gray under the winter sky.

It was nearly dark by the time we got back to the house. Heather had returned from the city, and my mom was up from her nap and puttering in the kitchen. She had a bag of small red potatoes that the Woodsman proposed to mash. I remember this so vividly because when my mother and I ate together and it was just the two of us, we almost never ate mashed potatoes—not that either of us disliked mashed potatoes; we liked them fine, we just never made them. But mashed potatoes sounded like fun, so the Woodsman was given license to mash away.

He boiled up the bag and chopped a whole head of garlic to season them. My mother snuck nervous glances at me as the Woodsman mashed up his mess, spattering a little in his enthusiasm. But by and large he kept the potatoes confined to a mixing bowl, and he added the garlic and some butter and milk. His mashed potatoes were ready just as the rest of the food was finished cooking, and the four of us sat down at my mother's kitchen table with the big bowl of mashed potatoes in the middle.

Despite the strangeness of our little gathering, dinner got off to a nice start. Heather had had a pleasant visit with one of her high school friends, now an architect who had had something to do with construction of the new baseball stadium in San Francisco. My mother loved baseball and had been to a couple of games at the new stadium, where a home run could clear the bleachers and plop down between boats in the bay. Her boss, Merritt, owned a couple of buildings in the area where the stadium was sited, the baseball traffic was doing good things for the neighborhood, and so on. The mashed potatoes were a hit, and everything was going just fine until all of a sudden it wasn't.

My mother may have opened the door by asking Timmy something innocuous about his parents. Or he may have taken us there all on his own—however it happened, in just a few leaps of conversation he was telling a story about a pile of dirty magazines he had had when he was a kid, that had been found by his parents, but that wasn't the story; the story was about how he had acquired the magazines from a neighbor five years his senior, fourteen or fifteen to his nine or ten, who had taken Timmy into his garage and shown him the pile of magazines and said that Timmy could have them if Timmy would suck his penis.

So right about there I tried to get us back onto baseball, but that mariner the Woodsman would not be stopped, because here came the punch line—Timmy only got *half* the magazines, because the neighbor kid thought he didn't do a good job with the penis sucking. And in retrospect, knowing what he knew now, the Woodmsan said he had to agree with the neighbor, because all he had done was put the penis in his mouth and kind of roll it around for a second or two, not, like, you know, really *suck* it. The neighbor's penis had tasted salty—but also, he blithely finished, kind of like soap. Heather and I looked at one another aghast. My mother was the first to speak.

"Sometimes things happen," she said softly, "that it's better not to talk about."

I didn't take this as a criticism of the Woodsman, and I am sure she didn't mean it as one. She knew he was crazy, and she wasn't going to hold anything he said against him. I believe my mother had in some part resigned herself to dying—not given up on the fight to stay alive but been compelled by her sickness to deeply acknowledge mortality—and her response to Timmy's revelation made me wonder what sad things might have happened to my mother that she had never talked about and I would never know. Nothing like that, surely, but we all have our sad secrets, the ones so sad we plan to pull them down behind us.

The Woodsman didn't take my mother's comment as a scolding, either, but looked back at her frankly and replied that maybe she was right. Maybe the story he had just told was one of those things, and if it was, he was sorry he had talked about it. Dinner ended in quiet conversation on other topics. We washed the dishes and went to bed. The next day Heather and I handed Timmy the Woodsman back over into Jason's care. Jason had custody of him over New Year's, and I gathered there were some shenanigans, but everybody made it to 2001.

Back down in Los Angeles, though, Timmy seemed worse off than he had been up north. He was back to nattering about THE BIG SHE and the helicopters. Jason was fried from the combined stresses of his own New Year's experience and trying to keep track of Timmy during it, so he handed the Woodsman back off to me and Heather.

A year earlier we had moved out of the apartment in Venice and into a duplex, when the landlords at the first place found out about the dog. Scott Mitchell had made the move with us, stayed another six months, and then moved into his own place, but almost immediately his spot had been taken by Clancy Pearson, one of the guys from SciArc who had designed the *Human Number* site. He and his partners had shared occupancy of the Venice Quiddity office at the end, and now they had desks in the CRAPtv warehouse.

Clancy was an obscenely talented artist—painter, architect, musician, designer, everything—a hilarious guy, and in general a happy one, but at this point he was caught in a severe post-postgraduate downward spiral, and he was spending most of his time at our place either asleep in his room or upright on the couch cuddling a warm forty-ounce bottle of malt liquor. The back room stank of boozy despair, and the layered grime of Mitchell's machine dirt and Clancy's hair product deposited over a combined year had already created a bathtub ring where the bed met the wall. I figured we could keep the Woodsman there at least until Clancy got back; Clancy was still at his own parents' for the holiday, and he was sympathetic to the Woodsman's plight.

The first night we had Timmy, I woke at dawn with the feeling that something was terribly wrong. Heather was softly asleep. Nemo whined from his chair and regarded me with worried eyes. I got up to go to the bathroom and on the way noticed that the Woodsman's door, which I remembered as having been open when we went to bed, was closed. I figured I'd look in on him just to make sure he was okay—something just felt weird; I have no better explanation—but the door was locked. I knocked, and there was no answer, only a scuffling movement. I started banging on it and yelling Timmy's name, but he didn't respond, so I kicked the door hard above the doorknob.

It cracked open to reveal the Woodsman standing on the edge of the bed, one end of a leather jump rope coiled around his neck and the other tangled in the ceiling fan. He leaned off as I entered and I caught him around the midsection, pushing him back over the bed from which his legs now swung free. I had most of his weight, and the wood-handled rope was clattering loose from the fan above us. He had done a crappy job of tying it off. Heather stood in the doorway regarding us in sleepy horror.

We lay on the bed, the Woodsman gasping as I reached up and uncoiled the rope from his neck. I noticed that his forearms were bleeding, and looked around to see that all the kitchen knives in the household were scattered over Clancy's desk. As an added comic touch, a cheap knockoff Samurai sword I had salvaged from the garage in Playa, too dull to be of use as anything but the biggest butter knife in the world, lay unsheathed on the floor. The crime scene resolved itself: First he had tried to slit his wrists, but all our kitchen knives were old serrated ones that made irritating messes out of tomatoes, and he had been unable to saw his way through to a vein; then he had attempted hara-kiri with a stage prop; and then he had tried to hang himself with the jump rope. Already he was apologizing and developing a little run about the knives, how he might as well have been trying to snuff it with a bunch of spoons, and what kind of shop were we running here, where a guy couldn't even find a real knife when he wanted to snuff it?

Snuff it—that was what the Woodsman called committing suicide. However disorganized this second attempt, certainly it qualified as an attempt. Heather and I proposed to check him into Freeman immediately. But going back to Daniel Freeman was not in the Woodsman's game plan. I didn't know what one was supposed to do at this point. A part of me wanted to have him hauled away—but by whom?

To where? He wasn't going to get in an ambulance if we called one. If we called 911, the LAPD might eventually drop by to Taser the Woodsman and haul him off to County, but it was hard to see how that was going to help anyone.

He promised he wouldn't try to snuff it again—and also reminded me, in case I was thinking of doing anything sneaky, they hadn't been able to keep him at Freeman last time. I woke Jason and Ward and Brody with phone calls as the Woodsman chatted with Heather and started cleaning up his mess, coiling the jump rope, washing the knives, jumbling them back in their drawer.

That day we all walked for miles, ambling with the Woodsman south along the bike path from Playa del Rey to the plant where all the sewage of the Los Angeles basin is treated and pumped out into Santa Monica Bay. Jets bellied off from LAX. The wind came in chilly off the ocean, and down by the treatment plant, hang gliders practiced on a shallow bluff where they could skim the seaward slope with running feet. Timmy trotted ahead of us and followed one of the gliders off the bluff, baying nonsense instructions at the old lady in the glider harness. By the time I got down to them he was helping her undo her straps, and she was smiling uneasily. We helped her get the kite turned around and rolling back up to the top of the hill, where he proposed that it was his turn now, and he tried to get into the harness, but the instructor came over and put a stop to it.

On the way back to where our cars were parked, Timmy picked up a plastic bag from the beach and started an impromptu cleanup operation. There was no conceivable end to it, to the buried cans, bottles, and tattered plastic pennants in the sand here at the end of the world. But we joined him for an hour or so, scouring half an acre down to pieces of trash small enough to pass for shells and pebbles. In the evening Brody took Timmy and me up to a yoga class in Santa Monica, where we stretched and strained among leotarded ladies, breathing, in and out, in and out. The Woodsman comported himself admirably, keeping quiet and doing as he was told.

But by nightfall we had reached no substantive resolution. Clancy wouldn't be back until the next day, and we decided to meet again then to come up with a real plan, ideally one that would end with the Woodsman deciding he was ready to check into the psych ward. If Timmy promised not to hurt himself, he could sleep at our place again.

Heather kept Timmy occupied with making dinner while I went out to rent some movies. Among my choices was perhaps a bad selection, *The Dogs of War,* in which Christopher Walken plays a career mercenary who engineers a coup d'état in Africa. After Heather went to bed, the Woodsman and I stayed up on the couch watching something innocuous and then, when he showed no signs of being ready to go to sleep, *The Dogs of War.* There were helicopters, and that was pretty bad, and there were also some nasty torture scenes I had forgotten. The Woodsman cut me sideways glances and raised his eyebrows significantly. When it was over, I gave him an extra blanket, went into my bedroom, and lay down.

Once there, I was afraid to go to sleep, certain that if I let myself doze off for even a moment, Timmy would try to hurt himself again. I was about to get up to check on him when he saved me the trouble, appearing in the doorway wrapped in his blanket and asking in a stage whisper if he could sleep with us in our bed. Heather had to go to work the next day, but she was a good sport about it, and my mind was put much at ease as the Woodsman snuggled down between us on top of our blankets. Heather gave me the quizzical sleepy face when she noticed he was naked under his comforter, but I just shrugged and put my finger to my lips, because it looked like he was finally settling down. His eyes were closed and he was breathing evenly, and I closed mine thinking that if only we could make it to another day, we would be able to figure out what to do with him.

I woke a moment later to find that he was gone. I jerked out of bed and ran to the other room. Despite my having kicked the door open once, it still had a functional lock. Without knocking I kicked the door again, and when it cracked open, this time splitting the hasp from the doorjamb, its swing was stopped by the desk and file cabinet Timmy had wedged against it as a barricade. I put my shoulder to the door and shoved these out of the way just as he stepped off the bed again, this time truly dangling for a moment as I clambered over the furniture, leather rope and metal creaking and wood and plaster snapping, before I could get to him and hold him up, yelling for Heather until she could come in and get the leather rope untied from the ceiling fan that now hung cockeyed from its mooring. The Woodsman tried to play it off again, but this time he knew the jig was up. I drove him down to Daniel Freeman Marina Hospital and checked him in.

3

Over the course of the Woodsman's stay at Freeman, I came to think of the psych ward as existing in the perpetual twilight of visiting hours. Considering that it was a locked ward catering to the indigent as well as the insured, it was a nice place, clean, comfortable, with adequate supervision. It was still a psych ward and therefore depressing, but most of us had been held in hospitals ourselves, so the rules and routines were familiar.

Timmy's diagnosis was frustratingly vague. The psychiatrist assigned to his case, a coolly clinical Indian woman, told us he could be classified as suffering from borderline personality disorder, schizophrenia, or bipolar disorder marked by psychotic episodes. Each of these was more a description of clustered symptoms than a treatable disease. But the symptoms might be mitigated by medication, and it was certainly good for the Woodsman to be away from unprescribed drugs and alcohol, which seemed to trigger his episodes. He was put on Depakote, an antiseizure medication that was also used to treat the manic phase of bipolar disorder; Risperdal, a powerful antipsychotic; and a third medication I cannot recall. By the end of the first week THE BIG SHE was out of the picture, and by the end of the second even the thud-thud-thud of LAPD helicopters overhead was cause for no more than a meaningful glance at the ceiling.

Throughout these trials Timmy retained the insight, humor, and sense of absurdity that represent the highest hallmarks of engaged intelligence. Intelligence is of little use against psychosis, but the Woodsman tried to get his shit together. Jason stayed and talked with him long after visiting hours were over, the two of them patiently finding points where Timmy's version of reality and a version that could be agreed upon touched and working to solidify those points of contact.

The one cliché of insanity that did not abate satisfactorily was the Woodsman's conviction that what was happening on television had something to do with him. He spoke of television, as did others on the ward, as a single power that spoke, in a million encoded voices through a million flickering panes, to each person individually. In this, of course, the Woodsman was correct.

He was no longer naming HER, but I had been unable to stop thinking about THE BIG SHE. In spite of being a crazy fuck, Timmy was onto something there. Big Brother was a scary construct, but Big Brother was such an overbearing dick—no more convincingly your pal than Saddam Hussein, with all those oversized billboards of himself. Naked totalitarianism gave you a concrete enemy, definitely terrifying, but ideologically fixed and doomed to topple eventually. THE BIG SHE was subtler, softer: spreading, adaptive, inviting. Attack her, and you are enveloped. Soothed. SHE was inescapable, SO BIG SHE WAS LIKE A GANG, a networked, perpetually lactating intelligence, keeping us a nation of babies bloated on HER poisonous milk and striking with a mother's fury if we tried to leave HER breast.

But even setting aside the fundamental correctness of the Woodsman's conviction that SHE was addressing him personally through the television, we had our work cut out for us explaining to the doctors that his situation was a bit more complicated than that of the others on the ward who were troubled by the same belief. For instance, while several other patients were also under the impression that they had deals to make TV shows as soon as they got out of the hospital, the Woodsman really did have a deal. And while several patients were under the impression that they were already on television, the Woodsman *was* already on television, and not in a way that made him feel any more sane or less a victim of HER malevolence.

The previous fall Jason had taken Timmy to a party up at Trey's house. There were parties up there pretty often, and in general these events formed a civilized counterpoint to the vomitous humanitarian disasters that were the parties at CRAPtv. In the years since *South Park* had hit, the parties had undergone an evolution from their origin as keggers for strippers and amazed nerds, through a short and somewhat lame phase of celebrity guest-list hyper-security, and then to pleasantly heterogeneous gatherings of friends and colleagues.

The best Hollywood party I ever attended was held there at the terminus of a transcontinental journey by the *How's Your News?* crew, a group of mentally and physically handicapped reporters led by a friend of mine from Stanford, Arthur Bradford, who had just finished crossing the continent in an RV and putting to the America they found along their route the titular question of their film. (Now available on DVD. Five out of five bananas.) Matt, Trey, and Tony Mindel financed the movie. America's news was just okay, but the *How's Your News?* crew's news was all good. Trey was an amazing piano player, and he accompanied reporter Susan Harrington through a rousing rendition of Aretha Franklin's "Respect." Newsman Sean Costello took the piano bench and played an original piece for the right hand. Heather performed half-improvised soap opera scenes with celebrity interview specialist Ron Simonson, who was also an actor—Ronnie knew the scenes, and she didn't. He opened the first one by yelling, "Elizabeth! Why did you get the abortion?!" and every scene ended with a big kiss. There was dancing, and I had the pleasure of being tackled from behind by and wrestling on the carpet with Mr. Robert Bird, a gentleman reporter with Down syndrome whose work I had admired for years.

But this party the Woodsman attended was not that *How's Your News?* party, just one of the regular parties, and I had left early, so I don't know specifically what the Woodsman did that night, only that it strained the hospitality of his hosts so severely that Dave Goodman, who lived up there at the time, could hardly speak of it. Jason's memories of the night were hazy, but there had been running around and yelling, maybe some karate-kicking of cocktails, almost certainly crawling and pants-down, and definitely a seizurelike spazz attack designed to make a pair of less seasoned drug-abusing guests think that they, too, were going to overdose and maybe die. Jason got yelled at and was made to drag the Woodsman out—by the armpits, because when Timmy didn't want to leave a place, he simply went limp. Very soon afterward and with the usual plausible deniability—but, come on—there appeared on *South Park* a new character whose name was Timmy and whose sole mode of expression was to shriek his own name at top volume.

Jason was quietly pissed. This wasn't the first time a piece of his world had been held up for America's amusement, and while the drinks were free, nobody was mailing him character payments. It has to be mentioned here that Trey's voice as Cartman bore a distinct resemblance to Trey's impression of Jason. Everyone has the right to take his material where he finds it, and the transformation of that material from dumb fact into comedy—or even, dare it be said, into art—cuts any trailing ties. That transformation is the job, and Trey was better at it than anyone else we knew. Jason knew that as well as anyone, and he never griped about occasionally being on the pointy end of it, even in private. He had been silent, silently—and gracefully, I thought, in light of its not really having been a choice.

Even setting aside all the hospitality, the parties and dinners, and, for some, the jobs and loans and dental care, it was outrageous how much Matt and Trey had done for all of us, individually and as a group, with their general support of our vague endeavor. The introductions, the associations, appearing on our silly panels—who knew how many times people had been willing to meet us or hear out our pitches just because they mistakenly thought we had something to do with *South Park?* Jason had made two movies and two pilots with Matt and Trey, but I was just some guy, and their simply declining to impugn us—because no doubt Comedy Central had made a call to them before calling us back about doing a pilot—showed tremendous generosity.

On the other hand, now Trey was rich practically beyond belief, with a weekly show and all the vocal amplification that came with that. Jason, by contrast, had his whole future staked on a homeless street performer. Timmy had been a cock, and Jason had probably shown bad judgment in bringing him to the party in the first place. But was it really necessary to name the new character Timmy?

It was Timmy the Woodsman's misfortune that Timmy the kid in the wheelchair became instantly, wildly popular. Flat *South Park* merchandise sales spiked as they had not since Mister Hanky's debut, and now it was not hooting calls of "Hi-de-ho!" that you might overhear from time to time from a neighboring aisle in the grocery store, but Timmy the Woodsman's shouted name, "Timmay!"

* * *

Timmy the Woodsman was uninsured, of course, and four-teen days was the limit of Daniel Freeman Marina Hospital's largesse. The Woodsman's options were walking out the door and doing his best, with what assistance we could provide, to get further treatment at outpatient facilities for the indigent or arranging to be incarcerated—and it was not too strong a word—in a state mental hospital. This was not a difficult choice. Timmy hated the logginess his sledgehammer meds induced, but they were definitely working. He was no longer suicidal, and he was perfectly capable of carrying on a regular conversation. And he was still funny, which made it possible that relatively soon he might have regular employment as the star of his own television show.

The Hot Show now looked like not just Timmy's best chance of success, but his best chance of survival, for with a pickup would come money to pay for housing and ongoing care. Jason's scheme for meeting the Woodsman's supervisory needs now was for the show to be a hit, which would mean that we could slip into the production budget some sort of assistant to Mr. Woodsman, a kid whose sole job would be keeping track of him. The assistant would live with Mr. Woodsman, drive Mr. Woodsman wherever he wanted to go, carry Mr. Woodsman's wallet, make sure Mr. Woodsman took his meds, and call us before calling the cops or anyone else when things were getting out of hand. Jason had the whole thing mapped. Being the assistant to Mr. Woodsman would be one of the more demanding gigs in Hollywood, but for the right film school graduate, it would be a matchless educational experience. Maybe we'd call Larry laBeouf back from Arizona.

Lapdance meanwhile was just two weeks off. Right up to that moment Josh Younger had been all over the phones telling us everything was lined up, and then he just disappeared. Josh Younger's disappearance wasn't a huge surprise, but still it was distressing. No answer at his office, no answer on his cell, and when we called the front desk at the place where he worked in Los Angeles, they didn't know where he was, either. He still had voice mail, so I left him a series of progressively dickier messages, but it had been a tough couple of months, and I really wanted to yell at him in person. Finally, I called his boss at the music management company in New York. The boss went back and forth between reviling Josh Younger in familiar terms and claiming hardly to have met him, and finally he said Josh Younger was no longer with the company—not that he ever had been, officially, or that the boss was willing to be held liable for any representations Josh Younger might have made—and that he had gone to live in Florida.

That wasn't quite the end of it. The day before Jason was scheduled to leave for Utah—sponsorship or no, it was too late to cancel Lapdance—a truck arrived in front of our office and off-loaded an entire shipping pallet of remaindered porn magazines, a cardboard box of dildos, and another cardboard box of plastic shopping bags from the Hustler store. All the driver knew was that he was supposed to drop this stuff at this address, and here it was, but I think the idea was that these were supposed to be our gift bags. Welcome to our party. Here is a bag containing three back issues of *Barely Legal* and a plastic dong. Enjoy.

Later that day, Josh Younger went past pissing me off and endeared himself to me forever by leaving a message on my voice mail—I was very sorry to have missed this call—in which he calculated the "street value" of the in-kind sponsorship he had secured for us to be in the neighborhood of ten thousand dollars, and said that if I called him back, he would give me an address to which I could send a check for 10 percent of that amount. When I called back to get the address—and got his voice mail again, of course—my voice must have given away my intentions, and I never got to send him the box of dildos.

Jason went to Utah a week before Lapdance was scheduled; Brody and Ward a few days later. I arrived the afternoon of the event. Jason had brokered a tangle of shady trade deals that put equipment in place for our screenings, and he had even managed to sell some small cash sponsorships. We already had free liquor in place—some yucky red stuff called Redrum, but nobody cared what it was, as long as there was plenty of it—and Ward had put together a separate sponsorship package in collusion with the marketing douchebags employed by the drink manufacturer SoBe. SoBe would supply, in addition to fruity beverages, money to pay for the services of "Naughty Nurses," who would wear white plasticized minidresses and carry oversized syringes that could be loaded up with shots of Redrum or SoBe's gross Red Bull–clone caffeine drink, Adrenaline, for squirting into people's mouths. Ward had pulled in a Vivid Girl named Sky to be our main Naughty Nurse. Let it not be said that CRAPtv put on anything but a high-class soirée.

But on the front end we were still short on cash, so Jason and Ward had come up with one final—and, I thought, terrible—idea for getting a thousand more dollars: an individual Pimp Sponsorship. The Pimp Sponsorship would allow its purchaser to wear his laminate on a special pink feather boa lanyard and occupy a makeshift throne throughout the event, and the SoBe nurses would serve him drinks all night from their syringes. I said nobody would pay a thousand dollars for something so dumb. They told me somebody already had, and I instantly formed a low opinion of this person, whoever he was.

We were all crabby. They had been working for days on end, coming down with nasty colds and trudging around in the slush, and once again they didn't exactly appreciate my dropping in at the last minute just to say it looked like another fucking mess. For my part, I wasn't sure where they thought I had been—on vacation in the tropics? Two days earlier my mom had tottered bald and wizened on my arm into the waiting room at the oncology clinic and vomited into a trash can. She didn't cry, but I almost did. Now she was done with the second CVP protocol—they got worse at the end, when her body was poisoned as comprehensively as it could be without killing her. Her hematocrit was in the shitter. The office staff and chemo nurses were as kind as ever, but I detected a new set to Jen Lucas's jaw, one I didn't like. She remained upbeat. But of course she remained upbeat; it was her exhausting job to remain upbeat. She had to remain upbeat, or she wouldn't be able to get out of bed and go to work each day.

The low-rent squalor of the party preparation wasn't the only depressing thing about Lapdance that year. A group of young succubi from the CRAPtv bulletin board had made a plan in that forum to subdue and ravish members of our affiliation group—Jason and Dian were specifically targeted for sexual destruction—in Park City. For the past week they had been plying Jason and Dian with liquor, hard drugs, and freshly killed meat (one of them was a butcher) in the hope that they would be rendered defenseless. Jason had an incredible tolerance for everything, but I am afraid Dian may have fallen under that assault, and it was also possible that in bringing our event to Utah we had unwittingly launched multiple new vectors of a genital plague known as the Rash.

Yes, the Woodsman had been brought along—it wasn't like he could be left behind—and I found out that for the past week nobody had been keeping track of his meds. After he checked out of Freeman, Brody had purchased a pill dispenser, one of those plastic tackle boxes with little cells arrayed in rows of seven. Even down in Los Angeles it had been a job to see that he took them with any regularity—and they were the kind of meds that you were supposed to take with serious regularity, not as you thought you might need them. But somehow the pill dispenser had been left behind, no one had bothered to get his prescriptions filled locally, and, to make matters worse, the Woodsman was now embarked on a full-blown binge of the type expressly contraindicated.

Already there had been consequences. Once more Jason had lured E! into taping a segment with CRAPtv. The silly bit they came up with sounded like a perfectly good one unless you knew anyone involved: CRAPtv would compete against *Playboy,* which had a promotional presence at Sundance, in a snowmobile race. A couple of Bunnies would ride double on one snowmobile against whatever champions we put forth on another. Riding for CRAPtv were Brad the Clown, a filmmaker who had just finished an edit of his sad self-documentary project, *Behind the Red Nose,* and the Woodsman, who would compete bundled up in Danny Diamond's one-eyed bear suit.

It wasn't supposed to be a real race. It was supposed to be a pretend race—a camera setup for the start, a couple of shots of the two snowmobiles "racing" side by side, and another setup for the dramatic slow-motion finish. For all the obvious reasons, plus the fact that the only way to see out of the bear head was to peer through a screened peephole under its chin, Brad the Clown was instructed in no uncertain terms not to allow the Woodsman to do any driving. At all. The bear was to be a passenger *only,* and Timmy was to confine his drollery to pratfalls off the back of the snowmobile, where the only person he could hurt was himself.

But Brad the Clown was an easy mark, and by the time the camera crew set up for the start, the bear was at the snowmobile's controls. None of us, for the record, was present when these events transpired. Danny Diamond was taping but could not as a cameraman have been expected to exert any control over events. When someone said to start, the Woodsman gunned his engine and with unerring blind precision found a stump from which to launch and thus propel the snowmobile, himself, and Brad the Clown through the air and into the only large tree in the area. The Woodsman was insulated from the collision by the bear suit, but the rented snowmobile's steering mechanism was wrecked, and Brad the Clown hit the tree face-first. His foam nose did little to soften the blow. When I ran into Brad—days later, at his sparsely attended screening on the day of the Lapdance party—he had scabs all over his face and was rubbing his neck and complaining that he thought something in it might be broken.

I thought he was just being a sad clown, but X-rays indicated that he had cracked a vertebra. Technically, it had been E!'s production, which as a general rule meant that it would be their insurance that was supposed to pay for anything bad that happened. But E! was understandably pissed off, and their attorneys were saying they wouldn't pay for Brad's care. Because of the sad eyes and general air of indigence Brad the Clown wore even out of makeup, I was worried he would be unable to pay for treatment. But it turned out Brad the Clown's dad was head of an HMO in Connecticut. Brad the Clown got flown home, and no lasting grudges were held in any direction, except maybe by Brad's dad.

This year we simply could not lose money. I had finally learned the lesson that if the twenties didn't go straight into my pocket, they would never make it into our bank account, so I ran the door, checking laminates and stuffing twenties from the people who didn't have them into my parka. I quickly lost count of how many people I let in, and a narrow stair led down to the club proper, so I couldn't tell how full it was. It seemed like I had let in a couple of hundred people, though, and there were a couple of hundred more waiting out in the cold. We had no idea what our deficit was at this point, but my pockets were filling up with bills. Maybe we were going to be okay.

At the heat of the crush, when the yammering publicists outside were reaching the peak of their fury (I remember one little troll in particular who waved her arms in my face and squalled, "Sopranos! Sopranos!" until finally I couldn't take the sight or sound of it anymore and just let her barrel past me with a minor pretend mobster, the short fat lispy one, in tow), I was joined from below by a moon-faced kid with steamed round glasses. He greeted me familiarly by name and started helping out with the door, holding the line at bay with good humor, telling the people at the front of the line that it was a nightmare down there, and if they wanted a good time they should go somewhere else. When it got to the point that people we had let in were having difficulty getting down the stairs from the foyer into the party itself, we stopped letting them in and leaned back against the bucking doors. I figured the moon-faced kid was somebody Jason had tricked into being a temporary intern. It was not until we took this break that I saw he was wearing the pink feather boa Jason and Ward had said was for the Pimp Sponsor. This, then, was our Pimp.

His name was Mattt Potter. Not a typo, or at least not mine. It was later that I learned the curious spelling of his first name and that it was an error on his birth certificate that he had elected not to correct. When I asked him why he wasn't downstairs getting his Pimp treatment, he made a sour face.

"That chick Sky smells like ass."

It was a standing-on-the-arms-of-the-Pimp-Throne lap-dance from our Naughty Nurse that had sent him scrambling for the relative safety of the front door. I replied that giving lap dances was sweaty work, and the Naughty Nurse costumes didn't look like they breathed that well, so you had to forgive a little body odor, and so on. He shook his head.

"Not BO, dude. Poo."

Now I thought maybe he was angling for a refund on his thousand dollars, and helping out with the door had been a move toward softening me up, so I hemmed and hawed some more about how where there's smoke there's fire, if it's hot in the kitchen, and what have you.

"I don't want my money back for this dumb Pimp Sponsorship," said Mattt Potter. "Jason said you were way over budget, so I called my girlfriend in Seattle, and she let me do a cash advance on her credit card to help bail you out. Don't you know who I am?"

I still didn't, but as we stood there, he told me some things that helped me put it together: This was a kid who had e-mailed us a couple of really funny Quicktime submissions we already had posted on the site. I took a closer look at Potter. Beneath the Pimp Sponsorship regalia—in addition to the pink boa lanyard, there were a bunch of fake gold necklaces and a paper Burger King crown—he had the look of a genuine film geek: the greasy hair, the steamy goggles, a slumped navy blue parka, oversized black T-shirt, stone-washed jeans pegged down to poofy black high-tops, now sopping from slush and spilled SoBe. Upon hearing that we had sold the Pimp Sponsorship, I had figured it had gone to an idiotic jet-setter or maybe an executive on an expense account. My impression here was not of some lame hipster who was faking the funk, but of a bona fide basement-dwelling nerd who had selected us, the lowest portal into the lowest storm drain, as his point of entry into Hollywood.

By one or two in the morning, more people were leaving than arriving. Potter and I left the door open and wandered downstairs for the party's denouement. From the mess, it looked to have been a good one. We helped the bands roll the PA and instruments back to their van and tour bus. Danny Diamond poked forlornly in the Dumpster out back looking for the bear head, which had been misplaced or stolen in the melee. Potter rode back to the hotel with me and Heather and a few other members of our group—staying with us turned out to be another part of the Pimp Sponsorship, but that was fine with me. He had paid us a thousand dollars for something he didn't want, and he was funny.

The rest of that Lapdance trip sucked. Perhaps the less said about it, the better, so just a few low points. A quick accounting in the morning established that we had lost money again. We had a fiasco of an impromptu second party in partnership with Slamdance, sort of, at the Silver Mine the next night, and when we got up the next day I was supposed to be writing a press release about what a wonderful success Lapdance had been. Instead, I got into a huge blowout with Brody over money and said I was flying out on standby. Brody stomped off and slammed the door of the hotel room, and in a few minutes my cell phone blew up with screaming calls from Jason's completely insane then-girlfriend, who was supposed to be our new publicist and wanted the press release she had heard I was refusing to write. I grumpily typed up the press release and didn't fly out on standby, but we all had behaved badly toward one another, and the next couple of days, which were supposed to be relaxing, were only more depressing.

We vacated the hotel rooms and went down to the house we had rented for the Lapdance filmmakers and volunteers. The house had been pretty well trashed, and the Woodsman was out of his head, doing naked snow angels in the back-yard. The girl who was a butcher had left us twenty pounds of bloody ground venison, and deer burgers sounded good, but they turned out to be disgusting. After we fried them up on the electric stove, nobody wanted to eat them and the whole house smelled like burning hair. The Woodsman took control of the stovetop to make a "cooking show," and I was too tired even to raise an objection when it devolved into his flinging meat around the kitchen and standing on tiptoe to stretch out his cock and scream while he seared it on the electric stovetops's evil spiral eye.

4

We still had three long months to go before preproduction for the *Hot Show* was supposed to start. Pop.com kindly paid us fifty cents on the dollar of what remained of our stillborn deal, but if the Comedy Central date pushed at all, we would have to move out of our offices. As much from habit as anything else, and to keep from biting one another's heads off in the grimy warehouse, we spent the time flogging two projects that had been languishing on our development slate, *Lovestyles* and *Incredibly Strange Wrestling*.

Here is *Lovestyles* in all its idiot glory: a dating show that draws its participants exclusively from the membership of an online dating service. It was a simple idea, but I thought a deceptively simple one in that its revenue implications might be significant. The bubble had popped, but big media companies were still trying to figure out how their broadcast and online divisions could work together. Most of the ideas in play were nonsensical, pie-in-the-sky technology applications that wouldn't be feasible for five or ten more years.

Unlike many types of Internet business, dating sites were actually making money. The primary cost of operating one, once the technology was paid for, was marketing. That cost here would be borne by a daily TV show that would, in effect, serve as a free daily infomercial for the site. In fact, it would be better than free, because it would earn license fees like any other TV show. It seemed to me that the *Lovestyles* concept took existing elements, the dating show and the dating site, and paired them to create a genuine revenue feedback loop.

Not exactly the marriage of relativity and quantum physics, but that was the point. *Lovestyles* wasn't that complicated either in concept or in execution. Yet we had been unable to raise any substantive interest in it during our first round of pitching, back in 1999 and 2000. The response at the places we pitched, most of which had both broadcast and Internet holdings that were supposed to be "synergizing," was a collective spaniel-like cocking of heads. Executives seemed not so much not to like the idea, which would have been one thing, as not to understand it. I had pretty much thrown up my hands at my failures as a communicator when we hit this lull in 2001 and revived the *Lovestyles* pitch.

Rosenberg put us in touch with a start-up called ICU. "I see you" was the idea, but the homonym summed things up. ICU was developing a video bulletin board. This was a very bad idea; the result would not be a useful environment for even mildly complex communication. Additionally, we discovered when we conducted basic research prior to our first meeting with ICU, a company called iClips had already developed a video bulletin board—and they were offering it for free from their Web site.

We opened our *Lovestyles* presentation by directing the ICU business development team to the fully functional iClips site. They had never even heard of iClips, and the blood drained from their faces as visibly as if we had stabbed them.

In immobile grief they listened to our pitch, and at the end of it they agreed to finance a pilot presentation and develop the dating site we described, with the addition that it would be video enabled.

They gave us thirty thousand dollars to make the presentation—not enough for a broadcast-ready pilot but plenty to make a sales reel on Mini DV and keep the lights on for a couple more months. Production was the usual CRAPtv debacle—we had to reshoot all the studio segments for a couple of reasons, significantly because I did such a shitty job in the control room, and we wound up replacing the original hostess with Jason, a decision that led to heavy recriminations. But a reasonably good time was had by most, and the result did articulate the idea. To round it off, ICU even delivered a beta site just as they were preparing to empty their offices. But still no broadcaster we met with was interested in *Lovestyles*.

We squeezed one more production in under the wire. Les Claypool had put us in touch with an organization called Incredibly Strange Wrestling based in San Francisco. We had wanted to do a wrestling project for years, and ISW was the perfect wrestling league we had only dimly imagined. To paraphrase the welcoming patter of their MC: It was incredible, it was strange, and it was wrestling.

ISW combined the acrobatics and theatricality of *Lucha Libre* with mascot costumes and punk rock. ISW shows were interspersed with band performances, and the league had spent a summer on the Warped Tour, playing a side stage and building a small following. Audra, the league's impresario, also ran Stinky's Peep Show, a San Francisco club night institution in which big, beautiful women battered customers in the face with cream pies and their own humongous boobs. Audra's day job was booking the Fillmore, so that was ISW's home venue.

There were more than thirty characters in the cast, played by maybe twenty amateur wrestlers. From memory, standout performers were The Poontangler, Macho Sasquacho, El Homo Loco, The Snackmaster, El Pollo Diablo, Suzie Ming, Sixty Nine Degrees, The Mexican Viking, and Rasputin. Audra said that at the league's first performances there had been some ice throwing, which was not good. Imagine getting nailed in the head by a chunk of ice flung from a theater balcony. Instead of trying to make her crowds quit throwing things, Audra had simply distributed items it would be okay for them to throw: day-old corn tortillas. A big bag of day-olds cost only a couple of bucks, and now Audra didn't even have to supply them. The kids knew to bring them, and they brought them by the bagful.

On the night we taped *Incredibly Strange Wrestling* at the Fillmore, the air positively swarmed with swooping, skimming corn tortillas. By the end of the night the mat, the floor, the wrestlers, and the crowd were covered in a layer of warm, delicious dust. Danny Diamond cut the footage into a highlights reel, and Clancy laid out a gorgeous book of all the characters. We tried to sell the package as a series to MTV, but they were already in business with the WWE and saw no reason to invest in a smaller, sillier wrestling franchise. Comedy Central was the other obvious outlet for the show. We thought *Incredibly Strange Wrestling* would be a great lead-in or follow-up to *BattleBots,* which taped in the Bay Area, and the *BattleBots* arena could easily double as a wrestling venue.

But Comedy Central wasn't interested in ISW, either—perhaps because they didn't see it as a strong property. Or perhaps, I worried, because it was we who were bringing it to their attention.

Could they know? More to the point by now, could they *not* know? Was it possible that after months of talking to us, they still hadn't realized we were a bunch of bumbling numbskulls or heard from any of a hundred different sources that our principal talent was not merely unpredictable but completely out of his handsome blue-eyed head? Apparently, they didn't know, because if they had known, surely they would have pulled the plug on *The Hot Show*, and they didn't pull the plug. In April of 2001 they set us up with a show runner and cut the first check.

Here it was. The moment we had been waiting for, the moment when Jason and I would be borne up together from the humiliation of our failures on the warm winds of success. Ladies and gentlemen, *The Hot Show*.

The poor bastard assigned to us as a show runner was smart and funny, but it was an unenviable task to be the liaison between CRAPtv and an employer. To his credit he immediately realized that Timmy was both funny and completely insane, and he responded well to Jason's proposal of a female cohost/bartender with strong improvisational talents. Timmy's talents were *entirely* improvisational—that is, there was no way he was ever going to say or do the same thing twice, so whomever he was dealing with would have to be comfortable with that.

The show runner brought in a statuesque blonde named Sirena Irwin, who in her audition socked Timmy in the face, threw him to the ground, and rode him around the warehouse like a pony, so that was a lock. We still wanted to do everything on Mini DV in a really loose environment, where shoot time was not a big issue—we were still talking about the cardboard-box desk on the beach in Venice—and Comedy Central still wanted a professional studio shoot (on our budget, essentially a one-take environment) on a talk show set. The show runner sold us out on that one, but I couldn't really hold it against him. It was much more likely that Comedy Central would still exist after the pilot than that we would.

The Hot Show ended up as a hosted variety and sketch format, with a musical number backed by Les and a runner about a celebrity interview that was always just about to happen. We used shorts and sketches from the CRAPtv Web site and made a few new ones. There were probably twenty different segments for the show, and I won't go into them or the many disasters that struck during their production—I'll just mention one in memoriam.

The celebrity runner was developed from a short film called "Mama's Little Baby." It chronicled our celebrity guest Whitney Houston's cracked-out attempts to get to the studio, as seen from the fish-eye point of view of a baby in the backseat of her car. A filmmaker named Lawrence Elbert made the short and sketch, and a beautiful genius named Mario Gardner played Whitney Houston to a tee. Mario died of a drug overdose not long after the shoot, but his Whitney had the savage pathos of immortal comedy.

The Woodsman, for his part, was a champ. As far as I could tell, he was taking most of the meds he was supposed to take and not taking many of the ones he wasn't supposed to take. I wish I could say that *The Hot Show* turned out great, but in all honesty it turned out not even okay. The sketches felt disconnected, and none of the studio stuff shot on BetaCam—we had five cameras on jib arms, a truck outside, the whole deal—had the raw intimacy of the original tapes of Timmy on the street. We did a final Avid edit and sound-sweetening and handed it in. The network asked us to cut it down to twenty-two minutes, hoping the flat feeling was just the result of stretching material too thin, but nobody thought cutting it down was actually going to help.

During the edit my mother gave me the news, vague and sugar-coated, that her blood counts had dropped again. She gave me permission to call Dr. Lucas and speak with her directly regarding my mother's course of treatment. I left a message at the oncology office, and Dr. Lucas reached me when I was driving out of the Fox lot. Jason and I had just finished a disastrous pitch there; for some reason we had driven separately. Waiting at the red light in front of Rancho Park Golf Course, looking west into the lowering sun, I asked Dr. Lucas if it was time for me to move home. She asked how difficult it would be for me to do that—not today, but in the next few weeks—and that was answer enough. I asked what the plan was right now, and she said she wanted to start my mother on Rituxan, the monoclonal antibody therapy that had been considered as a possible first course of treatment, immediately.

It was entirely possible that the Rituxan would be effective in countering my mother's lymphoma. But I understood when my mother started the CVP protocols that Rituxan was regarded as marginally less likely to work than CVP, and it was no more likely to work now, just because the chemotherapy had not. Deaths from administration of Rituxan itself were rare, but they did occur. Generally, if they were going to occur, they occurred during the first treatment, so I should come up to be there for it. It was overwhelmingly likely that the first infusion would go fine, but that was the situation.

The first infusion did go fine. It was administered just like the chemotherapy, by IV, and, as with the chemo, my mother was administered a temporarily immunosuppressive antihistamine that made her sleepy. I remember very little of that summer. Only snippets. I know I spent a good deal of it up north with my mother. The nurses started letting her take her infusions lying down in a bed in one of the offices. I often lay down on the bed with her, and we talked or read until we nodded off. I continued to drive up and down between Marin and Los Angeles, with the balance tipping toward spending more and more time up north.

The Woodsman was living in the warehouse, up in the loft. It wasn't like we were going to kick him out, but we didn't really know what to do with him. He was off his meds again. A few weeks after we got the official news from the network that the show wasn't getting picked up, his birthday came around again. Several of us were standing in the kitchen when police rushed into the warehouse. We didn't even know he was in the building at the time.

He had made a call from the loft to his father up in the Bay Area and said something bad. His father had called the LAPD and dispatched them to our warehouse. With the cops we went over to the stage side and called for him. He came down from the loft. He hadn't hurt himself, but he acted crazy with the cops, and they took him away. He consented to spending nine months in a state-run inpatient mental health facility, and we emptied the loft. It was a horror show up there—the usual stinky Woodsman detritus, damp clown clothes and bedding, drifts of remaindered porn, Larry laBeouf's *Star Wars* memorabilia, a seven-foot fiberglass marlin, but also forty-ounce beer bottles filled with piss, and blackened tinfoil crack pipes. Cleaning it out was a tremendous bummer.

After that I was mostly gone. Jason and Brody and Ward did their best to keep things together at the warehouse, but there just wasn't that much to keep together. Mattt Potter, who had come down to work on *The Hot Show* and now was firmly ensconced, convinced a friend who could draw in a realistic style to come out from Iowa, then put him and one of Danny Diamond's cohorts, a graphic artist who had burned out as a Disney animator—to work drawing Trekkie erotica for a pay site that Potter was going to build. Potter said there was a big market there, in drawings of Borgs and Klingons boning down. The Trekkie erotica business didn't go so hot, though, and it transformed into some other vague partnership with Danny Diamond—an auction thing, reselling computers Potter got from somewhere else at wholesale prices.

Danny Diamond meanwhile was still trying to figure out how to get his own production business up and running. There was no reason he shouldn't have been able to make a go of it. He was a talented kid. But he got a little too creative in his efforts to put financing together. In midsummer he stepped off a plane in Louisville, Kentucky, carrying three thousand hits of ecstasy and was searched by federal authorities. He had been flagged for buying his ticket just the day before, with cash. Danny was of age, and the ecstasy was a Class D felony. Because of his involvement in the computer-reselling business, its PayPal account was frozen, and that had an unfortunate domino effect. Customers who hadn't received their merchandise complained, and the FBI initiated a mail-fraud investigation. They seized Potter's home computers up in Seattle, some of which were editing boxes containing CRAPtv video projects. Those projects went on indefinite hiatus, and Danny wound up doing two years at Lompoc.

At the end of August, Heather booked a job with the music video production company AFMN, where she had been free-lancing as a production coordinator. The job was going to be in the Bahamas, which sounded nice. It would be a technically demanding job, featuring a dance troupe on a moving catamaran, but maybe she would take a day or two after it wrapped to relax in Miami. We both needed a break—not from each other, just a break.

I hadn't seen my father since the previous fall, when he came out to visit Margaret. Her condition was stable now, and her hematocrit had even risen to a reasonable level —low by normal standards but not scary. We were just waiting to see if it would drop again. If it dropped before November, six months after she started the Rituxan, that would be bad. It would mean that the next time she would have less than six months, and the next time less than that, and so on. But if she made it longer than six months without her red count dropping, that would be very good. Sitting around and staring ghoulishly at each other wasn't going to change the outcome one way or another, and my mom encouraged me to go visit Bert and Happy in Colorado.

I drove, pleasurably suspended between places and events. For work in Colorado I brought along a draft of *The Jockey* and notes Ted Demme had given Jason and me almost two years earlier. With all our other projects on the rocks, we had gotten back in touch with him. As always he was welcoming, and we called at an opportune time. He was between directing projects and in the middle of setting up a fund to make low-budget features on HD, a new video format. Because shooting horse races would require lots of cameras and hence lots of film, *The Jockey* would be an expensive movie to make on 35mm—probably prohibitively expensive, because no studio would likely be interested in financing it. In addition to not trading on a star, it was a weird, dark story; basically, it was about an alcoholic Little Person's fight for self-respect, a subject in line more with the 1970s auteur movies Teddy loved and had just finished contributing to a documentary about *(A Decade under the Influence)* than with anything a studio might consider financing. So Teddy said it would make sense for him to bring *The Jockey* in under the umbrella of this new HD fund, which as far as we were concerned was great news. I figured I could have something finished by Labor Day.

Several days into my visit, I got a call from Heather in the Bahamas. She said that there had been a plane crash, and she wanted me to know that she hadn't been on the plane. She could speak only for a moment, because there was a long line for the phone—cell phones weren't working on the island—but I would see the horrible thing play out in the news over the next few days. The job she was on was the last Aaliyah video. The singer and seven others died when the chartered plane leaving Abaco crashed shortly after takeoff. Heather was at the hotel when the crash occurred. Her boss, Scott, helped pull bodies from the wreckage. The only survivor died in his arms on the flight to a hospital on another island.

Scott stayed in the Bahamas and attended to the grisly task of identifying bodies. His partner Brent went back to Los Angeles to take the calls. Heather and Chris, the production manager, flew to Miami to wrap the job. Closing out the books was complicated by the fact that the production company of record, based in New York—the director's personal production company, which didn't actually produce, just looted the budgets and contracted AFMN to do the work—unplugged its phones and pretended not to exist. Paparazzi found out where Heather and Chris were staying in Miami and rammed their rental car with a van to get a photo.

But Heather was okay, and I realized driving back to California that that was all that mattered to me. Nearly four years had passed since I had returned from Texas. In those four years I had produced only work so bankrupt that no one could ever say I had tried my best and failed: corporate branding, porn and snuff, bad comedy. But even at those I had failed. One of my companies was finished, and the other nearly so. And, I realized with a surprising lack of disappointment or self-pity, I was no longer young.

Rather than sparking the immolating despair I had been so sure this realization would someday bring, it gave rise to a sensation of tremendous relief. Concomitant with the realization that I was no longer young—I was thirty-two; it hadn't quite hit me at thirty—came the realization that all the expectations I had held so dearly, my own fondest hopes for myself, had been for what I would accomplish while I was young. Fame, wealth, success in whatever form—it was hard now even to remember what I had imagined, but whatever it had been, an image of myself as prodigy, wunderkind, l'enfant terrible—it simply was no longer possible. I was, at least by any reasonable measure of age, all grown up. Strong, healthy, even of somewhat sound mind. But not young. I had comprehensively failed to deliver on whatever promise I might have had. This release from the tyranny of my own expectations was a sweeter relief than I can describe. The drive back to Los Angeles felt like it was all downhill, as it was.

A few days later and without regard for the function their actions would play as an objective correlative to the end of my youth, Islamic extremists hijacked four airliners and crashed them into the World Trade Center, the Pentagon, and a piece of ground in Pennsylvania. Heather and I were at home, asleep, when the first plane hit. We were awakened by a phone call, saw the second plane hit on television, then watched reports of the third and fourth and saw the towers disintegrate. I didn't yet know for certain that no one I knew had been killed or that the sky over Los Angeles would not at any moment erupt in thermonuclear white. But my primary feeling at seeing those towers come down was neither grief nor fear. It was a terrible elation at being alive myself, privileged to witness the End of the World.

5

We had a CRAPtv meeting on the books for that night, to make plans for the coming year. As a further sign of our extended childhood, we still thought in terms of the school calendar, in which fall is the time of new beginnings. Despite the unreality of that entire day, I don't think it occurred to any of us to cancel the meeting. We were all glad of an excuse to get away from our televisions.

On the drive back from Colorado I had decided to resign my post as CEO. Not that the job had many onerous duties, but the realization that my youth was over had brought with it a desire to work, to actually go back to making things instead of figuring out how to finance them or, when that had been done inadequately, how to keep them from pulling our company under. It wasn't I who was keeping CRAPtv afloat, anyway. Jason brought his limitless optimism to each new unlikely undertaking, and Brody kept the lights and phones turned on. Rosenberg, despite being a pain in the ass, brought in what few deals we had, and Ward had developed a real knack for convincing other companies to give us free stuff. I wasn't sure what I did anymore but write up pitches for shows I knew would never sell, revise my fantasy Business Plan, and write nasty e-mails to people when whatever we were doing with them went wrong.

The warehouse was desolate. Jolon and Martha were having a baby, and Kung Fu had moved out during the summer. Their intern had taken the warehouse cat. Two days before the meeting, I had dropped in and found Clancy working alone. He was squatting in front of his monitor on the seat of his chair, covered with welts. He had moved out of our house and into the warehouse, where he was sleeping on one of the couches, but it turned out the cat had had fleas, and without a cat to eat, the fleas were starving. A hatch exploded out of every carpet remnant and sofa in the warehouse, so many fleas that if you put your head down and looked across the floor, you could see them swarming like the air over a carbonated drink. I set off eight or ten bug bombs, and most of the fleas were dead now, but the building still smelled like insecticide.

We met in the conference room around the oval table Dave Hardy had built for the Quiddity office. We talked a little about the day's events, but there wasn't that much to say except that it was hard to believe, and conversation eventually turned to our business. I was feeling guilty about my plan to resign, but I thought I had come up with a good way to soften it, to make it seem like I wasn't just quitting. I proposed that I would relinquish my title and business responsibilities, and that moving forward I would concentrate on developing original properties. I would develop four properties for the company per year: feature screenplays, pilot scripts and show bibles, and so on. In exchange, the company would provide me a place in which to work. I wouldn't work exclusively on those four projects, because I had to make some money, and obviously the company didn't have any, but the company would have its pick of my projects, and I would do my best with them. I wanted the big room in back that tucked behind the stage side, which had been Jolon's office.

Jason was rightly thinking that we were going to have to sublet parts of the warehouse—definitely the stage side, and maybe the back, as well. Ten people could probably work in the back room I proposed to take, if you packed them in, and a tenant could probably be found for it. There was the smaller room, really a storage closet, next to the back exterior door under the loft. Maybe that would work.

I said that no, it wouldn't, because I wasn't sure what I would be doing to make money over the next year. Maybe some more brand strategy bullshit, I wasn't sure, but whatever it was, it would probably require that I have a place in which to meet with clients. The storage closet was eight feet by ten, with windowless cinderblock walls and a blank steel door. And—here was where I started being a dick—the rest of this place was a disaster area, which was why I wanted to move out of the main room. I wanted an office that was clean and quiet, that would look when I returned to it each morning as it had looked when I left. In fact, I wanted to start using the back door. I was sick of walking through the kitchen in front, where there was always some gruesome mess someone hadn't bothered to clean up, and tired of kicking my way through trash to get to my desk.

I had thought Brody would be my ally in this line of complaint, because she hated the mess as much as I did and we often ganged up on Jason about it. But I hadn't taken into account how much my plan sounded exactly like what it was. Granted, my asking price was small, a big clean room, but one way of looking at it was that I was proposing to leave them responsible for handling everything dull and difficult while I had fun in my private playpen. She asked me snottily if I thought I was really special. I asked her in the same tone if she was a dirty cunt, and that was the end of the meeting.

The next morning I dropped off some flowers, but she didn't respond, and in all honesty my heart wasn't really in it. However quickly I had loosed the c-bomb in response to a conventional strike, my proposal had been pretty reasonable, and if they didn't think so, I was finished working there. I spent the day trying to figure out how to disentangle myself from the morass of contracts and operating agreements that had come to define our relationships. By evening

I realized the solution was less complicated than the problem. I was just done, done with all of it. The following day I collected my computer and a box of personal crap, and a few weeks later I gave Jason a letter assigning all my phantom equity in everything to him, to hold or reassign as he wished.

In the days and nights after September 11, 2001, the skies over Los Angeles were empty. On the ground, nothing was different but the unusual courtesy people showed one another at intersections. But the silence and emptiness of the skies, usually crossed with roaring jets, transformed our stretch of beach. I ran on it at night. The waves were deafening, each crunch and foaming hiss distinct. The air over the water, normally hung with inbound blinking flights, was blank. The lights of Palisades and Palos Verdes still twinkled north and south, and the steam and refinery towers still winked up high above the sludge plant, but it was easy on those quiet nights to imagine what this place had been before the lights, and what it would be after.

Jason and Brody tried to keep the company going for a couple of months, but eventually they had to give up the warehouse, and that was pretty much the end of things as they had been. Brody moved back to New York to take a job as head of production at the place she had worked before she came out to Los Angeles. Potter was back in Seattle, and he took over managing the CRAPtv Web site from there. He redesigned it to operate on steeply reduced terms, basically as a fan site.

The Jockey was the last project Jason and I had together. We drove over to Hollywood a few times to meet with Teddy. His fund was closing, and we planned to shoot the following summer. The first couple of times we met at his office in an old complex called the Lot, and the last time we met at a restaurant called Barney's Beanery. He was expecting a second child, and Amanda had given him a text-messaging device that he was trying to figure out how to operate. We said good-bye in the parking lot. He merged into traffic driving a ridiculous Escalade on massive polished rims that we had all just laughed about. That was the last time we saw him. In January of 2002 he died of a heart attack while playing basketball. Jason and I attended a memorial service on a soundstage that had been transformed into a dim cathedral.

I needed a job, so I asked Matt Stone how to apply for one as a writer on *South Park*. He laughed and said you couldn't really apply, you sort of had to be asked, but a couple of weeks later he called and asked if I wanted to come write for a while. They hired me for the sixth season of the show, and I was tremendously grateful for it. They didn't need me. The other writers were hilarious, and the credit was all I required for entry into ongoing service to THE BIG SHE.

Rosenberg's empire unraveled in February of 2002, the week I started work at *South Park*. He and the financier in New York who managed money for the Lauder heiress had been arguing, and one day he received notice that he was fired from the company he had started. His removal had the appearance of suddenness, but it could have been accomplished only with the complicity of his partner. He asked me to call Collision and say that the couple of projects I was starting with them would be on hold until the situation was resolved. I was happy to make the call and made it, but I think I was the only one of the dozen or so writers and directors with whom Collision was working who did so.

They say this town is a killer, but I never witnessed anything like what I saw in the next few months, as Rosenberg came unglued. He brought all his old files up from the garage, boxes and boxes of them, and embarked on a scrapbooking project that ranged over an entire decade. He compiled the grosses of all the films he'd ever worked on, which came to over a billion dollars, and catalogued his manifold grievances to create a sprawling indictment of Hollywood. He hired a cartoonist to make the cover for his stack of binders, an illustration entitled "The Producer." A little Rosenberg, arms piled with treasure, is beset by bandits at the gates of a castle, which is supposed to represent the studio. Executives shoot arrows at him from the battlements. It was an epic justification of himself, for which, so far as I know, he and I were the only audience. I went over to his house in my spare time and ghostwrote letters to people he felt had wronged him, rambling monologues of supplication and threat.

Enough time had passed by then that I was prepared to record my own memories of the strange doings that had taken up my days since my return from Texas, to chronicle my adventures in independent media, corporate branding, Antichrist impersonation, and emergency psychiatric intervention—my interrogation of the question "What will I do when I grow up?" I outlined these pages that summer, thinking it would take me a few months to fill them in. It has taken a little longer than that, typing away during breaks from work, in a small office I rented at the Santa Monica Airport. And in the meantime, life has continued past the final page of the outline. Still no answer to the question, I'm sorry to report. But I have kept myself occupied.

At the end of my season at *South Park,* Dave Goodman and I took a sitcom pitch out together. We didn't sell it, but in the spring Goodman & Phillips were hired as a writing team on the DreamWorks CGI animated sitcom *Father of the Pride.* The show was about Siegfried and Roy's white lions. It aired a season on NBC. You may have seen it. If not, the DVD is now available. We had a ball; there are few better ways to spend the day than around a table with ten or twelve comedians. Twice, the mogul Katzenberg took us all on his private jet to Las Vegas, first to see the show and meet Siegfried and Roy and then, a few months later, to have dinner with them at their secret hideaway, the Jungle Palace. We dined al fresco by the pool surrounded by white lions, but I can say no more. The mysteries of the Jungle Palace forbid me to divulge its secrets.

In November, as most people know, Roy was eaten by a tiger. Heather and I were down in Laguna when it happened, spending the weekend with Bert and Happy. Happy's sister, Corinne, was dying of lung cancer. I had just had another wisdom tooth removed, and once again I was high on Vicodin. I developed an unpleasant condition called "dry socket" after the surgery. I told the oral surgeon it still hurt, but he thought I was just trying to hustle him for more pills, so I got another scrip from my regular dentist. I was up to fifteen a day and still not having fun when that side of my face went numb as a result of a bone infection. A broad-spectrum antibiotic cleared it up, and I quit taking the Vicodin cold turkey. It didn't even occur to me that I might have become physically addicted. It took me a whole day to figure out why I was weeping, and there followed five more of frozen sweat and long, junky-kick walks with Nemo. Corinne had died at fifty.

After the Woodsman was committed to the state psychiatric facility in the summer of 2001, Jason became his conservator, the person licensed to act as his advocate before the state. With a level of organization I had never seen Jason exhibit on his own behalf, he arranged for Timmy to receive state disability payments and opened a bank account in which they could accrue until Timmy was released. When in due course the Woodsman was released, the two of them made a plan that Timmy would move to Hawaii, where if you insisted on sleeping in shrubbery, at least you wouldn't freeze.

Hawaii didn't go so hot, but it wasn't Jason's fault. Almost immediately, Timmy ran into traffic (after a bouncing ball, naturally) and was hit by a car. He wasn't seriously injured—a broken arm, I think—but Hawaii sent him back, and after that we lost track. But we do hear from him from time to time. About a year ago he called me in good spirits from Marin General, where he was being monitored and rehydrated after collapsing "on maneuvers" up on Mount Tamalpais. I know Jason has seen him more recently than that. So far as I know, the Woodsman remains at large.

And what about Jason, the only one of us THE BIG SHE was able to neither break nor corrupt? Matt Stone bought a place in Topanga Canyon, nine acres looking west toward the ocean, and Jason lives up there now in high style. Matt makes it to that house only for a weekend every now and then, so for the most part Jason has the place to himself. He has his projects, far too many and marvelous to enumerate; we're even talking about starting a new one together. We play soccer up there on Sundays, six or seven of us going to bellies and back fat, run ragged by a handful of younger guys who can really play.

During a break between television writing seasons, my mother and I went down to Baja with friends to paddle kayaks between the dunes and mangroves of the coastal lagoons. We saw birds and dolphins, and we watched gray whale calves from so close in Magdalena Bay that once we were able to touch one. It rolled up beside the boat and watched us back from one black and sentient eye. Its skin felt like suede or velvet, something gently furred, and then it sank away. Margaret was fine. More than fine. She was better than she had been in the year before her diagnosis, better than she had been for as long as I could remember. The six-month mark had come and gone, and then a year; and then, another.

And now, another. We spoke yesterday on the telephone. She had just had her checkup and reported proudly, like a kid with a good grade, that her hematocrit was higher than it had ever tested before. We are grateful—so grateful that it's hard even to know where to focus it. Toward Dr. Lucas, of course. Toward Genentech, however confusing it is to be grateful toward a biomedical behemoth. But mainly just grateful. They say that it's still inside her, waiting. But it's inside all of us, waiting, and in the meantime, we may as well pet the whales.

Acknowledgments

I would like to gratefully acknowledge all my business partners, first for having the patience to work with me, and then for acceding with such grace to the publication of this account. I would especially like to thank Jason McHugh and Alex Frankel, both of whom offered suggestions and factual help in addition to their continued friendship. David Goodman was my television writing partner almost the entire time the time I was working on this, and he was unstintingly generous in encouraging me go off to my little office and pursue my private project.

The first seeds of *The Royal Nonesuch* were a couple of letters I wrote to *McSweeney's* back in 1998 or 1999. I didn't keep my promise to be a regular correspondent, and most of the events in this book occurred after I wrote the letters, but to a certain extent this book is an extension of that epistolary project, and I would like to thank *McSweeney's* for the start and encouragement. In the same vein of late thanks, I would like to acknowledge the Stanford University Creative Writing Program and all my peers and betters there for support much earlier in my writing life.

I owe more recent debts to Laura Gutin, who read and made very polite notes to the manuscript before I submitted it anywhere; to Jill Mason, whose close copyediting saved me from innumerable errors (remaining errors are mine); and to Jamison Stoltz, my editor at Grove Atlantic, who provided thoughtful editorial engagement of the type that just isn't supposed to exist anymore.

Thanks also to Matt Stone, Trey Parker, Jonathan Groff, and Jon Pollack for employment over the last few years. You are Medicis. Gail Hochman, Brett Hansen, and David Krintzman: I am so grateful for your kindness, advocacy, and counsel. Thank you.

People who can never properly be thanked are Heather, my family, and Timmy the Woodsman.